ON THE "QUESTION" OF WOMEN IN TANZANIA

Women in Tanzania

An Analytical Bibliography

By Ophelia Mascarenhas &
Marjorie Mbilinyi

N-T

PB 500

**AFRICANA
PUBLISHING
COMPANY**
A division of Holmes & Meier Publishers, Inc.
30 Irving Place, New York, N.Y. 10003

holm

Addresses to the authors:

Ophelia Mascarenhas
Senior Librarian
University Library
P O Box 35092
University of Dar es Salaam
Dar es Salaam
Tanzania

Marjorie Mbilinyi
Professor of Research
Institute of Development Studies
P O Box 35169
University of Dar es Salaam
Dar es Salaam
Tanzania

© Ophelia Mascarenhas & Marjorie Mbilinyi 1983

ISBN 91-7106-216-5

Printed in Sweden by
Motala Grafiska, Motala 1983

ACKNOWLEDGEMENTS

We would like to express here our appreciation to the numerous
individuals and institutions who have provided us with assistance
and encouragement. These include the East Africana and Periodicals
sections of the University Library; Bureau of Resources Assessment
and Land Use Planning, Economic Research Bureau, Departments of
Education and History, Institute of Development Studies and the
IDS Women's Study Group of the University of Dar es Salaam (1980-82),
the National Museum Library; the Tanzania Society, and the Department
of Research within the Ministry of Information and Culture, and in
particular the Jipemoyo Project staff and associates; the Ministries
of Agriculture, of National Education and of Health; the Prime
Minister's Office, Ujamaa na Ushirika Division in Dodoma and Dar es
Salaam; U.W.T. Headquarters at Dodoma and in Dar es Salaam; Tanzania
Food and Nutrition Centre; the Moshi Cooperative College; the Inter-
national Cooperative Alliance (ICA) Regional Headquarters at Moshi;
FAO Offices in Dar es Salaam and the UNFPA/FAO/PMO Population/Family
Life Education Project Headquarters at Arusha; Institute of Adult
Education; Tanzania Family Planning Service (UMATI), YWCA; Swedish
International Development Authority (SIDA), UNICEF and others.

The production of this book was made possible by a grant from
SIDA, which also covered its translation into Kiswahili so as to
reach as wide an audience in Tanzania as possible. We are especially
indebted to Anna Runeborg, formerly Programmes Officer in SIDA's Dar
es Salaam office, for her constant encouragement. We would also
like to express our appreciation to Dorrit Alopaeus-Stahl for her
fine job of copyediting, and helpful suggestions on reorganization.

We have included the contents of an earlier work in this text,
entitled Women and Development in Tanzania, An Annotated Bibliography
published by African Training and Research Centre for Women (ATRCW),
Economic Commission for Africa, Addis Ababa in 1980 as Bibliography
Series No. 2. This first stage of our work was funded by the Ford
Foundation, Nairobi, through the ATRCW office. We are extremely
grateful for the encouragement received from ATRCW to expand the
earlier work and include it here, and in particular to Nancy Hafkin,
ATRCW Publications Officer, for her painstaking work in processing
the 1980 publication.

Joyce Kibanga, Anita Kidinilo and Daines Mary Kuhanga typed this
draft with great care and patience, during many long sessions of
work.

Our work has gained from the contributions of the many colleagues
who provided criticisms and suggestions, including the BRALUP Workshop of Women's Studies and Development (1979) and the IDS Women's
Study Group (1980-1982). We are particularly grateful to Ernest
Wamba-dia-Wamba for his critical comments on Part One of the text.

We have developed greater clarity about "the question of women"
as a result of the learning we received from peasant women and men
in Diozile I Village, West Bagamoyo, and in Iringa Villages where
Mbilinyi and Mascarenhas respectively conducted research. It is
our hope that the way in which we have tried to pose the question
of women is a correct reflection of the interests of women and
peasants of Tanzania.

NOTES ON SOURCES

Many of the materials referred to in this text are not published
commercially. These include governmental reports, and research and
discussion papers produced at the University of Dar es Salaam and in
Government and other departments. These are available at the
original source, and some are found in the East Africana Section of
the University of Dar es Salaam Library. A Women's Research and
Documentation Project is in the process of formation, which will
set up a research/documentation centre where others will be found.
Nearly all of the unpublished M.A., and Ph.D. theses submitted to
the University are found in East Africana.

     We have concentrated our attention on materials produced in
Tanzania or else available here. There are probably many relevant
articles and books published elsewhere which are not included, simply
because these are not distributed within Tanzania, and have usually
not entered into the debates on the question of women here. This
is partly the result of the appropriation of knowledge about
Tanzania's history, and in particular, the history of the struggles
of Tanzanian workers and peasants. Lengthy annotations have been
produced for certain crucial materials so as to ensure that the
issues raised in them will not be irretrievably lost. Throughout
the text annotations are referred to by section and item number.

     As we noted in the 1980 publication by UNECA (Women and Develop-
ment in Tanzania), "the text is a resource in and of itself. In
the production of this work, we as well as those who provided
materials to us are engaged in an act of sharing knowledge with the
readers. We trust that those who make use of it will share their
work with us in a similar way". Materials which relate to the
problems or issues posed in the book would be highly appreciated.

ABBREVIATIONS

(Used in annotations as author, source or location)

ATRCW	African Training and Research Centre for Women, UNECA, Addis Ababa.
BW	BRALUP Workshop on Women's Studies and Development, University of Dar es Salaam, September 24-29, 1979.
BRALUP	Bureau of Resource Assessment and Land Use Planning, University of Dar es Salaam.
CCT	Christian Council of Tanzania.
EAF	East Africana Section, University Library, University of Dar es Salaam.
ERB	Economic Research Bureau.
FAO	Food and Agriculture Organisation of the United Nations.
ICA	International Cooperative Alliance.
ILO	International Labour Organisation of the United Nations.
IPPF	International Planned Parenthood Federation.
NGOs	Non-Government Organisations.
PMO	Prime Minister's Office.
SIDA	Swedish International Development Authority.
Tanzania	United Republic of Tanzania.
TFNC	Tanzania Food and Nutrition Centre.
TNR	Tanzania Notes and Records, The Tanzania Society, Dar es Salaam.
UMATI	Tanzania Family Planning Association.
UN	United Nations.
UNFPA	United Nations Fund for Population Activities.
UNICEF	United Nations International Children's Emergency Fund.
UNRISD	United Nations Research Institute for Social Development.
UTAFITI	National Scientific Research Council.
UWT	National Women's Organisation of Tanzania.

8

TABLE OF CONTENTS

INTRODUCTION

The purpose of this book is to pose "the question" of women in Tanzania, to clarify the issues being raised in research and in programmes of the government and other agencies, and to critique the different positions which are taken, be they explicit or implicit. The volume consists of two parts. Part One seeks to clarify the relationship between ideological and political struggles over the question of women and the concrete struggles waged by working class and peasant women. Part Two consists of critical annotations of selected materials and introductory essays to the separate sections in which these annotations are found. The introductory essays identify the major issues which arise in each section, and elaborate questions which require further analysis and action.

Fundamentally we are grappling with the problem of how to pose the question of women and whether it should be posed at all as a separate question. At the same time, we critique those who have either ignored the oppression and exploitation of women, or have dismissed it as a secondary or residual problem. There is no "question" that women are oppressed and that the oppression of women is fundamental to imperialist and capitalist exploitation. Our understanding of these problems is partly derived from an earlier work (XIV:393) and on the critical feedback we have received. It is also based on research activities in which we have separately engaged during the same period of time as the writing of this volume, and on study group activities.

The arguments developed are tentative in nature, and require more concrete empirical investigation. Our own conceptualisation of the problem can be clarified by a reassessment of the two central concepts of our earlier work (XIV:393), which were patriarch relations and the sexual division of labour. The concept of patriarch relations was based on analysis of precapitalist social relations of production situated at the level of clan or extended family. Although it was briefly noted that these relations changed as a result of the development of feudal and later capitalist relations, they appeared to have a transhistorical character. In the former analysis, for example, patriarch relations of production were constituted at the level of household in contemporary peasant production systems, with the male head of household being the patriarch. The logical outcome of such analysis would be that classes can be identified at the level of the peasant household - for example, male patriarch exploiters and exploited wives.

In certain precapitalist social formations patriarchal relations were the basis of class formation, and related to complex groups not reducible to the kinship or lineage relations characteristic of their phenomenal forms, their appearance on the surface (II:35, IV:99, 106, 107). Both women and men were exploited by patriarchal relations, as wives, "junior" men, pawns and others. However, these and other precapitalist relations of production have been subjugated to capitalist relations and transformed. This process of subjugation has taken centuries in certain areas of what is now called Tanzania, beginning with the penetration of merchant capital; but has relied

on more concentrated, intense and violent mechanisms of subjugation
and transformation during the colonial and post-colonial periods
(argument and other references. II:47). The domination of peasant
production systems by capital and the state is unevenly developed,
is still in process and constitutes one arena of major class struggle.

We use "reconstituted patriarchal relations" to refer to the way
that production and reproduction is organised within a peasant household. Peasant production systems can not be reduced to the household
level, however, which is clarified by the studies of villagisation.
Villagisation practices represent a mechanism to create new forms of
cooperation in production with increasing state management of the
labour process in production and reproduction. In this sense,
villagers increasingly are becoming like the "collective worker",
situated in a commodity production system geared to the international
capitalist market, with varying degrees of differentiation and the
development of agrarian capital (XIV:393).

The central question has therefore become the way women and men
are allocated to different (or the same) positions in production and
reproduction in the context of the national and international social
division of labour. The question of women is understood to be a
class question. Women's subordination and oppression is fundamental
to imperialist exploitation in Tanzania. In seeking to clarify the
material basis of women's subordination, we have given great emphasis
to the problem of reproduction as it relates to biological reproduction (section XI), maintenance of the labour force of peasants and
workers (especially sections IV, V and XII), sheer survival of
classes in peril as revealed in high infant and child mortality rates
and the prevalence of malnutrition (section XI on biological reproduction and XIII on health and nutrition) and the reproduction of
social relations themselves, and ideological struggles in particular
(sections VII "Ideology" and VIII "Education").

The identification of materials which provide basic information
is also important. These include information about the structure of
the government, especially the Prime Minister's Office which is
responsible for organisation of projects and government at village
level; U.W.T. activities; the legal system, especially as it relates
to marriage relations and employment; sources of statistical data;
sources of financial assistance for local level and other projects;
and about technological development which would reduce labour time
demands in directly productive and domestic labour activities, or could
contribute to higher levels of productivity especially in food production. Only certain materials were selected, in order to indicate the
range of possible sources of practical information and the possible
location of additional ones. The form of annotations is critical and
often "long" to provide a substantial summary of a given item. The
annotations are particularly crucial for materials which are
inaccessible due to their unpublished nature or language (Swahili
items for non-Swahili speakers; English items for non-English
speakers). Although we have retained the annotations from earlier
work (XIV:393), changes in our conceptualisation of the question of
women are reflected both in the selection of new items and in their
annotations and in the introductory essays to each section.

There are fourteen sections, beginning with a general analysis
of women in developing countries, Africa and Tanzania and then moving
on to materials categorised by major themes. It is obvious, however,

that many items could fit different sections. For example, issues concerning women in production in sections II, IV and V also relate to the issues raised in "Education" or in "Ideology". Although a separate section, "Education" is clearly a fundamental aspect of "Ideology". The reader is therefore advised to search for materials relevant to a specific problem area in the text as a whole, and not to rely solely on one section.

The present text was completed in 1981. Since then, we have identified earlier work which was inadvertently overlooked. Moreover, a great deal of new work directly relevant to analysis of the question of women has been produced in Tanzania during 1981/1982. It has not been possible to incorporate these materials in the present text. As we noted in our earlier work, this is an on-going project. We invite others to share in the challenge of developing a critical examination of women's studies and related work.

Ophelia Mascarenhas

Marjorie Mbilinyi

1982

PART ONE

STRUGGLES ON THE QUESTION OF WOMEN IN TANZANIA

I. THE OPPRESSION OF WOMEN

Struggles over the correct strategy of development in Tanzania have
heightened during the last few years, during a period of severe
economic recession in the international and national economies.
These struggles centre around those who take the capitalist line of
development, and those who take the socialist line. President
Nyerere noted in his July 7th, 1981 speech, that the government and
party (CCM) remain committed to socialism, despite the struggles of
external and internal enemies to preserve and strengthen exploitative
capitalist relations. However, commitment to socialism does not make
a country socialist. In "Ten Years after the Arusha Declaration",
President Nyerere said, "Tanzania is certainly neither socialist, nor
self-reliant" (Nyerere 1977:1). Indeed contradictory practices of
government and party leaders have often confused the people about
what socialism really is.

In the Arusha Declaration (1967) it says:

A truly socialist state is one in which all people are workers
and in which neither capitalism nor feudalism exists.... In a
really socialist country no person exploits another; everyone
who is physically able to work does so; every worker obtains a
just return for the labour he performs; and the incomes derived
from different types of work are not grossly divergent.
(Nyerere 1968:15).

Socialism is created by the revolutionary class struggle of the
workers and peasants and their allies against the dominant capitalist
relations and remnants of feudalist and other precapitalist relations
which exploit and oppress the masses. Government nationalisation of
the major means of production has contributed to that struggle, but
is not in itself socialism. England, for example has state-owned
productive enterprises, but it is still a capitalist country. The
situation in Tanzania is made more complex by the fact that the
government is dependent on foreign finance capital represented by
the World Bank and IMF in particular. Even the state enterprises
and state financial institutions depend on foreign sources of
finance, which allows imperialist interests to penetrate the national
economy and direct development strategies towards a capitalist
direction.

The Party Guidelines of 1971 ("Mwongozo") clarified the nature
of the revolutionary struggle "to wrest from the minority the power
they exploit for their own benefit (and that of external exploiters)
and put it in the hands of the majority to promote their well-being"
(par. 2).

The greatest aim of the African revolution is to liberate the
African. This liberation is not sent from heaven, it is
achieved by combatting exploitation, colonialism and imperialism.
Therefore, the experts of this liberation are ourselves, we who
are being disregarded, exploited and oppressed. There is no
nation in the world that has expertise to teach Africans how to
liberate themselves. Our duty is to liberate ourselves and the
necessary expertise will be obtained during the struggle itself
(par. 3).

Which classes in Tanzania are "disregarded, exploited and oppressed"? The exploited classes are the poor and middle-level peasants and the workers. A capitalist farmer or a rich peasant who exploits hired labour is not the "exploited". Wage employees who are able to enrich themselves on the basis of their control over factories or commercial enterprises as managers are not the "workers" being referred to here, but rather an embryonic state bourgeoisie. Not all high level wage employees are in a position to be exploiters, however. Many provide basic social services or skills as government or other employees, and are categorised as members of the "petty bourgeois" class. The basic social force upon which the struggle against capitalism and for socialism depends is the peasants and the workers, together with their allies among the petty bourgeoisie. The significance of the peasants and the productive workers was pointed out in President Nyerere's Speech in Parliament on July 18th, 1975 (p. 9):

> ... ultimately we all depend upon the production of goods by the farmer and the workers. The teachers, nurses, doctors, soldiers, office workers, - and politicians - can only do their work if their wages give them access to food, clothes, and houses which are produced by the peasants and production workers.

Mwongozo also raised the question of social relations at the work-place, and the relationship between the government and the Party and the people.

> The truth is that we have not only inherited a colonial govern-mental structure but have also adopted colonial working habits and leadership methods. For example, we have inherited in the government, industries, and other institutions the habit in which one man gives the orders and the rest simply obey them (par. 13).

> For us development means both the elimination of oppression, exploitation, enslavement and of being disregarded and the promotion of our independence and human dignity ... The duty of our Party is not to encourage people to implement plans which have been decided upon by a few experts and leaders. The obligation for our Party is to ensure that the leaders and experts implement the plans that have been agreed upon by the people themselves (par. 28).

The years after the Arusha Declaration, relations between the leaders and the people remained a major problem:

> The truth is that despite our official policies, and despite all our democratic institutions, some leaders still do not LISTEN to people. They find it much easier to TELL people what to do, meetings are too often monologues without much, if any, time being devoted to discussion; and even then the speech is usually an exhortation to work hard rather than an explanation of how to do things better.
> (Nyerere 1977:43-44).

A central aspect of socialist principles of organisation is criticism, self-criticism and counter-criticism.

> Our leaders at all levels must make more effort to reach decisions by discussion. They must encourage the people to criticise

mistakes which have been made, and they must be willing to work
with the people in rectifying past mistakes and avoiding new
ones .... The leaders of Tanzania must accept that democracy is
at the heart of socialism.
(Nyerere 1977:44).

In "Socialism and Rural Development" (1967), the question of women's
oppression was posed in relation primarily to "traditional" (or
precapitalist) society and to present-day peasant production systems.

> ... it is true that the women in traditional society were
> regarded as having a place in the community which was not only
> different, but was also to some extent inferior. It is
> impossible to deny that the women did, and still do, more than
> their fair share of the work in the fields and in the homes. By
> virtue of their sex they suffered from inequalities which had
> nothing to do with their contribution to the family welfare.
> Although it is wrong to suggest that they have always been an
> oppressed group, it is true that within traditional society ill-
> treatment and enforced subservience could be their lot. This
> is certainly inconsistent with our socialist conception of the
> equality of all human beings and the right of all to live in
> such security and freedom as is consistent with equal security
> and freedom for all others. If we want our country to make
> full and quick progress now, it is essential that our women
> live in terms of full equality with their fellow citizens who
> are men.
> (Nyerere 1967:3, emphasis ours).

The basic argument of this book is that women's oppression is a
fundamental aspect of the dominant capitalist relations of production
and reproduction in Tanzania today. The oppression of women in the
home and in the productive sector is necessary for the reproduction
of capitalist relations. To clarify this, it becomes essential to
penetrate below the surface level appearances of "family" understood
as "private" and irrelevant to capital. For example, the wage that
workers receive is in exchange for the value of reproduction of their
labour power, which includes the goods and services necessary to
maintain themselves and their families on a daily basis. The work
to prepare and cook food, to take care of children, to fetch water
and so on, which is primarily women's work in the home (domestic
labour) is a vital part of the value of reproduction of labour power.
It is "hidden" however because of the appearance of a private,
separated domain called "the home" or "the family". The family is a
social creation, however, which takes different forms in different
kinds of societies. Capitalist relations allocate women and men to
different positions both in production and reproduction. Women's
oppression contributes to the maintenance of these positions, for
example, by cheapening the value of labour power through the
organisation of the domestic labour process based on an oppressive
sexual division of labour, and by creating a pool of cheap female
labour, which allows the wage to be lowered for all workers and
provides capital with a labour force which can be hired and fired
as it wishes.
Women's oppression is fundamental to the exploitation of
peasants as well. In peasant production systems, female labour is

not only vital in the domestic labour process, but is also a major component of food production and export crop production. The way in which peasant production and reproduction is organised is highly profitable for capital, in that the prices paid for marketed crops are much lower than the value of reproducing labour (power) in the peasant family. Hence, it can be argued that subsistence production based to a large extent on female labour subsidizes the production of marketed crops, although it never enters into the calculation of market prices.

According to the Party Creed of the CCM Constitution.
The Party believes:

(a) that all human beings are equal;
(b) that every individual has a right to dignity and respect as a human being;
(c) that socialism and self reliance is the only way of building a society of free and equal citizens.
      (Article One, 4).

One of the basic aims of the Party is "to protect the rights of peasants and workers; in particular to ensure that every individual receives a just return for his (her) labour (No. 7). Another is "to ensure that the government and all public institutions give equal opportunity to all citizens, women and men alike, irrespective of race, tribe, religion or status" (No. 15). Number 16 aims "to ensure that in our country there is no injustice, intimidation, racial discrimination, corruption, oppression or favouritism". The meaning of these aims depends on the class position or line being taken. The socialist line reflects the interests of the workers and the peasants. There are many different ways of posing the question of women or of women's oppression. In order to understand which positions represent a "socialist" position, it is essential to "listen" to the people, by examining the concrete struggles and demands of peasant and working class women themselves. As paragraph 3 of Mwongozo illustrates, objective knowledge about the nature of women's oppression is the product of these struggles, not of theory removed from practice in a university classroom or a library. Such an analysis will contribute to a deeper understanding of the dominant exploitative and oppressive relations of production and the strategies to be adopted in the struggle for socialist transformation. Only the bare outlines of such an analysis can be produced here, drawing on items included as well as press reports to supplement them where necessary.

Posing the question of concrete struggles necessitates the problematisation of the forms which struggles take, and the way that they are viewed by the actors in the struggle. Practices of struggle may be individualised or joint forms of action. They may be spontaneous or highly organised. They may consist of acts of seeming non-action which appear to others to be passiveness or an absence of struggle. To discern the political content of these practices requires attentiveness to the way in which groups of people articulate their needs and demands, how these are understood by these groups themselves, the strategies of struggle adopted and who they are directed against. Such analysis has also got to be carefully periodised in relation to the wider context in which the struggles are situated.

II.   STRUGGLES OF WORKING CLASS WOMEN

The majority of Tanzanian working class women who work for wages are found in the lowest paying, unskilled and often temporary jobs in the organised and the informal sector (II:28, 29, 47. V:148, 150, 152, 158, 159). There are different segments of the working class, and in our analysis we rely on whatever relevant information is available about particular segments. Much of the research done about women workers has focused on structural analysis to document the sexual division of labour in the workplace and the problems specific to women workers. There has been less of a tendency to engage in a political analysis of positions taken in concrete struggles, to analyse women's participation in strike actions, and so on. Newspaper reports have therefore been an important supplement.

The Right to a Decent Wage

One of the primary struggles of working class women has been over security of wage employment, the length of the working day and the wage. Women in the cashew nut industry, for example, have struggled against periodic firing of certain categories of women. In 1975, women forcibly "retired" from the Mbagala factory in Dar es Salaam because of "old age" protested that they were still capable of working and that the amount of severance pay did not take into account their long years of work (Daily News, October 23rd, 1975). Women cashew nut workers were recently laid off again in the process of mechanisation, on the grounds of inadequate skills (education), and struggled to retain their jobs or else receive severance pay in line with their length of work experience. Large numbers of women have previously been employed on a temporary basis in the cashew nut industry for many years, contrary to the relevant employment acts (V:159). Women are a highly exploitable segment of the labour force, vulnerable to the changing demands of capital for labour. The more recent expulsion of one group of older and less educated women, and hiring of more educated women coincides with mechanization of the industry (see also V:148, 149). Barmaids are another segment of the labour force which is highly exploited and in practice not protected by legislation on the length of the working day, minimum wages, weekly days off and leave benefits. Employers of barmaids are able to exploit their "sexual function" as well, ensuring prostitution services for clients and using the possibility of such earnings as a rationale for maintaining low wages. Women have been forced to accept the resulting high rate of exploitation on the grounds that no alternative forms of wage employment are available to them (V:154). Moreover, there are such a large number of women desperate for work, thereby pushing the wage downwards. At the same time, barmaids have jointly quit in protest over wages way below the legal minimum wage, as in 1971 when ten quit from a "public institution" over a 60 % wage (compared to the minimum wage then of 180/=).
    Another category of working class women who are unorganised and tend to be highly exploited are domestic servants. Despite the

existence of a statutory minimum wage for such work the majority
receive only a fraction of the wage. There is a form of differentiation among domestic servants, however, such that some make use of
JUWATA to secure the minimum wage and other rights. These tend to
be employed by expatriates or by the highest paid petty bourgeois
and bourgeois salariat. For many, the wage is paid in kind, with
the provision of housing, meals and cast-off clothes. A large
number are children, often brought from villages to work as "ayahs".
The working day extends to 12 hours or more for a seven day week
without regular holidays and leave benefits. The isolated nature
of such work, and the availability of large numbers of girls or
women seeking wage employment in towns have blocked organised
struggles of domestic servants thus far. Moreover, young girls are
often brought to town under special arrangement with their peasant
parents, so that "obedience" to the employer is enforced by
patriarchal ideologies of subordination. Domestic servant struggles
take the form of absenteeism, "absconding" from one employer in
search of better conditions in the household of another, stealing
subsistence needs to complement the low wages, a "go-slow" performance of tasks (often defined as stupidity or laziness by
employers), and eventual search for alternative forms of employment
of subsistence, including prostitution, concubinage or marriage
(V:143, 150, 151 and 162 document such actions from the point of
view of working class and other employers).

The issue of domestic servants is complicated by the fact that
working class women themselves must usually hire somebody to take
care of children, cook and keep house so that they can go to work.
A minimum or low wage earner is obviously not in a position to pay
someone else the same wage. Women workers perceive the problem of
substitute child care and other aspects of domestic labour to be one
of their major problems (V:143, 144, 148, 150; VI:165, 170). On the
one hand, young girls are not satisfactory substitutes at home. On
the other, the kinds of day care centres being set up are too few
and do not meet the specific needs of working class women. They are
not accessible because of transport problems, only cater to children
three to seven years old, only operate for a half-day and are often
too costly.

The Double Burden

The problem of the "double burden" of "paid" work and "unpaid" work
in the home also affects women's work performance. If a child is
sick or the domestic worker leaves her employment, the woman worker
has little choice but to take the child to the hospital or to remain
at home, even at the risk of losing her job through being late or
absent. Even if a "husband" is present in the household, he is not
morally obligated or ideologically expected to undertake such
responsibilities. For women, the tasks of being wife and mother are
defined as "duties", as moral obligations, by the patriarchal
ideologies which govern the sexual division of labour in domestic
labour. The impact of the "double burden" on women's work was made
very clear in discussions held with Tanita Cashew nut and Bora Shoes
workers about doing the "night shift" (The Nationalist, February 12th,
1972). The problem was not the night shift itself, but the fact that
being on night shift interfered with women workers' capacity to do

domestic labour at home, and was also felt to be injurious to pregnant women due to transport difficulties. Organisation of child care, especially of young infants, and cooking for the husband and the rest of the family were the major issues noted. As one women said,"she works nights only because it is the only way she can earn a living".

Domestic labour is an essential aspect of the reproduction of the labour force on a daily basis, as noted above. The worker's "personal consumption" is primarily dependent on the labour input of women to cook, care for children, take care of sick members of the family and so on. The wages or other sources of income which family members receive are not in an immediately consumable form. In order to subsist, the wage must be transformed into housing, clothing, food, water, medicine, and care of the children and other dependent family members. The kind of work which women do in the home is therefore absolutely essential to reproduce the labour force – but it is not essential that women do it, or that it be situated in "private" families rather than in other institutions. The fact that schools have taken over the formal education of children which was carried out within extended families in the past exemplifies the way other family tasks could be socialised and transformed. Women workers' identification of the double burden as a major problem and site of struggle at home and at work is therefore extremely significant. The way in which capitalist relations organise the reproduction of the labour force is fundamental to the overall re-production of capital labour relations. On the one hand, the present system cheapens the value of reproduction of labour power; on the other hand, it contributes to the creation of a large segment of the labour force which is vulnerable and highly exploitable, namely women. Ideologies of women's subordination contribute to the process of allocating women to the more temporary, least secure forms of wage employment, to be hired or fired according to the needs of capital.

Control of Sexuality and Fertility

Struggles over maternity leave benefits have clarified the signi-ficance of the question of biological reproduction and how it is socially organised, as well as child care, one of the basic aspects of domestic labour. Heated debates began in 1971 over whether or not paid maternity leave should be extended to unmarried mothers. It became the focus of organised discussion in factories and offices, in branches of TANU, NUTA and UWT at that time, in the National Assembly and in the press. Women workers, many of whom were themselves unmarried mothers, argued that the practice not to pay maternity leave to unmarried mothers was contradictory to socialism and was creating two classes, one of married women and the other of unmarried women. Workers were particularly concerned about security of employment, including the wage received at the time of maternity leave, and the continued payment of a full wage during the full 84 days of leave. Without such conditions, women were forced to return to work soon after delivery, thus endangering the health of mother and child. Even one month leave without pay endangered the subsistence of the household.

Lohana Simba, a binder at Printpak and an unmarried mother, argued forcefully:

"I want my name to appear wherever you want so that the Government
can consider paying maternity leave salary to all women ... My
third child passed away mainly due to grossly inadequate care.
I could not help myself, nobody was supporting me and though the
disease which consumed him was not a very serious one, he became
very weak". Lohana recalls in grief. "The Government should
give unmarried mothers maternity leave pay because when those
women resume duty, some of them do not even get bus fares to and
from their places of work. How can you afford to pay for an
ayah, and for milk for your child and food for both him and
yourself, with the 180/= salary you got before proceeding on
leave?"
(Sunday News Magazine, September 12, 1971).

Both workers and government and party leaders pointed out that there
was no legal distinction made about "illegitimate" children, and that
all of the children of the nation were a social responsibility. The
Junior Minister of Health and Social Welfare, Lucy Lameck, explained
that the exclusion of unmarried mothers from maternity leave
benefits was partly the result of

"Traditional cultural values and norms and the fear that this
would encourage our young girls to give birth to children outside wedlock .... Even if we go on discriminating against our
unmarried mothers, this will not deter them from conceiving or
giving birth.

No provision in our laws points out that there are illegitimate
children. The mother gives birth to a baby and not 'illegitimacy'
... by denying the mother paid maternity leave, we are denying
the child of some of his/her rights such as infantile care. This
is indeed a reflection of the contradictions within our system".
(Sunday News Magazine, August 8th, 1971).

The arguments against maternity leave benefits for unmarried mothers
centred around issues of social control of female sexuality and
fertility. Unmarried mothers were labelled as prostitutes. Moreover, as Lameck pointed out, there was concern that providing leave
benefits to unmarried women would encourage young girls to engage
in sexual relations with men and conceive children without getting
married. The arguments against provision of contraceptives and
sexual instruction to young girls and women are exactly the same
today.
    The line taken by the women workers themselves was that women
had the right to be unmarried and to bear children, without being
subjected to patriarchal relations of women subordination, and
that as workers they had the same rights to maternity leave benefits
as married women have. This line contradicts the way both precapitalist relations and capitalist relations have allocated women
to the process of social reproduction as subordinated reproducers
of the labour force. This was not the line initially adopted, by
the U.W.T. and the debates within the national women's organisation
over this issue clarified the different class lines being taken in
the organisation at that time. Women workers accused the UWT of
being an organisation of "big wives" (i.e. wives of party and
government bureaucrats) which did not represent their interests.
This class division was a focus of struggle at the UWT Conference

held on Mwongozo (TANU Guidelines) at the University in 1971 as well.
Women workers explained their non-participation in terms of its
irrelevance to their interests and needs (X:261 is a summary report
of this meeting).

The line corresponding to the interests of women workers was
finally adopted by the UWT at its Annual Conference at Mbeya in
1971. This was announced by the National Chairperson of UWT, Sophia
Kawawa, at a meeting of the UWT branch at Muhimbili Hospital, and
was received with cheers. Notably, however, on the same occasion
the Muhimbili Medical Superintendent stated that:

> "All women medical employees at Muhimbili Hospital should
> discard their inferiority complex and negative attitudes
> which made most of them abscond from work or shirk their
> responsibilities".
> (Standard, August 9th, 1971).

Sexual Harassment

At the UWT Conference on Mwongozo, the whole issue of sexual harassment at work came out as a major problem for women workers. Two
lines were taken on the question of sexual relations "at the workplace". One identified as a line of older married "big wives" was
that the women workers seduced their husbands in order to get money
or other forms of payments. The line identified with women workers
themselves (young and old, unmarried and married) was that the
bosses in factories or offices ("your husbands") demanded sexual
services from women workers in exchange for employment, on-the-job
training placements and consideration for a higher wage. They
talked about the every day occurrence of sexual harassment at work,
and the predicament women workers faced who needed a wage to
subsist. Examples were given of women who were fired from their
jobs, or were forcibly moved to less desirable work, because of
resisting bosses' demands.

Commenting in the press on problems of working women in towns,
a community worker noted that:

> "... an older woman looking for employment also has to face the
> problem of men's bad intentions. But her experience is even
> worse. The man who is supposed to give her a job may not be
> attracted to her personally. He may consider her too old to
> be pleasing or too complicated for him because she is married.
> Or, perhaps, the woman is not willing to comply with his
> wishes because she does not want to compromise her marriage".
> (The Nationalist, September 11th, 1971).

In the same article, a young unmarried office worker in the UWT talked
about the problems of unmarried girls.

> "All girls primarily move to towns because they want jobs and
> they think they will find them there. Yet they find that the
> one stumbling block to their ambition are men who won't give
> them job unless they agree to their other propositions of
> which the No. 1 is having pre-marital relations with them.
> This is number one problem facing girls in towns.
>
> Worse still are those men who give a job to a girl for one
> or two weeks then dismiss her. Apparently there are some men

who think that they can easily get girls to agree to what they
want when they are under their power. Finding that they are not
willing even then, they dismiss them before their first
salaries".

Sexual harassment and rape are mechanisms of social control
historically practised in class society. It underlines the subordinated place of women within the exploited labour force, and
defines women as sexual objects rather than, or in addition to,
being producers. The threat of sexual harassment or rape is
extremely powerful in controlling women's movements and even defining
what kind of work they are "safe" to do. For example, in the
discussion on night shift, the women kept pointing out the hazards
of walking home alone from the bus-stop late at night. As a Bora
Shoes worker noted, "Many a times the woman from her night duties
has been rebuked, scandalized, chased and even assaulted".
(The Nationalist, February 12th, 1972).

Rejection of "Patriarchal" Marriage

A growing proportion of urban women are single and have never married
or else have married and are now divorced, according to demographic
and census statistics (II:54; XI:302, 304, 312). Case studies and
surveys have shown that many female factory workers and urban petty
traders are female heads of households with children of their own
and other dependents to support (V:148, 150, 159, 162). Some women
divorcees have completely rejected the patriarchal form of marriage.
Their explanations stress the costs of having a husband in terms of
family maintenance costs, which include his personal consumption
(namely of alcohol and women) as well as the maintenance of his
relatives; and oppressive family relations expressed in wife-beating,
subservience to the husband and his relatives, and constant ridicule
or being put in one's place as an inferior member of the household,
despite the substantive contributions made of wages, other incomes,
and domestic labour (V:143, 144, 159).
    Access to a wage or other source of cash income "frees" women
from having to submit themselves to a patriarchal marriage, and
allows them to engage in other forms of sexual relations on different
terms. Very often these relations are contradictory, in that the
women is expected to provide labour and sexual services, in return
for gifts or contributions towards daily subsistence. Nevertheless,
the woman has a different bargaining position, from which she can
reject unsatisfactory or extremely oppressive actions and retain
the children she bears (sections XI and XII). Frequently women are
forced to seek work as a result of being divorced by the husband.
Once employed, however, their consciousness may change as a result
of being able to subsist independently and the experience of
organised labour itself, outside of the home situation. What is
significant is the way that women are through their actions
redefining marriage and other forms of sexual relations, and the
public alarm this has aroused.
    These changes are in advance of the Marriage Act of 1971, which
on the whole reconstituted patriarchal relations of marriage as the
legitimate form of state organisation of marriage. For example
polygamy, bridewealth and female child marriage have all been
legalised (see section IX). Deference to "customary law" with

respect to custody of children has also meant in practice that most
women are dispossessed of their children as a result of divorce or
death of spouse if the widow refuses to be inherited. During
debates in the National Assembly, and even before, the UWT lobbied and
also organised a march to protest against polygamy and bridewealth.
Bridewealth has recently been again a major issue in the national
press. The debates surrounding these issues in the National
Assembly and elsewhere reveal the tenacity with which particular
groups have clung to and imposed patriarchal ideologies and forms
of marriage relations on others, including daughters, wives and
male youth. Ultimately through the legal system and the courts,
the state has constructed the definition of woman as "motherhood",
subordinate and dependent on males for existence and exchangeable
as a commodity through the medium of bridewealth.

As we have tried to show in this essay and in the rest of the
text, this "definition" relates to the way that women have been
allocated to relations of production and reproduction under the
dominance of capitalist relations. It is essential to investigate
the extent to which state practices are a response to the
"resistance" of precapitalist patriarchal relations to subjugation
by capitalist relations, or the reconstitution of patriarchal forms
as new mechanisms of social control and reproduction. These
phenomena lead to forms of consciousness which block the development
of class consciousness. The arrogant pride necessarily aroused when
surrounded by several "dependent" wives and their offspring; the
exchange of women as commodities; the dominance inherent to social
relations between a young sixteen year old girl and a husband ten
years or more her senior - such objective relations induce a form
of consciousness in men which aligns itself with oppressive and
exploitative relations in the work place and the village through
extension of "I" the patriarch at home to "the BOSS", or the
political/government leaders, the patriarchs of work and politics.
Subjection of women from childhood to such relations may lead to
internalisation of oppressive self images, thus destroying their
capacity for revolutionary action against oppressive and exploitative
relations. At the same time, however, women, and in particular
working class women of all ages, are rejecting patriarchal forms.
The unruliness, "bad behaviour" and sexual promiscuity of young
girls being talked abount in towns and villages suggests that old
relations are breaking down (XI:284, 310; XII:333). What will take
its place is an important question, related to the issue of socialist
morality as opposed to patriarchal or capitalist/bourgeois morality.

III. STRUGGLES OF WOMEN PEASANTS

Peasant Differentiation

It is necessary to problematise the concept of peasants in order to
take into account class differentiation among agricultural producers.
The objective conditions of production and reproduction of poor
peasant families are entirely different from those of rich peasant
families, due to the different positions their members are allocated
to in the social relations of production. The concepts of "poor"
and "rich" do not refer to differential amounts of wealth, but rather
to position in the social division of labour measured by differential
ownership and control of the means of production, the market
orientation and scale of production, and the extent of exploitation
of hired labourers.

The nature of class formation in the countryside varies from one
area to another, and relates to social relations beyond the locality
of a village per se. For example, traders in Lugoba trading centre
in West Bagamoyo have particular relations to poor peasants in
neighbouring villages like Diozile I which in themselves may be
relatively undifferentiated. Some members of this class of poor
peasants hire out their labour on a temporary or permanent basis to
a neighbouring state parastatal, as well as to richer households in
the same village or in neighbouring pastoralist and other villages.
Peasants are organised to produce export crops through state mediation
and supervision. For example, the Diozile I village government
provides hybrid maize seeds and cotton seeds to villagers, and
purchases their farm products (IV:108-110, 111,[1] 136). In this brief
analysis, the ensemble of social relations at ward level (Lunga Ward)
is made up of the state administrative apparatus, state production
enterprises, petty traders, poor peasants, an embryonic rural
proletariat and an embryonic middle class of peasants (concerning
peasant differentiation in Tanzania, see Kirimbai 1981, Mbilinyi
1974 and Section IV). Women poor peasants are among those economically compelled to hire out their labour to others. Often their labour
power is exploited by middle and rich peasant women. It is therefore absolutely essential to avoid generalisations about "peasant
women" who may have entirely different interests as a result of
different class positions. Empirical investigation is necessary
which considers social relations at household level as they relate
to village, ward, regional, national and international levels.

Impoverishment of peasants is related to the objective
deterioration of the capacity of peasant production systems to
provide an adequate basis for subsistence as a result of capitalist
penetration (II:47). Women and men migrate from villages in search
of wage employment or other sources of income, despite state
policies against migration. For example, Sachak (IV:125) found in
Dodoma villages that the largest proportion of out migrants were

1)   Ulla Vuorela clarified to members of the IDS Women's Study
      Group's Peasants Sub-Group the significance of ward-level
      analysis of peasant class differentiation (1981).

married women who went to Dodoma town to work as domestic servants
or to make and sell charcoal. The women explained that they were
compelled to leave their husbands and children behind because
farming provided them with inadequate food and cash income to maintain their children. Peasant men complained about women migration,
and said that the women went to town to seek a "softer", easier
life. The women refer to a shift in "responsibility" from men to
women. Women increasingly provide school uniforms, school costs
of other kinds, kerosene, medical services, purchased foods, etc.,
on the basis of their limited earnings from production and sale of
food, beer, pottery, firewood, charcoal and other products; hiring
out their labour to other peasants or petty commodity producers; or
working as migrant labourers or permanent wage labourers in towns
(IV:87, 90, 108-111, 125).

Relations of Distribution and Consumption

Within a patriarchically organised family, women are not "free" to
distribute their labour product as they wish, but rather are
compelled to provide food and cash needs of the household unit. Men
are not subject to the same constraints over distribution of their
own labour product as well as that of other family members when
they have jointly produced export crops. Male "control" over major
cash flows in the household, and the way men engage in "personal
consumption" (drinking, paying bridewealth for additional wives,
purchasing radios and bicycles are most frequently mentioned by
women) is recognised and bitterly resented by women themselves.
Moreover, the women perceive village distribution of proceeds of
village economic activities as an extension of "male" control -
village government leaders are usually men (IV:108-111). Women
peasants react to patriarchal consumption relations by refusing to
work on their husband's shamba or lowering the amount and quality of
labour put in; by expanding production of food crops over whose
sale they have more control; by hiding the amount produced and
earned so as to avoid its being "appropriated" by the husband; and
ultimately by rejecting the patriarchal form of marriage altogether
(IV:86, 90, 96, 108-111, 117, 121, 122).
        Underlying the so-called shifts in responsibilities for
providing family subsistence needs perceived by women peasants is a
fundamental transformation of the organisation of peasant production
and reproduction systems. Peasant men continue to provide
subsistence needs for their families, as well as their personal
consumption needs. What has changed is the way all family members
are now compelled to engage in petty commodity production or to sell
their labour power to provide for family subsistence. The basis of
reproduction of peasants is clearly changing, but in ways specific
to the classes in formation. Kirimbai (1981) found in Dodoma for
example, that both women and men in poor peasant families engaged
in subsistence food production. The women traded food produced by
themselves and their husbands for cash to purchase family needs.
Likewise, in West Bagamoyo, children, women and men members of poor
peasant families were all engaged in various forms of commodity
production to provide subsistence needs (IV:108-110). In rich
peasant families, on the other hand, Kirimbai (1981) found that only
women cultivated food for subsistence whereas the men engaged in

cattle-keeping and cultivation of grapes, tomatoes of other "cash" farm products geared solely to the market on the basis of hired labour.

Sexual Division of Labour

The issue of consumption relations is continually related to the sexual division of labour in the organisation of production and reproduction by women peasant informants. Labour time studies have documented the fact that the length of the working day for women is one and one-half to two times that of men, including domestic labour activities (cooking, toting water and firewood in particular) as well as directly productive activities (see section IV and Kirimbai 1981 for documentation of the significance of differential domestic labour times through labour time and other forms of research). Women peasants in certain areas have refused to contribute labour for village self-help activities or to adopt new technologies requiring additional labour inputs as a result. At issue is the greater labour demands made on women in combination with the appropriation of their labour product by husbands at household level and by village governments at village level.

Opposing Class and Gender Interests

The fact that food subsistence production and/or domestic labour is primarily women's work leads to problems of consciousness among poor peasant men. They do not recognise the centrality of the question of the organisation of the labour process of production and reproduction to their exploitation as a class because domestic labour and subsistence food production is so often women's work. Moreover it appears in their immediate interests to struggle to preserve the sexual division of labour. Women are more able to recognise the significance of this issue because of their immediate role in production and reproduction. Given the phenomenal forms of patriarchal ideology and practices, backed up by force like wife-beating, and of the real "appropriation" of female labour by men in consumption relations, women tend to "blame" men or husbands for their exploitation, however. This is referred to as "male colonisation" in Kagera and Bukoba, for example, and as "German-type male colonisation" in Dodoma.[2] What is difficult for women and men peasants to grasp is nearly impossible for many intellectual researchers to understand. This is revealed for example, in arguments about "articulation of modes of production" with the implication that precapitalist relations of production are being reproduced either at household level or within peasant production systems as a whole (I:7; II:28, 29; IV:106-108 for the household-level argument, and Hyden 1980 for the systems-level analysis; for a counter-argument, II:47). It is also revealed in the argument

---

2) This has been found by Zinat Bader (IV:86) for Bukoba, Magdalena Ngaiza for Kagera and Mary Kirimbai for Dodoma; the latter shared this information during discussions of the Peasants Sub-Group of the IDS Women's Study Group, September 1981.

that women's oppression is a "secondary" contradiction, separate from that of class exploitation, or in analyses of economic relations which ignore the organisation of reproduction and within that, the question of domestic labour. The lines being taken in villages over planning and implementing village infrastructure reveal the significance of class exploitation.

In Dodoma, Sachak (IV:125) found that women were demanding more labour-saving devices like flour melling machines. Given the fact that some women were acquiring income in cash or kind by pounding millet and other grains of other women, such machines might lead to a loss of income for poor peasants who would also be unable to pay for their use in any case. Provision of clean water sources near to residential areas is a fundamental demand of poor peasant women, more so than men who do not engage in water toting activity themselves (IV:108-111). Moreover women rich peasants or traders hire labour to tote water, for example in Dodoma (Kirimbai 1981) and West Bagamoyo and rich peasants or traders also organise the trade in water (IV:136). Hence, their interests are likely to be different from that of poor peasant women on the water issue.

Struggles over Land and the Product of Labour

The struggles taking place over allocation of land, labour and the labour product at village and household levels are particularly significant. The village act requires each village member, male or female, to be allocated separate plots of land and to cultivate crops which are designated in local village bye-laws. If practiced, this would contribute to a transformation of land tenure systems based on old precapitalist relations of production.

This is revealed for example in the way patriarchal relations have been reconstituted at the level of nuclear families or a much contracted extended family network. Whereas centuries ago, land was controlled and allocated to household or extended family heads by patriarch leaders of clans or feudal/semi-feudal chiefs, today land is owned by the state and allocated by the village government to village members. However, in many areas of the country, the practice of village government is to allocate land to male household heads, who then allocate land to wives and unmarried sons and daughters, as well as to young, newly married sons. Even where land is allocated on an individual basis, however, land usage continues to be organised in a patriarchal way (section IV).

Peasant women have historically struggled over the related questions of allocation of land and labour. In Lushoto during the colonial period, for example, women resisted the reallocation of land for export crops, on which food crops were formerly cultivated by women (IV:106). Post-independence settlement schemes in Morogoro partly failed because women peasants resisted the transformation of matrilineal land tenure systems into patrilineal systems (VI:88, 89). Women simply refused to cultivate as initially planned by the colonial government, and finally large numbers left the schemes and returned to their home areas to retain matrilineal rights to land and the product of their labour. Agricultural production organised on the basis of "family cooperation" collapsed without the necessary female labour. Another indication of resistance to patriarchal relations is the migration of youth from villages to urban centres (IV:108-111, 136; VIII:201, 215, 216, 228).

    The movement of women peasants out of patriarchically organised
production systems into wage labour of a temporary or permanent
nature has already been discussed. In Bukoba some women peasants
have accumulated capital on the basis of prostitution, and then
invested in land, coffee trees and hired labour, thereby establishing
themselves as "independent" middle to rich peasants in their own
right. These women household heads have all been formerly married,
but now reject patriarchal marriage as "male colonisation". They
may have permanent liasions with men, but retain their land and
houses and refuse to "marry" in a formal, "traditional" way. They
perceive themselves as liberated, compared to "enslaved" wives
(IV:86). In Morogoro, divorced women engage in beer brewing as a
means of subsistence (IV:96). The same has been found in Dodoma
(Kirimbai 1981) and Kilimanjaro (IV:91; V:153) where the "rich"
female beer brewers are able to accumulate on the basis of
exploitation of female hired labour. Differentiation is found in
beer brewing, as in cultivation and other forms of petty commodity
production. Poor peasant women and men supplement their incomes
and food subsistence by petty beer brewing and trade. Others,
usually women, hire their labour directly to rich beer brewers, or
produce in a putting out system of cottage industry organised again
by rich beer brewers or traders or pombe shop owners.
    In other villages, women peasants have protested at village
assemblies about the appropriation of their labour product by husbands
and the village government (IV:108-111). They have also refused to
contribute labour to village government construction projects,
claiming they are already over-burdened with work. Researchers have
concluded that women villagers are "excluded" form village production
activities (IV:134 in Mara, IV:128 in Bukoba), on the basis of
measurements of labour time inputs in household, and village
activities. It may well be, however, that the women refuse to
contribute labour to such activities, perhaps with the connivance of
husbands as well. Class and patriarchal contradictions can be seen
to converge here, at both women and men poor peasants resist
appropriation of the family labour product by the village government.
Struggles over crop choice in West Bagamoyo were engaged in by both
women and men poor peasants, who resisted forced cultivation of cotton
in preference to food crops. Similar struggles over cultivation of
coffee, cashew nuts and other export crops elsewhere and the resulting
falls in output reveal the widespread nature of this form of struggle.
Peasants explain their rejection of certain export crops as due to
relative falls in prices in combination with the generally worsening
terms of trade. Whatever the crop grown, the prices received can not
provide basic subsistence needs (IV:108-111).
    The recent rise in food prices may not lead to the expected rise
in marketed output, due to class differentiation among agricultural
producers and the patriarchal organisation of the labour process
itself. Poor peasants are not in the position to mobilise expanded
labour inputs necessary to produce more, because of the lack of the
capital needed to hire labour and the resistance of wives and youth
to patriarchal appropriation of the labour product. First priority
for poor peasant families as a whole will continue to be provision
of adequate food for family consumption, rather than reliance on the
market for food subsistence needs. Labour is a major constraint in
peasant production systems which is not understood by policies which
assume an unlimited and unproblematic supply of family labour. These

policies are usually based on farm systems or econometric analyses
which ignore the contradictory social relations underlying peasant
production systems (II:57; IV:133).

Crisis in Food and Health for the Poor

The prevalence of malnutrition and extremely high infant and child
mortality rates, especially amont peasants, is a significant indication of the growing incapacity of poor peasants as a class to
reproduce themselves. Areas like Handeni which were identified as
extremely rich in food surplus during the late 19th century now
experience recurrent severe famines. Inadequate food consumption is
a generalised phenomenon, as revealed in the 1977 aggregate figure
for average daily calorie supply per capita of 89 % of requirements
in 1977. Twenty-five per cent of all children aged 0 to 4 years
suffer from malnutrition (XIII:381), due to an absolute lack of
sufficient calorie food intake and not protein deficiency alone.
Malnutrition causes 50 % childhood deaths and also increases
vulnerability to other diseases like measles, malaria and infectious
diarrhea among children (XII:356, 381).

Tanzania, like other countries of Africa and the Third World, is
facing a food production crisis. Falls in food production as a
result of commoditisation and capitalist penetration in peasant
production systems have been identified by the Tanzania Food
Nutrition Centre as a major cause of the food crisis (XII:381). Low
birth weights have been found to be related not to maternal food
consumption as much as to high labour demands during pregnancy, even
if for only a short period of time (XI:268). Differential food intake of infants and children is related to indicators of class
position in the countryside and these are all associated with infant/
child mortality (XI:305). Studies of MCH clinics indicate that the
medicines needed for preventative treatment either are not stocked
in sufficient supply or are found in deteriorated conditions and
are likely to be ineffective (XII:367, 379, 380). The clinics are
also a long distance from most villagers, and 60 % of the 8,200
villages in the country lack any health facility at all. Despite
the fact that the vast majority of the people rely on rural health
centres, and dispensaries, these receive the smallest proportion of
medicines compared to urban hospitals. Tremendous disparities are
also found in allocation of hospital beds and doctor services. For
example, at a recent MCH evaluation preparatory workshop, it was
noted that there was only one doctor to 65,000 - 84,000 persons in
the countryside, compared to one doctor to 25,000 persons in urban
centres (reported in Daily News, September 4th, 1981). The recurrent
expenditure of one hospital seeing 137,000 out-patients a year
equals the recurrent expenditure of 53 dispensaries seeing a total
of 1,060,000 out-patients per year (Louda 1981:17). Despite the
glaring inequalities already existent in health services, more
large hospitals are being built, diverting funds from the health
services oriented to the masses.

Higher maternal mortality rates have been found for rural
medical centres as compared to Ocean Road Hospital in Dar es Salaam
(XI:275). The major cause of death is post-delivery bleeding,
often after home delivery. The majority of peasant women deliver
their infants at home, in the absence of modern trained midwives or

doctors (be they traditional midwives provided with upgrading in
skills and knowledge or "modern" nurses) and the necessary sanitary
and other conditions (XI: 275, XII:339).

Struggle for Survival

These health phenomena are not to be taken as given - they must be
problematised. We can learn from the struggles of poor peasant
women whose primary demand is for health centres or dispensaries to
be established in their villages and clean water sources near their
homes (for example, IV:108-111). The demand for dispensaries,
water and schools has been a major part of the politics of villagisation throughout the country. Their continual struggle to retain
land and labour for food production has already been noted. Anxiety
about the survival of their children is matched by their expectation
that a relatively large number will die. Fertility rates reflect
the reality of high infant mortality rates - poor peasants calculate
the number of births necessary in order that at least some children
may reach adulthood and take care of the parents in old age as well
as provide child labour in production beforehand. For example, in
Rungwe with a 30 % infant mortality rate (50 % greater than the   '
national average), peasants (women and men) calculated that if they
bore seven children, there was an 80 % likelihood that one son would
survive to when the father was sixty-five years of age. People's
calculations are probably not based on national averages, nor even
on local peasant averages. They are based on the worst possibilities
revealed in the experiences of other peasant families, where out of
ten children born, three survive; out of five children born, none
survives; out of twelve children, four survive (IV:108-111).
    The way high fertility rates and strategies to reduce them have
been isolated from other, more fundamental issues distorts the
objective reality of peasant (and working class) lives. The key
issue, as peasant women have clarified, is infant child mortality,
strategies for survival of children and the related question of
female labour intensification and exploitation. At the same time,
bearing and rearing many children does have a tremendous impact on
women's health and labour burden. This has led to women peasants'
demands for distribution of contraceptives to the villages so they
can control their own fertility (IV:119, 120).

Gender and Class Politics

Peasant women speak of their frustration over being excluded from
village government and exclusion from decision making at baraza/
village assembly level. As women in one village of West Bagamoyo
noted, "If we are called to a village baraza, there must be work to
do that day. If they are discussing money, we are not called"
(IV:108 - 110). They also point out that fear of wife beating and
public ridicule intimidates poor peasant women from speaking out at
village barazas. The husbands will be "shamed" by the "unfeminine"
behaviour of their wives, defined according to patriarchal
ideologies of female subordination. "Who are you to speak? You are
only a woman." Or "What do you know? How much education do you
have?" Patriarchal and bourgeois ideologies thereby divide poor
peasant women and men from joint political action which is in their
shared interests. Moreover, the class consciousness of men peasants

is blocked by their dominant position and the oppressive forms it
takes in family relations (the lack of female participation in
village government is widespread; see IV:102, 103, 119, 120, 128,
134).

The revolutionary potential of women poor peasants in particular
has usually been ignored by progressive analyses of the contradictions
in villagisation policies. During the early phase of "ujamaa"
villagisation, and pioneering collectivisation which preceded the
1967 policy in Ruvuma, women poor peasants were often the most
enthusiastic to join ujamaa villages and to work in collective
production systems (IV:102, 103, and Awiti 1972). Their own
explanation in Ismani was that for the first time they received
cash payment in exchange for their labour (Awiti 1972, and in seminar
discussion of his paper). Women organised collective day care
centres for their children on their own initiative (IV:102 and press
reports 1969, 1971). In Mbarika Ujamaa Village in Mwanza, the
villagers had even established "communal meals" one day per week,
where men and women for the first time ate together (though all the
women cooked the food which was then consumed collectively!) Women
perceived that joint militia training helped "to put women on an
equal footing with men," ("We Lead a Much Better Life Now" The
Nationalist, June 26, 1971). Women were also in favour of the
creation of village food stores which covered subsistence needs
during famine. During the contemporary phase of villagisation,
women peasants tend to favour investment of village funds into
collective village projects which will benefit the majority, rather
than their distribution to individuals (see items IV: 108-110; X:258).
Their struggles against patriarchal land usage systems and
consumption relations is a progressive position. It has also
contributed to a militant stand with respect to village government
appropriation of their labour or labour product, when it is perceived
to be against their interests.

The line taken by the UWT, The Prime Minister's Office and international agencies towards development and in particular the improvement
of peasant women's lives is the promotion of income-earning
activities like cooperative shops, poultry raising, beer brewing and
beer selling "clubs" (I:25; X:255, 262, 264). According to the UWT's
own evaluation as well as research by others, these "cooperative"
enterprises have been a failure. The reasons given are usually lack
of sufficient capital, inadequate skills and knowledge, and lack of
material support from government and parastatal agencies providing
credit, raw materials or other inputs (IV:90; VI:167, 170-173;
X:255). Programmes of education and funding have been mounted, but
failure continues. By paying attention to the issues raised by
women poor peasants themselves, which have been noted already, it is
possible to explain such failures and to identify the weaknesses in
the line adopted in the first place.

Under the conditions outlined above, such as a severe food
crisis and worsening terms of trade, poor peasant women will refuse
to withdraw labour from food production oriented to family subsistence needs unless returns are absolutely assured and cover
subsistence needs. Given the way female cash proceeds are either
appropriated by the husband or are totally spent on family subsistence
needs, married poor peasant women do not benefit themselves from
increased cash earnings, and therefore lack incentive to increase

their earnings above the level necessary for family subsistence.

One of the major explanations for failure of UWT, and other women's cooperatives is attributed to lack of adequate capital. Women members of the poor peasant class do not have such financial resources, and are thereby blocked from participation (IV:119, 120). The petty bourgeois nature of such cooperatives was brought out in Bader's research in Bukoba (IV:86), where poor peasant women explained that they lacked the money to join UWT cooperatives and the organisation itself. Moreover, they said they would not be welcomed in the local branch, which was dominated by rich peasant and traders' wives and local school teachers who despised them for their manners, dress and lack of education.

Chale and Ngonyani found that women's cooperatives in rural (and urban) areas were often organised in an exploitative way (VI:165). They were controlled by women rich peasants and others who hired the labour of poor peasant women. Wages tended to be far below government minimum wages, with the justification that the often younger members are learning a new skill from the employers (VII:201). The "co-operative ideology" also distorts the true nature of the commercial enterprises like shops and pombe clubs which are owned by women rich peasants or traders and not by all the women of the village (IV:94; VI:165; X:254). Exploitative relations underlying the cooperative activities are likely to be a major cause of failure.

To what extent has UWT succeeded in identifying with the class interests of poor peasant (and working class) women? It is essential to pay attention when large numbers of women poor peasants (or workers) say that UWT is "not useful" or is "a waste of time", as recently found in a survey of eight Morogoro villages (IV:119, 120). The reasons for joining UWT are also revealing: "to discuss problems with other women" and to better "women's conditions" were the most common replies. The usefulness of UWT includes (in order) learning family planning techniques and child care, women getting the opportunity to express themselves, "to fight shyness", learning household skills, training female leaders and helping women to organize themselves. Earning money was mentioned very rarely by women. In comparison, male peasants gave only two major advantages of UWT: teaching household skills and earning money. Not one man mentioned any of the uses related to women's organisation to raise their position noted above. Poor peasant women on the other hand clearly wanted a women's organisation which defined its task as the mass mobilisation of women, and not the creation of money-earning activities.

Struggles of poor peasant women are ultimately directed to fundamental social transformation of exploitative capitalist relations and oppressive patriarchal relations. This has also been found to be true of women workers' struggles. These struggles can be compared to the principal aims of the Party, which include the building of socialism (number 2); the right to effective participation in political practices and freedom of expression (number 8); "to safeguard, develop and perpetuate the revolutionary spirit among Tanzanians" (number 10); "to ensure that the wealth of our nation is used for the development of the people, particularly for the elimination of poverty, ignorance and disease (number 14); to eradicate "injustice", intimidation, racial discrimination, corruption, oppression or favouritism" (number 16); "to continue to fight against colonialism, neo-colonialism, imperialism and all kinds of discrimination" (number 17), including we would add, sexual discrimination.

Following the aims of CCM, and the struggles of women workers and poor peasants, the correct line of a socialist women's movement would necessarily be women's emancipation (not merely "improvement" or "development"), in the context of class struggles against capitalist exploitation and patriarchal oppression at every level, which is at the same time a struggle for socialist transformation.

IV. STRUGGLES IN THE CONCEPTUALISATION OF "WOMEN" AS A PROBLEM OF
ANALYSIS AND ACTION

Fundamentally different positions have occurred in the way that women
have been posed as a problem in research as well as in other social
practices such as programmes and projects of the state and international agencies. These positions reflect different class interests,
and have developed in response to struggles of different classes of
women themselves. The tremendous amount of attention given in the
last decade to "women" as an isolated category requires a substantive
critique, only the bare outlines of which are presented here.

Women as a Residual Category

During the colonial and the immediate post-colonial periods, women
were not posed as a "problem" requiring separate analysis or action
in a concerted way. Colonial state functionaries, including
anthropologists, state officials, and missionaries investigated the
patterns of "kinship" and chief or headmen relations in the supposed
"traditional" form as well as changes taking place during the
colonisation period. Some of the problems identified as crucial areas
included marital instability and adultery (of women), residence
patterns in urban centres, conditions of work on sisal plantations,
polygamous and monogamous tendencies in marriage, prostitution,
bridewealth, the middle school leaver problem and youth migration to
towns, social "disequilibrium" caused by male participation in
migrant labour or the imperialist wars, etc.

These research topics were oriented to the crucial problems of
colonial conquest, labour, and the contradictory consequences of the
subjugation of precapitalist relations to capital faced by the
colonial state and agricultural, commercial capitals situated in the
territory (see Mbilinyi, Vuorela, Kassam and Masisi 1979 and Vuorela
1981).

With respect to state practices, women were identified (if at all)
as a separate social category only as mothers or as potential wives
for educated or christianized men. A few domestic science programmes
trained women with great emphasis on child care, and they also included modern (or western) cooking, embroidery and housekeeping.
Women were excluded from agricultural extension education programmes
or training in industrial skills.

After Independence, problems of establishing the post-colonial
state and the hegemony of the new ruling class were reflected in
research on voting behaviour in elections, the schooling system,
tribalism and national unity, the economic psychology of peasants,
the agricultural extension services and settlement schemes. A
substantive critical examination of the form and content of research
in the social sciences during the post-independence period has not
been carried out to our knowledge, nor are we in a position to do so.
Rather we will focus attention on the development of research about
women posed as an isolated category of analysis - see relevant
sections of the book, from which our conclusions are drawn.

Women as a Problem

By the end of the 1960s there was growing concern in the government
about the nonenrolment of girls in school, school girls' pregnances.
the migration of girls and women (as well as boys and men) to towns,
prostitution, and sexual promiscuity among girls and women. Beginning
in the late 1960s, papers began to be produced on "the status" or
"role" of women. These were discriptive, positivist analyses,
typical of the dominant trend in the social sciences. Generalisations
were often made about all women, thus ignoring class differentiation
as well as the concretely different conditions of existence of
peasant women situated in different areas. Studies going beyond
the "role" question examined differential access of girls and women
to schooling education, later to wage employment, to agricultural
extension education, as well as the technical division of labour by
sex in farm practices and rural economic activities, and sexist
attitudes towards women. Such research was partly a result of
government concern (in the case of female schooling opportunities,
for example), as well as the increasing "fundability" of "women's"
research.

International and other funding agencies began to place a
special interest in women's research by the mid-1970s. This has
usually been related either to population issues or to the agricultural production crisis. In the 1970s, the villagisation
programme, falling levels of agricultural and industrial productivity,
worsening terms of trade on an international and national level, and
deterioration in the conditions of existence of peasants in
particular contributed to the growing concern about peasant production systems and the politics of villagisation. The major source
of state revenue remains peasant production; hence the importance
given to this problem area. Currently the state is engaged in an
effort to rationalise the organisation of production in agriculture
and industry and to increase production output as well as
productivity.

Women peasants as producers and reproducers have been identified
as a problem by the international agencies and by the state. Although
a gross simplification, one could say the problem is how to get
peasant women to grow more of the right kinds of crops (food and
export crops) and to produce fewer children. This is revealed, for
example, in the promotion of women's income-earning projects, which
lead to intensification of female labour in the production of "cheap"
products.

The growing interest in the "problem" of women is in part a
response to the struggles of poor peasant and working class women
analysed in the preceding section. Stagnation in peasant production
has many causes, but the primary one is resistance of peasant
producers (women and men) to coercive mechanisms of organising the
peasant process, diverting production from food to export crops, and
appropriating the labour product. Control of female peasant labour
in production and domestic labour is vital for capital in order to
ensure adequate food production and to "free" male labour for other
economic activities including small-scale industries as well as
export crop production.

Female domestic labour is also necessary for the cheap reproduction of working class households. Female resistance to patriarchal

marriage forms therefore becomes a threat to capital itself. At the same time, women represent a source of cheap labour in industry, and in commodity agricultural production as cash crop producers. Capitalist penetration has therefore had contradictory consequences, in that the transformation of women into commodity producers or into wage labourers has undermined the patriarchal organisation of reproduction. Much of the research referred to in this book focuses on problem areas reflecting these contradictions.

Women Studies

Research on women as a distinctive category has clearly not been restricted to only one or two concerns. Nevertheless, there are commonalities in the way the problems have been posed, rooted as they usually are in descriptive, positivistic research. As a result, there is a great deal of important information which documents the oppression of women. The valuable contribution of most of this research and/or analysis cannot be denied. The fundamental weakness of such work, however, is its inability to explain why and how women are oppressed and exploited as a function of their sex, through what mechanisms, and according to what differences for different classes of women.

The adoption of positivist, non-explanatory research methodology ultimately represents a bourgeois ideological position. An important feature of the conditions of production of knowledge about women is the increasing numbers of female university graduates and postgraduates, and women scientists, lawyers, writers, etc., at the University, in government or other positions. Although male social scientists have contributed to the investigation of women directly or indirectly, in the last few years such studies have been dominated by women. In posing the question, their work has often reflected their own personal and professional struggles as members of the petty bourgeoisie. These struggles are not to be discounted – sex stereotyping in education, in mass media, in drama; sex discrimination at work; the double burden of paid and unpaid work, lessened in their case by paid house help; access to further educational and professional opportunities. However, they do arise from a particular class position. A conscious effort has to be made to critique the way problems are posed and investigated, in order to clarify the class interests reflected. This is not a problem peculiar to investigators of the question of women, but to all social scientists, government and party officials and others, be it about education, villagisation, industrialisation strategy, or cognitive development and testing.

An alternative approach to the question of women has begun to gain ground since the late 1970s. The problem posed is not that of women or men per se, bur rather the social relations of production and reproduction which combine to oppress and exploit particular classes of women. The development of historical materialist analysis is partly a result of the debates surrounding the concrete social struggle which led to the Arusha Declaration in the late 1960s and heightened during the current economic crisis which began in the mid-1970s. Learning from the concrete struggles of peasant and working class women has been particularly crucial in clarifying the questions to be posed and the way to pose them. Women are not investigated as a distinctive category of analysis. Instead, the problem is that of the changing combination of class and gender relations and struggles in the context of the subjugation of pre-capitalist relations to capitalist relations and the development of different forms of capital-labour relations. Questions of reproduction, including biological reproduction and domestic labour, and women's oppression are inserted as fundamental to the analysis of social relations of production. It then becomes possible to under-stand such phenomena as the changing sexual division of labour in the production process, the differential positions women and men have in production and reproduction and patriarchal ideologies of male superiority and female inferiority. The way women's oppression objectively divides the working class and the poor peasants, and inhibits the development of class consciousness necessary to struggle against capitalism and for socialism becomes clear.

Clarity about the correct position to take concerning the question of women is partly the result of continual struggles surrounding whether it should be posed at all, and how to pose it. One position taken on these questions is that the issue of women's oppression and/or emancipation is "foreign" and irrelevant to the real existence of peasant women. To paraphrase one speaker at the Education Department Seminar (1981) where Sumra presented a paper on population policies and women's oppression (XI:309), "Why are people having to follow these foreign ideas? Our mothers in the villages are perfectly happy. The problem is that our educated women get these ideas from books or travel." Such criticisms also reflect the kinds of issues which are being raised by some of the bourgeois positions on the women's question. For example, petty bourgeois women's struggles to get access to the credit necessary to establish capitalistic commercial or production enterprises do not reflect the interests of poor peasant and working class women.

There is also a tendency to ignore the question of women's oppression, or to laugh it off as non-existent. The laughter often reveals a tremendous amount of personal anxiety aroused when questioning social relations having to do with the organisation of reproduction in the family, as well as production per se. Ideologies about male superiority have been internalised by women and men alike. To question ideologies of male dominance appears to question the very basis of existence. A third position found among leftist progressive intellectuals is the argument that women's oppression is a separate issue from that of capitalist exploitation, and represents a secondary contradiction to be resolved after the primary contradiction of capitalist exploitation has been resolved by the establishment of a socialist state. Alternatively, the position is taken that by posing the question of women's oppression, "class is substituted for by sex".

These positions do not grasp that women's oppression is an integral part of class relations and class struggles, an aspect therefore of the primary contradiction of capitalist exploitation. The relationship between the organisation of domestic labour and biological reproduction and class exploitation has also not been understood. Social relations in the family are therefore considered irrelevant to class struggle, due to the inability to grasp the reality underlying the phenomenal forms of the "privacy" of the family and the reproductive and ideological functions situated there.

There is also a tendency to reduce women's oppression to being an
ideological problem without perceiving the way women and men are
allocated in objectively different ways in the relations of production and reproduction.

The inability to grasp the objective reality of sexual divisions
lead our leftist critics to argue that the analysis of women's
oppression, and struggles around the question, will divide the
progressive forces in their struggles against capitalism. The
counter-argument is clearly that the progressive forces are
objectively divided along sexual and other lines, that capital has
contributed to the creation and reproduction of these divisions, and
that struggles against women's oppression are a part of the struggles
against capitalism. The question of women's oppression is a class
question.

The lack of clarity on the question of women's oppression has
also led to the inability to grasp the revolutionary potential of
peasant and working class women. Intellectuals divorced from political action do not perceive the significance of the question of women's
oppression in part because they are not forced to do so in the context
of political organisation of the masses. Samora Machel expressed the
argument in a clear and forceful way during the period of Frelimo's
national liberation struggle in Mozambique:

> The emancipation of women is not an act of charity, the result
> of a humanitarian or compassionate attitude. The liberation of
> women is a fundamental necessity for the Revolution, the
> guarantee of its continuity and the precondition for its victory.
> The main objective of the Revolution is to destroy the system of
> exploitation and build a new society which releases the
> potentialities of human beings, reconciling them with labour and
> with nature. This is the context within which the question of
> women's emancipation arises.

> Generally speaking, women are the most oppressed, humiliated
> and exploited beings in society, a woman is even exploited by
> a man who is himself exploited, beaten by the man who is
> lacerated by the palmatoria, humiliated by the man who is crushed
> under the boot of the boss and the settler.

> How can the Revolution triumph without the liberation of women?
> Will it be possible to get rid of the system of exploitation
> while keeping one part of society exploited? One cannot only
> partially wipe out exploitation and oppression, one cannot tear
> up only half the weeds without even stronger ones spreading out
> from the half that has survived.

> How then can one make a revolution without mobilising women?
> If more than half the exploited and oppressed people consist of
> women, how can they be left on the fringe of the struggle? To
> make a revolution it is necessary to mobilise all the exploited
> and oppressed, and consequently women as well. If it is to be
> victorious, the Revolution must eliminate the whole system of
> exploitation and oppression, liberating all the exploited and
> the oppressed. Therefore it must eliminate the exploitation and
> oppression of women, it is forced to liberate women.
> (Machel 1974:24).

40

Tanzania has arrived at a crucial conjuncture in its history. Class struggles are intensifying between finance capital (particularly in the form of World Bank and IMF), and the state and the masses on the one hand; and between the state and the poor peasants and workers on the other hand. Major contradictions have emerged in the state between those taking a "socialist line" towards strategies of development and those taking a "capitalist line". The capitalist liners are promoting the strategy of developing the productive forces at any cost, of increasing productivity and total output in agriculture and industry through the most efficient and quickest means possible. This has led to the official encouragement of capitalist agriculture, for example, and the orientation of financial credit systems to rich peasants, state farms and large-scale capitalist farmers. There is also strong pressure to resolve the question of worker discipline in a bourgeois, capitalist way. Villagisation has been shifted from its earlier direction of collectivisation in production and reproduction, and is now directed towards individualisation in block farming. Development based on technique has taken command, rather than development based on mass mobilisation in the struggle to transform exploitative social relations of production. Modernisation has taken the place of revolution.

The World Bank and IMF have intensified their demands that the state take the line of modernisation. The increasing financial debt of the state to these and other financial institutions is being manipulated to try and force the state to submit to their demands. Clearly there is a strong basis of support for the World Bank/IMF position among certain politicians and bureaucrats. At the same time, there is opposition among others who remain committed to a "socialist line" of struggle and transformation. (See the July 7, 1981 speech of President Nyerere).

These struggles must be perceived from the class position of the workers and poor peasants, the "exploited", "disregarded" and "oppressed". A correct stand with respect to the question of revolution or modernisation is inseparably related to a correct stand with respect to the question of women's oppression.

REFERENCES

Adhu Awiti (1972), "Economic Differentiation in Ismani, Iringa Region: A Critical Assessment of Peasants' Response to the Ujamaa Vijijini Programme." Dar es Salaam, E.R.B. Seminar Paper, University of Dar es Salaam.

Chama cha Mapinduzi (CCM) (n.d.), Constitution. Dar es Salaam, Tanganyika Standard (Newspapers).

Carmen Diana Deere and Magdalena Leon de Leal (1979), "Measuring Rural Women's Work and Class Position". Studies in Family Planning Special Issue: Learning About Rural Women edited by Sondra Zeidenstein. Vol. 10 No. 11/12 (November/December): 370-374.

Göran Hydén (1980), Beyond Ujamaa in Tanzania. Berkeley, University of California Press.

Mary Kirimbai (1981), "The Impact of Domestic Water Supply Projects on the Rural Population and their Role in Production and Reproduction in Dodoma Rural District". University of Dar es Salaam, unpublished M.A. Dissertation (This work was completed after finishing our annotations; it provides a detailed analysis of the different sexual divisions of labour found in poor peasant and rich peasant households, and the substitution of hired labour for women's labour in production and reproduction).

Tony Klouda (1981), "Prevention is More Expensive than Cure - Review of Tanzania's Problems in Health 1971 - 1981". Dar es Salaam, Oxfam Medical Adviser, mimeo.

Samora Machel (1974), "The Liberation of Women is a Fundamental Necessity for the Revolution" in Mozambique Sowing the Seeds of Revolution. London, Committee for Freedom in Mozambique, Angola and Guinea.

Marjorie Mbilinyi (1974), "The Transition to Capitalism in Rural Tanzania". University of Dar es Salaam, E.R.B., Paper 74.7.

Marjorie Mbilinyo, Ulla Vuorela, Yusuf Kassam and Johana Masisi (1979), "The Politics of Research Methodology in the Social Sciences". Paper presented to 1979 Participatory Research Network of African Region, Mzumbe.

Julius K. Nyerere (1967), Socialism and Rural Development. Dar es Salaam, Printpak Tanzania Limited.

Julius K. Nyerere, 1968 (1967), "Socialism and Rural Development", in Ujamaa, Essays on Socialism. Nairobi, Oxford University Press.

Julius K. Nyerere (1975), "President Nyerere's Speech in Parliament, 18th July, 1975". Dar es Salaam, Tanzania Information Services.

Julius K. Nyerere (1977), "The Arusha Declaration, Ten Years After". Dar es Salaam, The Government Printer.

Julius K. Nyerere (1981), "July 7th Speech". Broadcast on Radio Tanzania and summarized in the Daily News and Uhuru.

Tanganyika African National Union (1971), "TANU Party Guidelines, Mwongozo wa TANU". University of Dar es Salaam, Institute of Development Studies, translation into English of "Mwongozo".

Ulla Vuorela (1981), "Participant Observation in Colonial Tanganyika". Paper tabled at IDS Regional Workshop on Research Methodology, Usa River, March 30 - April 11.

PART TWO

WRITINGS ON THE QUESTION OF WOMEN

I.   APPROACHES TO THE ANALYSIS OF WOMEN'S OPPRESSION

In this section we have mainly included materials which illustrate
the different positions being taken on the women's question in
other African countries, in the third world and in international
agencies which focus much of their attention on "developing
countries", including Tanzania. These have been necessarily
restricted in number, given the major emphasis of this book on
Tanzania.
      The major issues raised in the texts concern the changing
sexual division of labour in production and reproduction; the
way in which women are specifically situated in the labour force
as peasant producers or as wage-earners; the international division of labour and methodological questions concerning research
on these issues.

Sexual Division of Labour

Historically women in Africa have contributed a major proportion
of total labour input into agricultural production, as well as
into the maintenance of the household or broader community. Jean
Henn's work indicates that the sexual division of labour in agricultural production was not the same all over pre-colonial Africa
(I:8) and varied according to a combination of factors. These
included the nature of precapitalist production relations (for
example: lineage-based patriarchal relations, semi-feudal and
feudal relations); the specific forces of production dominant
at any given time; ecological conditions and political and
ideological relations which were closely combined with economic
relations. Hence, the impossibility of generalising about "women
in Africa", especially when focusing on the pre-colonial period
consisting of centuries of social transformation (see also I:10).
      Analyses of the sexual division of labour in contemporary
peasant production systems, in organised industrial production
and in the informal sector indicate that women represent a cheap
labour supply throughout Africa. Moreover, the unpaid work which
women do in the home and in the fields contributes to the
cheapening of the value of labour/labour power. Wages do not
cover the costs of maintaining families, nor do peasant prices
(I:7, 9, 17, 22, 24 for different approaches to this problem).

Women in Wage Labour and Peasant Production

Women in general have been found to have the lowest paid work
in industry, which tend to be unskilled manual, "dirty" work.
They represent a large proportion of temporary workers, not
covered by most worker benefits and not protected by "right to
work" laws (for example, I:5, 9, 10 and sections which follow).
      In capitalist agriculture production, women agricultural
labourers again are relegated to low paying, unskilled work.
Women peasants provide unpaid labour in the production of cash
crops, which is usually not "counted" by statisticians and
economists or is categorised as "unpaid family labour" (I:3,
11, 15, 24).

The International Division of Labour

The process of the internationalisation of capital and labour allows us to explain the development of multinational export industries in third world countries. Labour intensive textile, leather and electronics industries have moved in search of cheap labour supplies, and this has often meant migrant women (I:5). The interests of capitalist agri-business in creating a market for fertilisers, insecticides and hybrid seeds, as well as food, in third world countries partly explains World Bank policies towards Tanzania (I:25) in line with the Bank programme expressed, for example in its World Development Report 1980. The concept of comparative advantage permeates the analysis of the problems and strategies of development in the 1980s. It is argued that developing countries have a comparative advantage in the promotion of export manufactures and primary processing industry rather than in basic industry and export of unprocessed primary goods. The concept of comparative advantage takes as given the structure of the world market and the international division of labour, and is used to justify policies which would tend to adapt developing countries' economies to that structure.

The emphasis on trade and production for export as the means of development in fact encourages a pattern of ever-increasing dependence of developing countries on the world market and subordination of their economies to the demands of monopoly capital. Developing countries are not in a competitive position within the capitalist world market, nor can they build up an independent economic base within it. The specific policies which the World Bank promotes are generally against the interests of the developing countries as a whole, and in particular, against the interests of peasants and workers. For example, promotion of export crops rather than food crops would be suicidal under present conditions. The major supplier of food on the world market is the United States. The American government uses food as an international weapon. The refusal of that government to supply food to Mozambique in 1981 is a recent example of what could happen to Tanzania. The liberalisation of import-export controls and opening up the economy to foreign capitalist investment would lead to a complete "surrender" of the economy to monopoly capital situated outside of the country. Reduction of investments in schools and medical services would really mean their virtual closure, since they are already operating at extremely low costs. Moreover, adoption of such policies would lead to even more impoverishment among the masses, delegitimisation of progressive regimes like Tanzania, and political turmoil. Hence underlying the appearance of the World Bank as being a multilateral financial institution is the reality that it is a political institution serving the interests of monopoly capital, and in particular that of the United States.

The "soft line" of the World Bank, which is also presented in the report, emphasises the need to reduce poverty and to promote human development defined as health, nutrition, education and fertility. All four aspects of human development are shown to have had little progress. The relationship between increased penetration of capitalism and increased poverty, revealed in such

indicators as high malnutrition, high infant and child mortality
rates, high fertility rates and low quality schooling is totally
ignored. Rather, psychological and sociological explanations
are given, often "blaming" the ignorance of the poor, leading to
reformist and technicist solutions, such as the increased adoption
of pesticides to combat malaria (the pesticides produced by
multinational corporations, needless to say). The overwhelming
concern of the report seems to be population growth in developing
countries. Population growth is related not only to poverty but
also to the possibility given to the adoption of population
control measures to reduce the population, without relating
fertility rates to such problems as high infant mortality rates
and the reliance of smallholder peasant producers on children's
labour in production. Women are rarely mentioned in the whole
report, despite the significance of analysing the place of women
in small-scale peasant production particularly as food producers,
and in relation to issues of education, health, nutrition and
fertility. In one place, women are incorrectly referred to as
"the dependent poor" like children and the aged. This distorts
the role of the majority of women in developing countries as
peasant producers or as members of the working class.

The statistical indicators in the Annex include vital
statistics on Tanzania, such as infant mortality rates, education
with male-female breakdowns, nutrition levels, fertility rates,
male-female employment figures and so on. The World Bank represents one of the most powerful centres of research in the world,
with access to confidential sources of data as well as a large
group of researchers in its employ on a full-time or part-time
basis. While critical of the overall methodology underlying
World Bank analysis and policies, critics are dependent on its
source of data, which are often more up-to-date than what is
publicly available within the developing countries themselves.

The World Bank is extremely powerful in directing economic
and political practices worldwide and within developing countries
in particular. Its focus has in fact become the "absolute poor"
nations, one of which is Tanzania, and within them, the poorest
classes, poor peasants, workers and unemployed urban dwellers.
Tanzania has become a "test case" in the struggle of power
between monopoly capital, whose interests the World Bank is serving,
and progressive governments.

Problems of women peasants and workers in any one country
are related to the international division of labour. This
underlies the debate concerning the "New International Economic
Order" being discussed in the United Nations, and elsewhere
(I:9, 17, 22). The World Conference on the United Nation's
Decade for Women has successfully lobbied to insert the women's
question into developmental programmes and strategies. In this
process, a great deal of research has been generated on women
and work around the world. Moreover, it has been found that one
- third of the world's families are headed by women, not men,
indicating major changes in the organisation of families and
reproduction overall. Such analysis has called for technological
developments which lead to labour - saving machinery in agriculture production and post - harvest food transport, processing
and storage, as well as in cooking, water provision and energy

sources (I:11, 23). The fact that women are the major food producers in Africa has been highlighted in the effort to clarify problems in analysis and action thus far concerning the international food crisis. The concept of the "invisibility" of women's role in production and reproduction is often identified as the problem (I:13, 25). If this is the major problem, then the solution obviously becomes one of research and education to inform policy-makers about the important contribution of women in production.

This emphasis on visibility - invisibility is misplaced. It tends to mask the reality of exploitation and oppression underlying the way women enter into the labour force. For example, in Tanzania "everybody knows" that women cook, care for children, farm, milk cows, and/or work for wages. What is not clearly understood is the significant contribution such work makes to the cheapening of the value of labour power in wage earning or labour in peasant production - that is, to the cheapening of wages, producer prices and other sources of subsistence. To explore the latter issue means to investigate the underlying relations of production dominated by the capitalist relations. It has already been pointed out that multinational corporations are moving to African countries in search of cheap labour. Women represent the cheapest source of labour, not only in Africa, but worldwide. A major obstacle to women's movement into wage labour or into production of crops and other commodities for the capitalist market has been the combination of patriarchal relations and the "traditional" sexual division of labour. It is in capital's interests to "free" women from at least certain elements of patriarchal relations which confine them to the home or restrict their participation in schooling and occupations, or block their "independent" production of commodities. Moreover, the subsistence character of peasant household production which is primarily based on peasant women's labour input must be destroyed. As peasants become increasingly dependent on the market for subsistence and producer goods and services, they will be forced to produce more and more commodities for the market or else sell their labour/labour power. The process of destruction of subsistence production and reproduction is a dynamic aspect of the commoditisation of peasant production and reproduction and the creation of a massive surplus population, a potential industrial reserve army.

It is clearly in the interests of women to destroy patriarchal relations. But the contradictory dynamics of the process of social transformation being experienced in Africa today must be examined and appropriate strategies for action developed. Otherwise, social change will mean "freeing" women from subordination to a patriarchal household head only to be subordinated to capitalist and state owners of factories and farms. Moreover, certain aspects of patriarchal relations are not under attack, which contribute to mechanisms of social control not only of women, but of children and youth (see following sections).

Research Methodology

At least eight works included in this section focus on methodological issues in research concerning women (I:3, 5, 7, 10, 14,
15, 24). These issues go beyond mere questions of technique to
argue for particular ways of formulating the problem of women as
producers and reproducers, situated in a context of social
transformation. For example, Ulrike Von Buchwald and Ingrid
Palmer (I:3) stress the analysis of the different modes of production in which women are situated, and class formation
processes as they effect women. The dynamics of the international division of labour are stressed as a fundamental aspect
of the exploitation of women peasants and workers in several of
the works in this and the next section. The international
division of labour within research itself is becoming another
site of struggle (I:5, 16). The posing of these issues clarifies
the need for the further development of theory capable of explaining the processes of exploitation and oppression of women.
Descriptive research is not adequate to this task.

The need for both in-depth "micro-level" research and
statistical analyses of specific aspects of the problem of women
in production and reproduction is stressed (I:3). The significance of labour time and household consumption surveys in
quantifying the exploitation of peasant women is discussed by
Jeanne Henn (I:7). Her own research in Cameroon provides
a concrete example of such analysis (Henn 1978). Specific
research topics are provided in I:3, 5, 10, 14 and 24. The
Kenyan Government's statistical survey of educational trends
(I:6) illustrates the kind of statistical analyses needed to
clarify the differential allocation of resources like education,
medical services and social welfare to women and men. Ngwangwa
Shield's analysis of women in wage labour in Tanzania exemplifies
the kind of data necessary to clarify the segmented nature of the
labour force (V:158).

The issue of the distribution of knowledge produced by
researchers is raised in the report of the IDS (Sussex) Conference
on the Subordination of Women (I:5). This includes the question
of language and format of presentation, as well as feedback
mechanisms to the women (and men) included in research or affected
by the research outcomes. The production of small pamphlets and
other materials written in a simple, straight-forward manner and
directed to peasants and workers is one recommendation. Participatory research promotes the full participation of peasants and
workers in the research process itself, combined with political
organisation to promote their interests. Examples of participatory research are found in later sections, and is critically
analysed in the "Conclusions and Recommendations" of the IDS
Regional Workshop on Research Methodology. Such research is
situated within a historical materialist framework, and focuses
on concrete realities in specific countries, situated within the
wider worldwide context. Choices as to what kind of research to
engage in, and the manner of presentation and distribution of its
products, are political ones with definite personal consequences.
The issue of who does research posed in I:15 and 16 thereby
becomes in whose interests does one do research. The answer partly
will be revealed in the concrete practices adopted by the researcher.

REFERENCES

Jeanne Koopmen Henn (1978), Peasants Workers and Capital: The Political Economy of Labour and Incomes in Cameroon. Harvard University, unpublished Ph. D. dissertation.

IDS Regional Workshop on Research Methodology (1981), "Conclusions and Recommendations". Presented in the Summary Report of the above workshop held in Usa River, Arusha, March 30th - April 1981, University of Dar es Salaam, IDS Task Force.

----

1. AFRICA REPORT (1981), "Statistics on African Women" 26 (2) March-April: pp. 65-66, taken from Population Reference Bureau, Inc., "Women's Data Sheet", Washington D.C.

Provides basic demographic statistics on women in Tanzania, as well as other African countries. For example, forty-five per cent of Tanzanian women 15-19 years are married, compared to 34 % in Kenya and 32 % in Eastern Africa as a whole. The proportion of men and women living in urban areas is nearly the same, 10 % of the male population and 9 % of the female (1975).

2. BAUMANN, HERMAN (1928), "The Division of Work According to Sex in African Hoe Culture". Africa, I (3): 289-319.

Argues that hoe culture was first discovered by women, as a means of living a settled life. The men grew dependent on the produce of the women and gradually came to be legally and socially at a disadvantage. This became the basis for matriarchial societies. Introduction of the plough, draught animals and cash crops banished the women from control of cultivation of the fields to a little garden in front of her home. The new development was clearly associated with the development of patriarchial societies where the inheritance of land by the eldest son was the key feature.

3. BUCHWALD, ULRIKE Von and INGRID PALMER (1978), Monitoring Changes in the Conditions of Women - A Critical Review of Possible Approaches. Geneva, UNRISD, 94 pp.

The monograph is concerned with the methodology to be used in setting up national monitoring systems to monitor changes in women's conditions. The literature is surveyed on such issues as the impact on women and men of changes in agriculture production as a result of colonialisation and economic dependency; the patterns of industrialization and urbanization; and women's place in the social structure and production system. The limitations of current data and basic information usually used to study changes in women's conditions are explored, with emphasis on statistics on economic activities, education and training and health and nutrition. Alternative approaches and methodology which could be adopted are discussed, including the need for a balance between the use of aggregate statistics and special survey material. The argument for a monitoring service which regularly collects and evaluates pertinent data and information on women is given in the conclusion. UNRISD is engaged in developing preliminary research on monitoring changes in the conditions of women as one step in that direction. It is necessary to get beyond mere description of conditions to study the actual causes of such conditions and the impact of particular interventions. This reveals the need for basic and often micro-level research. The sample questions suggested as a possible "core" of monitoring efforts are given below:

"1. In which modes of production do women emerge via the impact of migration and unemployment when agriculture is passing through a technological revolution and urban areas are rapidly modernizing their production relations?

2. Are economic and occupational changes causing greater stratification of classes, reducing previous equality which existed among women under traditional economic patterns?

3. In which way do customary decision-making and division of labour within the domestic unit alter with developments in the economic roles of the sexes?

4. What elements of traditional culture have a detrimental effect on women's status in the modernizing sector?

5. What are the relationships between several sets of observable data (e.g. fertility, labour force participation, education) if examined on a class basis?"

The monograph is very valuable both to practitioners developing a critical attitude towards the statistics and other data concerning women which they use, and researchers engaged in producing meaningful material about and for women.

4. GOODY, J. and BUCKLEY, JOAN (1973), "Inheritance and Women's Labour in Africa", Africa, 43 (2): 108-121.

In Africa women play a "dominant" role in agriculture in terms of labour input, particularly in systems of hoe agriculture. The dominant role of women is most clearly seen in the Congo, East, Central and South Africa. In spite of their dominance in production, agriculture land was by and large in the hands of men. This has considerable repercussions on the types of economy, inheritance and descent. Woman's dominant role in agriculture is linked with two types of inheritance: firstly matrilineal and secondly with the form of vertical inheritance that Gluckman has called house-property complex found mostly in patrilineal and sometimes in bilateral societies. It divides male property among children on the basis of their maternal origin. In agricultural societies it gives to a woman's sons the land she has cultivated but can neither possess nor transmit. It is also found in pastoral societies where women play a part in tending or milking cattle. "The house-property complex there-fore constitutes a kind of social recognition of a woman's major role in the process of production though she is excluded from ownership of production themselves". Gluckman's concept of a house-property complex seems similar to Rigby's (forthcoming) concept of "matricentrality" in pastoralist groups.

5. IDS BULLETIN (1979), <u>Special Issue on the Continuing Subordination of Women in the Development Process</u>, Vol. 10 (3). Brighton, Institute of Development Studies, University of Sussex, 67 pp.

This is a report of the IDS Conference on the Continuing Subordination of Women in the Development Process organised by members of the Subordination of Women Workshop under the leadership of Kate Young. The report presents the conference resolution on a woman political prisoner, a Puerto Rican nationalist imprisoned by the United States Government, together with recommendations and research guidelines. The recommendations argue that research must be clearly situated in the context of theoretical analysis of the nature of development itself and the structures which maintain and reinforce class domination and gender "asymmetry". The need for an information network between those engaged in studies of women subordination is stressed, as well as closer contact between researchers and local women's groups, women's research groups and trade unions. Joint research and comparative research is needed, based on interdisciplinary work. All research project budgets should include money for translating the final report into the main language of the area in which the research project was carried out. The language or method of presentation should be such that local people can understand it, and the report must be accessible. Reports should be returned to the people in the form of education materials like films, photographs and casette recordings during the research period. Findings should be discussed continually with the people from whom the information is collected.
    Women in the first and third worlds must critically analyse the work of funding agencies such as FAO, UNICEF and others, as to their insertion of the women's question, and implications of funded projects and programmes not only for women but for different sectors of the economies concerned. Third world women need to have the opportunity to study first world women struggles and organisations. A set of research priorities is then listed under sub-headings of overall processes, patterns of investment and women's employment; women as rural producers; women as wage workers; women as unwaged workers; family and household; birth control; forms and organisation of control.
    The main body of the report consists of summaries of the papers and the discussions aroused by them on the following main themes: The sexual division of labour in rural production systems, the internationalisation of capital, social reproduction, the transition to socialism and organisation and forms of action. Four papers on issues of women and development are also included.

6. <u>KENYA</u> Central Bureau of Statistics, Ministry of Economic Planning and Community Affairs (1977), "Educational Trends 1973-1977", 85 pp., 65 tables.

Analysis of trends in primary and secondary education between 1973 and 1977 is accompanied by detailed statistical tables showing enrolment in primary and secondary school by district, sex and type of school, and examination performance at Primary 7 and secondary levels. Although the abolition of primary school fees in 1973 has led to expanded primary school enrolments, this has not led to equal rates of enrolment of girls as compared to boys. Boys tend to perform better than girls on all three multiple-choice papers of the CPE (Primary 7) examination, that is in English, Mathematics and General Knowledge, in both rural and urban areas, with the exception of the English paper in the urban areas where no sex disparity is found. Even where rural districts are clustered together by degree of educational development "there was less difference in mean scores among members of the same sex for the three groups than there is between males and females within a particular group".

Sex disparity is also found at secondary level. A higher proportion of girls attend the unaided sector of secondary schooling, which tends to have poorer examination results and school resources as compared to boys. The authors interpret this as a positive sign of parental willingness to invest in girls' education in the face of structural limits to educational opportunities for girls in the aided schools system. These structural limits are based on a fixed number of places for girls, especially limited in the sciences. (We would argue the need for a more cautious interpretation of a situation where two-thirds of all secondary school girls are educated within the less satisfactory, unaided sector). That growth in female enrolment occurs primarily in the unaided sector indicates that the unaided sector acts as a safety-valve and "streaming" factor releasing the aided sector from responsibility for providing more places for girls, and channeling them into a second-rate schooling system).

Female performance in EACE results (Form 4) in 1976 was higher than males as measured by the percentage achieving Division I and II. In addition, female candidates had a much lower failure rate. The authors note the importance of greater selectivity of female candidates as one explanation, but counter it with the fact that a greater proportion of female than male candidates attended unaided schools which generally perform more poorly on EACE than aided schools.

The detailed documentation and careful statistical analysis of school enrolment and examination performance by sex (and region, etc.) provided is exemplary. There is an urgent need for similar statistical analysis of the education system in Tanzania, which analyses enrolment and examination performance over time, taking into account sex differences in relation to breakdown by region, district, urban-rural, government-private, higher performing-low performing, and high resource-low resource (e.g. staff ratios, qualifications, experience and school equipment and facilities). Having an educational policy which explicitly states that the promotion of sex and regional equality in schooling is a fundamental objective is absolutely meaningless without such data to help monitor the education system.

7. HENN, JEANNE (1979), "Who Benefits from Peasant Women's Work? Insights from a Modes of Production Analysis". Paper No. 29, BW, 19 pp.

Analyses the articulation of the patriarch mode of production at household level, the petty commodity mode of production characteristic of smallholder peasant production system, and

the capitalist mode of production. These relations are
concretised through an examination of different labour time
inputs in household production and reproduction, situated in
terms of production for household use and for the market.
Labour time studies must be combined with analysis of differential consumption patterns to clarify who benefits from household
labour in the household, village, nation and internationally.
Measures of differential labour times and consumption will
clarify the major contribution of women peasants in agriculture
production and in the maintenance of peasant households.

8. HENN, JEANNE KOOPMEN (1981), "Women in the Rural Economy: Past,
Present and Future". University of Dar es Salaam, paper presented to IDS Women's Study Group, April 6th, and to Economic Department Seminar Series, 32 pp., to be published in S. Stichter and
J. Hay (eds.), Women in Sub-Saharan Africa.

This is a comparative analysis of the situation of women in
Africa, beginning with the pre-colonial period. Women are located
in the context of social relations within patriarchal household
production in a range of political systems in the 18th and 19th
centuries. Comparisons are made between patrilineal and
matrilineal cultivating societies, and pastoralist and hunting
and gathering societies. The dynamic of economic control and
accumulation was based on control over persons centred around
control over marriage. Women were subject to the double demands
of patriarchal and tributary modes of accumulation in semi-feudal
states. The changes unleashed during the colonial and post-
colonial periods are analysed, with focus on commoditisation in
agriculture production and migrant labour and their impact on
women peasants.
    The comparative approach adopted not only in this paper but
presumedly in the text as a whole requires close scrutiny. It
is definitely necessary to examine the different sexual relations
which developed within different societies ever time, and to
abstract common tendencies among them. At issue is the most
appropriate and correct method to do so, given the present state
of knowledge (or lack of knowledge) concerning such issues in
Africa. There is a dearth of significant materialist research
on the question of class and sexual relations, on which to build
comparative analyses. Hence, the author has had to rely heavily
on anthropological and other sources which require a very critical
re-reading. This is not to deny the value of such sources, but
it does require adequate space to grapple with the different
methodological problems implied. Otherwise, it is all too easy
to slip into a kind of "armchair" scholarship in women's studies.
    Women's studies in Africa is in desperate need of empirical
research at local, national and international levels. A good
example is the earlier work of Jeanne Henn herself, conducted
in Cameroon (1978 Peasants, Workers and Capital: The Political
Economy of Labour and Incomes in Cameroon, Harvard University,
Unpublished Ph.D. dissertation).

9. MAIR, LUCILLE M. (1981), "New International Economic Order: What
does Development Really Mean to Women?". IFDA Dossier 21 (Jan.-
Feb.): 56-68.

The Secretary General of the World Conference of the United
Nations' Decade for Women argues that women perform one-third
of the world's quantified work, as well as the "uncounted" and
unpaid work they do at home, but that they are basically
powerless and propertyless. Moreover, one-third of the world's
families are headed by women, in contrast to the usual textbook
assumption that in Africa and elsewhere all families are headed
by men. Women earn less than 1/10th of the world's income for
the 1/3rd paid work they do, and control less than 1/100th of
the world's property.

The situation of women is related to that of the poor classes
to which the majority of women belong. Seventy per cent of the
world's population receives only 30 % of the world's income.
Global tension has been intensified by global recession, the
energy crisis and the mounting debt burdens of developing nations.
Despite these objective realities which condition the life and
work of women in the "South", the women in the "North", i.e.
developed capitalist countries, do not identify with the struggles of the South in general and women of the South in particular.
Women of the South (i.e. the Third World) know that it is inadequate merely to set up women's bureaux. In order to achieve
the liberation of women, it is necessary to confront economic
issues and historical social struggles. Women cannot be straight-
jacketed into one set of issues or another.

10. MBILINYI, MARJORIE J. (1971), The Participation of Women in
African Economies. University of Dar es Salaam, ERB paper
71.12, 34 pp.

A general analysis of women in Africa. The impossibility of
generalising about "the role of African women" is stressed,
given different socio-economic conditions. Examines the nature
and extent of women's participation in specific economic sectors
during the pre-colonial, colonial and post-colonial periods.
Questions of differentiation in ownership and control of the
means of production, and control of the labour process and
distribution of its product are examined in the different
periods. Obstacles to wage employment of women include lack
of education, including vocational and technical training, and
very strong patriarchist values and attitudes. Modernisation
in agriculture has led to increased labour demands for women,
and loss of control over one's own labour. Analysis of education and vocational training shows the sex bias in courses
offered to women and the closed doors which exist at higher
levels. Conditions and measures necessary to free women to
combine work, family and civic responsibilities are presented.
They include the provision of adequate child care facilities
in urban and rural areas; food processing with cheap products;
provision of medical and other service schemes for women in
their own right at their places of work; equal pay for equal
work; women control of their own earnings and the encouragement
of single, independent women to join ujamaa villages as full
members, being allocated housing and land the same as all others.
The role of governments, intergovernmental organisations and
non-governmental ones is analysed as well. Guideline research
questions accompany the text.

11. MCDOWELL, JIM (1976), <u>Village Technology in Eastern Africa</u>. A Report of a UNICEF-sponsored regional seminar on "Simple Technology for the Rural Family" held in Nairobi, June 1976, Nairobi, Eastern Africa Regional Office. 63 pp. illustrations.

Discussions centred on the potential benefits of introducing appropriate technologies to the overall quality of life of rural mothers and children. Emphasis was placed on simple, easily constructed domestic gadgets to reduce the physical work load of women; as well as on improving the availability and quality of food supplies through better methods of cultivation and improved food storage, conservation and preparation. Special emphasis was also placed on improving the availability and quality of water supplies.
    A wide range of potentially appropriate village-level technologies are described and suggestions offered as guidelines for introducing appropriate technologies into the rural area and disseminating information about the concept.

12. NEWLAND, K. (1979), <u>The Sisterhood of Man</u>, A Worldwatch Institute Book., W.W. Norton & Company, New York, 242 pp.

Presents a global look at the problems and areas of change that are facing women in the world today. Discussions on women in Tanzania concern their situation as to polygamy, how dietary taboos are directly contributing to their standard of health, stipulates the reasons why women favour the ujamaa villagization programme and discusses how, theoretically at least, women's traditional rights to the land are recognised by the government.
    (Taken from: John P. Snell, <u>Tanzania</u>, an <u>Annotated Bibliography on Population Within the Context of Development</u>, September 1980).

13. O'BARR, JEAN (1975), "Making the Invisible Visible: African Women in Politics". <u>African Studies Review</u>, 18 (3): 19-27.

Examines preconceptions and assumptions prevalent about the political roles of African women-assumptions held by both political scientists and decision makers and which have led to the exclusion of women from analyses of political life. Identifies four sectors that effect the active participation of women in politics in contemporary Africa.
    Asserts that "Women's political activities are critical factors in understanding the politics of any developing society". In African societies where the domestic and public spheres are not widely separated, women are "political actors who initiate issues, condition their development, acquiesce in or resist their outcomes". Several studies are used to show how economic power spills into political power and how even the secondary role of women can be significant. For Tanzania the examples are taken from Mbilinyi's "The 'New Woman' and the Traditional Norms in Tanzania" and the writer's own work among the Pare.

14. PALA, ACHOLA O. (1974), <u>The Role of African Women in Rural Development, Research Priorities</u>. Nairobi, Institute of Development Studies, Discussion Paper No. 203, 31 pp.

Examines several studies to show that in pre-colonial economies in Africa, women played an important role in rural economies based on cultivation and/or cattle tending and trade. Little has been done to integrate this fact into rural development strategies although women are expected to join in the nation building.

The discrepancy between theory and fact are due to two facts. Colonial administrators and planners, by preferring men to women for commercial agriculture promoted the productivity of male labour at the expense of women. This trend has continued even after independence. Findings in Kenya and Tanzania show that extension services and research findings are more easily accessible to "progressive farmers". These are usually those farmers with comparatively large farms which are mostly owned by men. The subsistence sector left to women is usually neglected. Secondly, research on African women has been dominated by those outside African production and development or by Africans who are unwilling to approach rural development problems from the point of view of peasants.

Emphasizes that rural development must include the role of women as an integral part of rural improvement that is equal and contemporary to the role of men. There is need to analyse the nature of rural societies and the changing social and economic position of African women. In this context, the author identifies broad outlines of research areas, to aid the planning of rural change.

15. OKEYO, ACHOLA PALA (1981), "Reflections on Development Myths". African Report, 26 (2) March-April: 7-10.

Argues that the international recognition now given to the relative low and deteriorating status of women all over the world, with its negative impact on developmental goals, has led to the refinement of research methods and data collection concerning inequality. Stresses the removal of distinctions between market and non-market activities, such as production of food for the market and food for home consumption. At the same time, strategies and tactics must be developed by the women within each region. The African women's problem has been defined "externally" with reference to the international division of labour, with emphasis on ideological and socio-economic norms.

Analyses which stress culture are criticised for separating culture from political and economic forces and for assuming that there are no endogenous processes of change in cultural traditions. Women are separated as a category from socio-economic circumstances, and from the international economic order. The Western feminist position which views men as the enemy is based on the specific form of alienation found in the Western world where female is perceived as negative. This is not the same case in Africa where women have always engaged in productive work. Hence African women rarely consider men to be a problem. Moreover, when women struggle for advancement, it is not for themselves but rather for the welfare of their families which "does not in any way preclude the men in their lives". Hence, it is incorrect to say that "women's programmes may lead to conflict between men and women".

In order to oppose anti-feminist positions in African social
science, the author takes a compromising and apologetic position,
which becomes self-contradictory. There are ample studies to
show the extent of alienation experienced by peasant and working
class women who too often do perceive men as the enemy. That
this is an incorrect understanding of the social relations underlying the oppression of women is one thing, but to deny the
existence of the alienation objectively and subjectively is itself mystifying. As the author notes herself, "The sharing of
power, the challenging of dominant power structures - be they
embodied in class, sex or race - has never been a nonviolent or
nonpolitical act".

16. SCANDINAVIAN INSTITUTE OF AFRICAN STUDIES (1978), Women in
    Africa and Development Assistance. Report from a Seminar arranged
    by the Scandinavian Institute of African Studies, Uppsala, 20-21
    August, 1978. 55 pp.

The seminar focused on the following issues: What is the impact
of foreign aid on women? What type of assistance do women need
to improve their situation? Which methods can be used to improve
the effect of aid on the women's situation? The need for more
research on the situation of women was stressed, research which
was on-going, applied and action-oriented. Research took place
in the context of neo-colonial relations and the international
division of labour, where African women are a vital source of
cheap labour. The concept of a division of labour in research
which separated "Western" and "African" researchers was argued
by some and rejected by others who noted that "content of research
is more important than the question of who is doing it". It was
argued that "chicken-policy", basic needs orientation in research
and development programmes perpetuated the marginal or oppressed
position of peasant women in the economy. Women required
training and incorporation in the most advanced sectors of the
economy.

Zenebework Tadesse provided a "Statement about the Association of African Women for Research and Development (AAWORD)", a
network restricted racially to women researchers of African
ethnic background. Citizens of European or Asian descent born
in Africa and/or naturalized citizens are presently excluded
from membership. Underlying the ethnicity question is conflict
between feminist positions which perceive all women to share
the same subordination and need for liberation, and the opposing
position which argues for the need to situate women in the
context of imperialism and class struggles and to distinguish
the class position and class interests of women and women's
studies.

In her speech, "Women in Africa and Development Assistance",
the Zambian Minister of State for Economic and Technical Cooperation, Lily A. Monze, noted the need for international and
regional cooperation. New structures of the ECA have been set
up to facilitate decentralization and fuller participation of
member states in development programmes. A selected reading list
on "Women in Africa" by Birgitta Fahlander includes recent
bibliographies and periodicals.

17. TINKER, IRENE (1981), "Policy Strategies for Women in the 1980's".
    African Report, 2 (2) March-April: 11-16.

Provides background to the development of the concept of "women
in development" (WID), which became popularised during the last
decade. Argues that one result of the World Conference of the
UN decade for women in Mexico is the development of WID elements
in international and national aid programmes such as the USAID
special office on Women in Development. UN bodies passed
resolutions which require all programmes to include women as
actors and beneficiaries. Such developments have actually had
very little impact. Probably the most worthwhile achievement
of the 1970s has been the collection of data to refute development
theory and development planning tendencies, and the development
of small-scale women's projects. Research has shown that women
work hard, and they work whenever possible for money. Time
budget studies have included information on who controls
expenditure in the household as well as basic income figures.
For example, in the USA it has been found that women earn $ .59
for every dollar earned by men, due to occupational sex segregation if not outright sex discrimination. Women are kept in low
paying jobs at the bottom of the economic hierarchy as in the
case of women industrial workers in Tanzania.

Labour services of family members like wives and children
and seasonal hired labour have taken the place of former exchange labour in developing countries, and tend not to be
enumerated in analyses of the labour process. These include
food processing, fetching water, and weaving mats, which are
not counted as economic activities although they contribute to
production for the market. Substitutes for such activities like
mills for grinding grains and kerosene stoves are no longer
accessible to many due to rising costs. As a result women are
pushed back into labour-intensive drudgery, termed income-
substituting labour.

The strategy of women projects has separated women's efforts
from development planning, and treated women as subjects of
welfare programmes. Moreover, these tend to be small and
economically unviable projects. The focus in the 1980s should
therefore be on the promotion of projects which meet women's
priorities and needs and involve them as decision-makers and
implementers, but which are adopted as development programmes
for the whole community or nation. Women's projects or groups
are still necessary however to build up self-confidence,
leadership and to test project ideas. The women's "network"
has been weak on publicity and even weaker on political organisation to influence policy. Women's issues must be taken into the
"male world" and be heard.

This paper represents the more enlightened position among
WID proponents, showing awareness of basic problems and issues
relevant to women in developing countries, and tendencies in
government and multilateral agencies. The author has herself
been active in lobbying for WID conditions in American aid
programmes. The paper's position exemplifies a liberal feminist
one: never critical of the exploitative nature of "development"
itself, rather promoting the equalisation of opportunities for
women.

18. UNITED NATIONS (1979), <u>Convention on the Elimination of All Forms
of Discrimination Against Women</u>. New York, 15 pp., available
form UNDP Offices in Dar es Salaam and Arusha, together with
other UN documents.

In December 1979, the General Assembly of the United Nations
adopted the Convention on the Elimination of all forms of
Discrimination Against Women which sets out in legally binding
form internationally accepted principles and measures to achieve
equal rights for women. The thirty articles call for national
legislation to ban discrimination of all kinds, in political,
economic, social, cultural and civil spheres. It also recommends
temporary special measures to speed equality in fact between
women and men and action to modify social and cultural patterns
that perpetuate discrimination.
    Special measures include equal access to education and no
sex segregation in school curriculum, exemplified in girls alone
studying domestic science and boys mechanics; non-discrimination
in employment and pay; and guarantees of job security in the
event of marriage and maternity. It also stresses the equal
responsibilities and duties of men with women with regards to
family life and household chores. Social services like child
care facilities are needed to enable parents to combine family
obligations with work responsibilities and political participation. A machinery is being set up for international supervision
of the obligations accepted by states.
    Ultimately, the responsibility of ensuring that action is
taken against sexual discrimination, as well as lobbying for the
necessary legislation, is that of women and men in each country.
In the Tanzanian context, for example, it is the responsibility
of each citizen, female or male, to find out whether the
government has signed the convention, and the steps taken thus
far to put it into action. Finding out is one aspect of our
responsibility, another is to organise together in the work place
or the village in order to ensure that the necessary measures
are adopted by the government, the schools, the factories and so
on, and are implemented. As the evidence in this bibliography
shows, there is a great deal of sexual discrimination in Tanzania
and much to be done before it is totally eradicated. It will
only be eradicated if women and men organise together to investigate
sexual contradictions which prevent the full participation of
women in all aspects of society, and act to destroy them.

19. UNECA SOCIAL DEVELOPMENT SECTION (1967), <u>The Status and Role of
Women in East Africa</u>. New York, 65 pp.

The study examines the current situation of women in Ethiopia,
Kenya, Malawi, Tanzania, Uganda and Zambia, in order to identify
the role played by women in the context of economic, social and
political changes and factors that have shaped and continue to
shape, the status of women in these countries. Attention is
focused on education and training, employment, health and welfare,
legal rights of women, their participation in community life, as
possible factors affecting women's integration into the
mainstream of national life.

20. UNECA (1975), "Women and National Development in African
    Countries: Some Profound Contradictions". African Studies
    Review, 18 (3).

    In very early African societies women were providers. Even in
    contemporary African societies women participate heavily in
    agriculture. However, they are not well represented in modern
    sectors. In the rural areas the work load of women has increased
    because of male migration into wage labour or because of the
    introduction of cash crops. Mechanization in agriculture has
    resulted in less jobs for women. Women's ratios in management
    and administration are also very low. Factors affecting women's
    employment as well as the consequences of the neglect of women
    are discussed. The study includes several examples of the
    situation of women in Tanzania to support its arguments.

21. UNECA, African Training and Research Centre for Women (1976),
    "The Education and Training of Rural Women for National
    Development". Paper presented to the International Workshop on
    Education for Rural Women, Lushoto, Tanzania (PMO/UNICEF), 14 pp.

    The position of women is described in the rural areas, cut off
    from education and training, including agriculture extension
    services, which leads to their becoming second class citizens.
    Attention is therefore needed to train women farmers, women
    agriculture extension workers, other village-level field workers,
    and the expansion of formal schooling opportunities including
    secondary school agriculture training. It is noted that in
    Tanzania only 3 of the 36 agriculture secondary schools are
    girls schools. Women and girls also need training in animal
    husbandry at all levels; commerce and trade, small-scale
    industries and crafts, with emphasis here on production, quality
    control, management, diversification, use of equipment; training
    in food processing, preservation and storage to avoid waste and
    enhance the nutritional level of foods; retraining of traditional
    village midwives; training of day care and child and maternal
    health personnel; expansion of functional literacy programmes.
    The programmes of the African Training and Research Centre for Women
    (ATRCW) are described, which include the running of workshops
    such as the Workshop on Food Preservation and Storage at Kibaha
    in 1975 (ECA 1976). The African Women's Development Task Force
    identifies and sends trainers in particular skills and techniques
    from one African country to another. The establishment of
    national machinery such as commissions and bureaux for women
    are encouraged and assisted.

22. UNECA (1977), The New International Economic Order, WHAT ROLES
    FOR WOMEN? Addis Ababa, E/CN. 14/ATRCW/77/WD3, 54 pp.

    This monograph is based on research findings and analyses the
    knowledge gained by ECA staff (especially the ATRCW Unit) from field
    work and conferences, "It is intended to open discussion on the
    roles of women in the new economic order". The background to
    the movement toward the New International Economic Order (NIEO)
    is presented, and a brief description of economic trends in
    Africa and the place of women in their economies. Proposals
    for the NIEO at global and regional levels are critically

analysed in terms of the degree to which they have considered
the role of women in their programmes. Proposes some systems
for monitoring women's contribution and access to the essential
tools of development, which include the use of already generated
data and statistics as well as the need for surveys to produce
data which is necessary but not available. Model tables are
presented and discussed, which cover the following kinds of
data: <u>employment</u> (% of workers who are female, comparative wages,
hours of labour which are female in the informal sector); <u>educa-
tion and training</u> (female enrolment % at primary, secondary, and
third level and including fields of study; female participation
% in different areas of non-formal training - e.g. agriculture,
animal husbandry, etc.); <u>health and maternity</u> (female participation re: water supplies, health facilities); <u>law</u> (land ownership,
credit and loans); <u>rural technologies; decision-making</u> positions.

23. UNITED NATIONS PROTEIN ADVISORY GROUP (1979), <u>Women in Food
Production, Food Handling, and Nutrition, With Special Emphasis
on Africa</u>. A Report of the Protein-Calorie Advisory Group (PAG)
of the United Nations. Rome, FAO, 223 pp.

Focuses on the situation of women in various parts of Africa
including Tanzania because of their key position in African
production systems. Using an inter-disciplinary approach, it
takes data from the fields of history, nutrition, sociology and
social anthropology as well as from UN research and policy
documents in order to appraise (1) women's role in food production
and handling and nutrition in Africa; (2) the extent to which
conditions under which women live and work have a bearing on the
availability of food and the nutritional levels of their families
and communities. Deals with the background to Africa's under-
development and its specific effects on women; women's access
to resources and opportunities; how nutrition researchers think
women influence nutrition levels and their own role in the
conceptualisations of women's involvement in nutrition.
    Conclusions and recommendations are presented and their
implications for future research are discussed. Among its
conclusions are: (1) increased national food supplies alone
will not eliminate food shortages and malnutrition unless there
is a fair distribution of these supplies; (2) unless the woman
has the decision making power over the disposal of any increased
family income, it is unjustified to make any assumptions about
an improvement in family nutrition.

24. UNRISD (1978), "The Impact on Women of Socioeconomic Changes".
Geneva, 16 pp. (UNRISD/Board 1978/W.P.6/Rev. 1/).

Peasant women must be situated analytically in relation to the
international division of labour which underlies the poverty,
exploitation and oppression which they experience. A research
proposal is presented which will study the role of women in
economic production and the reproduction of the labour force,
the sexual division of labour and the effect of political reform
on women's status. Beginning with Africa, the research design
will be used in Latin America and Asia if financial support is
found. The historical background of Africa is briefly analysed,
in order to place the women's question in context. The role of

women in producing food and otherwise maintaining their families
is found to be general to most zones in Africa. Women's studies
must distinguish between different basic geographical and economic
conditions, such as those found in labour reserves as compared to
plantation areas. The working hypothesis is that the integration
of developing countries into the world market has aggravated the
exploitation and oppression of the family unit. The primary
function of the family unit in Africa is to provide a source of
cheap labour. Women are relegated to certain positions in the
production of cash crops and/or food, as a result of changes
which have occurred with modernization in agriculture. The major
parts of the study and the research topics to be worked on are
presented and discussed, which cover women's participation in
peasant agriculture, agricultural modernization, female agriculture wage labour, migration of women and industrial wage
labour of women.

25. WORLD BANK (1979), "Recognizing the 'Invisible' Woman in
Development: The World Bank's Experience". Washington D.C.,
31 pp.

According to the Preface written by Robert S. McNamara, then
President of the World Bank, there has been growing awareness
in the World Bank of the need to give explicit attention to the
effects of its projects on women. In line with this interest,
the Bank established the post of Adviser on Women in Development
in 1977, "to monitor and advise on the effects its projects were
having and would have in the future on the status of women".
According to McNamara, "expanding the social, political, and
economic opportunities of women beyond their traditional roles
of motherhood and housekeeping enables them to channel their
creative abilities over a much broader spectrum of activities".
    Some of the factors considered by the Adviser on Women in
Development when monitoring projects are: How can projects
respond to women's needs and make use of their abilities? Can
opportunities for women to participate and share in the benefits
be found? What is the current socio-economic role of females in
each project area, and what implications might that role have
for the design of the project? Might a project affect women
detrimentally? How can those effects be identified and prevented?
    Despite such highly relevant questions and a cohesive
insightful summary of findings, the concept of development which
has been adopted and the underlying objective of the World Bank's
programme for women, is that of capitalist development. This
concept separates women from the social relations and processes
of change in which they are situated. Whereas the destruction
of oppressive social relations in peasant production is
progressive in general, its liberating consequences will depend
upon the development of socialism, not capitalism. The
development of socialism is not on the agenda for the World Bank.

26. WRIGHT, MARCIA (1975), "Women in Peril: A Commentary on the Life
Stories of Captives in Nineteenth-Century East-Central Africa".
African Social Research, 20 (December): 800-819.

Based on re-reading of written autobiographical accounts of
three ex-slave women and one ex-slave man born during the second

half of the nineteenth century during a period of economic
change and social transformation. Individual life histories
are analysed to develop hypotheses about changes taking place
in general in women's situation in the context of broader
social transformation.

Women were transferred between one group and another through
several different mechanisms, only one of which was mediated by
bridewealth or payment of labour services. Women were also used
as payment for fines or compensations, were forcibly seized in
war, and were sold in the market place of the slave trade. The
offspring of female or male slaves remained expendable persons,
never fully adopted as lineage members, even if the parent(s)
had been married into a given group. The cases illustrate the
way expansion of wage and other employment opportunities in
mission and urban centres provided a means of escape for women,
and provided the basis for becoming independent household heads.
Nevertheless, in all cases women were forced to be "attached"
to a man with jural and social status, like a married son.
Moreover, women were always most vulnerable to capture,
enslavement and sale. Given their value as "multipliers of the
population, as labourers, as inheritable and disposable units
(they) were at a premium".

The analysis would have been strengthened if combined with
a thorough examination of transformations taking place in
society, taking into account the nature of the colonial state,
and the processes of proletarization and peasantisation which
accelerated at this time.

II. GENERAL ANALYSIS OF WOMEN IN TANZANIA

The papers included in this section can generally be grouped under
the following headings: the role of women peasants and workers in
society and national development; an analysis of the historical and
current forces that have contributed to this role; the contradictions
between avowed and actual policies for enabling women to participate
in national development, and the status of present data and research
on women. Many of these aspects are also covered in the sections
that follow, but with greater specificity as to whether the women
are peasants or workers, housewives or professionals.

Women's Subordination

Most of the studies which focus on women point out the subordinate
position that women occupy in Tanzania today, both at the household
level and the society at large. This position is highlighted over
and over in this book because of its detrimental impact on the welfare and development of women themselves, as well as the nation.
Discrimination against women prevents full mobilization of a major
section of its economically active population. If women are
discriminated against in matters of ownership of the means of
production, inheritance, or rights to children, then their position in
society becomes tenuous and their personal security and stability
threatened. What security can there be for a woman where "traditional" laws can turn her out of her land and house or force her to
stay in an unhappy marriage since the alternative would be to lose
her children? At the national level women's lack of access to
education, especially scientific and technical education and lack
of opportunities to participate in planning and decision making,
constrain them from participating effectively in national development programmes. In spite of the expansion of educational facilities,
the number of women able to use these opportunities is still small,
particularly as their role as producers and reproducers keeps them
tied to activities centred around the household - activities which
seldom get computed into the national GNP.

      This is starkly brought out by the Agricultural Census (II:55).
It shows that of the 2.9 million economically active women engaged
in agriculture, about 2.6 million are categorised as unpaid family
workers. The comparable figures for men are 2.5 million and 0.8
million respectively. Of the 2.4 million holdings, only 0.4 million
were owned by women although overall they constitute a far greater
proportion of agricultural manpower. These figures are indicative,
even though the census findings in general are subject to further
scrutiny.

      The production relations at the household   level are maintained
and reinforced by family structures and socialisation as well as
the ambiguities of the legal status of women (II:36, 37, 41, 42, 49,
53).

      There is a divergence of opinion about how women have reacted
to their subordinate role. Mary Kamm (II:34) argues that the women
are docile, fatalistic, passive and resigned to their position.
Bryceson and Mbilinyi (II:28, 29) point out that women are not
resigned to their fate. Resistances range from voluntary proletarisation and migration to towns to suicide. The National Demographic
Survey (1973) shows a high rate of marital instability which could

be partly interpreted as evidence of women's actions to resist
unsatisfactory marriages (see section XI).

Underlying Forces of Subordination

Historical materialist analyses enable us to identify the factors
that have contributed to this position. The main forces leading
to it are attributed to the process of primitive accumulation
reinforced by the imposition of colonial rule, the developing
dominance of the capitalist mode of production, the introduction
of cash crops and the links with international capital (II:28, 29,
37, 47, 53). Increased commoditisation has intensified demands on
women's productive efforts but has paradoxically reduced women's
control over their product.

Mbilinyi (II:29, 47) stresses that the question of women must
not be seen as merely a sex problem but must be situated in the
specific class situation in which women are located in changing
social relations. In this context the struggle against exploitation
is a struggle of women and men against exploitative and oppressive
capitalist and patriarchal relations, and not a struggle of women
against men. Attention is also drawn to the tendencies of
multinational corporations (MNC's) to situate large industrial
complexes in developing countries in order to raise their profits.
Women usually constitute the cheapest source of labour.

Some attempt is made to suggest ways to overcome the situation.
Koda (II:37) suggests labour saving devices and education. However,
it has already been stated that the restrictive nature of the household and agricultural activities prevent women from taking part in
educational and training programmes. Is there better hope then for
the girls now taking advantage of universal primary education?
During a very recent field experience in Mufindi, Ophelia
Mascarenhas found that the number of girls at upper primary levels
was still significantly low. At the post-primary technical school,
girls were still only enrolled in domestic science, while boys were
learning carpentry, welding, and other technical skills (Fieldwork
in three villages around a proposed large scale industrial project
in Mufindi District, Iringa Region). The changes necessary for
women's entry into history are those necessary for Tanzania's full
development as an autonomous socialist nation, a point stressed by
many authors here.

Contradictions in National Policies

The practical implications of these are yet to be explored fully.
At the national level, although the policy of socialism has among
its goals the security and welfare of all the citizens of the
country, the contradictions are still apparent and are reflected
in the scant regard given to the role of women in development
planning. The Third Five Year Plan, for instance (II:57) completely
ignores the need for mobilising women in its programmes for
increased agricultural productivity, better food storage and
preservation policies and the dissemination of research findings,
popularly known under the rubric of extension services. These
activities are a dominant part of women's lives in rural Tanzania.
Training programmes for improving village skills (II:60-62) and

still aimed predominantly towards men and have begun to show weaknesses because they are not aimed at those who are most involved.

Research in Tanzania

More research is needed which has strategy and well defined aims oriented towards the interests of the peasants and workers in Tanzania. Mascarenhas has pointed out the need for empirical data and applicability of analysis to specific situations of women being researched (II:40). There is also the need for coordination of and communication about women's activities and research. One effort at communication is this book itself, as well as Mascarenhas and Mbilinyi (XIV:393).

Another outstanding effort at coordination and communication was the BRALUP Workshop on Woman's Studies and Development, September 1979 (II:30). Participants included researchers as well as women working with women's programmes and women able to influence policy, either directly or through the mass media. The Workshop stressed the need for research, but also emphasised the importance of finding ways to implement the research findings in government and party policies with the aim of eliminating sex inequalities. The participants also agreed with the opening speech of the Minister of Justice, that research findings had to be translated into the national language, Kiswahili, popularised in the form of school texts and easily readable booklets as well as songs and plays; and incorporated in professional manuals and academic books (II:39).

The need for information cannot be overstated. Part of the problem for not inserting the women's question in national policy-making is the lack of adequate documentation as well as patriarchal attitudes of the policymakers themselves. The majority of planners are men and they too have been socialised to take for granted the work done by women and the work done at the household level. Appropriate analysis backed by statistical information is necessary to document both the significance of women's contribution to production and sexual discrimination in various spheres. Some positive action has already been taken. For instance, the Musoma Resolution stipulation that prospective entrants to the university must work for at least two years before joining the university was waived in the case of women. Enough evidence was presented to show that the stipulation in fact lowered the number of female students at the university, and was in danger of eliminating them entirely. The policy was finally changed in the case of women after lobbying from the national women's organisation (UWT) and other sympathetic groups.

Such cases clearly show the need for in-depth analysis and research. Some guidelines are presented in works discussed in section I above. Locally there are serious attempts to work out research programmes, such as the joint UWT/BRALUP study on rural women's cash earning activities (IV:90). Here, UWT felt the need to have assistance in scholarly and practical analysis that could be provided by academics at the university. Another important ongoing activity is women's study groups where women from the university and elsewhere are engaged in study and research activities designed to suit Tanzanian conditions and problems.

At another level, researchers are also pointing out the need for a reorientation of national statistical and other data. Sembajwe (II:50) examines the current available demographic data and recommends a more realistic assessment of women's full participation outside the sphere of the household. This aspect of national data collection including censuses has hardly been touched. Figures for "employment and earnings" have few tables giving sexual breakdowns. The Annual Manpower Report to the President is another example.

In this section, as well as in the book as a whole, it is possible to trace the development and qualitative change taking place in women's studies in Tanzania. The sheer number of works focused on various aspects of the women's question has risen, especially since the early 1970s. The growing interest in this field provided the basis for Ophelia Mascarenhas to engage in a critique of "women's studies at the University of Dar es Salaam" in 1979 (II:40). There has also been an important shift from focus on attitudes and roles (for example, II:34, 41, 42 and 49) to a more rigorous analysis of women's place in the relations of production and reproduction, situated in the context of the international division of labour as well as the Tanzania social formation (II:28, 29, 47 and 53). This has led to the critique of generalisations about "women's role", with stress on the need for specificity about which women we are talking about e.g. peasants, workers or petty bourgeois.

----

27. ALOPAEUS - STAHL, DORRIT (1979), Social Politics in Tanzania. Dar es Salaam, SIDA, 81 pp.

The main emphasis of the study is on the evolution of social conditions and social welfare services in Tanzania. It is particularly significant as one of the few comprehensive studies describing social services in Tanzania. Although not directly centred on women, it nevertheless touches on various aspects concerning women such as the urban and rural environment, security benefits for wage earners, etc.

   Of particular significance is the section on children, child care and rights of women to child care allowances in the case of divorce, widowhood, etc. The study is amply supported by statistics and data collected from field work.

28. BRYCESON, DEBORAH FAHY and MARJORIE MBILINYI (1978), The Changing Role of Tanzanian Women in Production: From Peasants to Proletarians. Dar es Salaam, BRALUP Service Paper No. 78/5 57 pp. Presented to the Sussex Conference on Subordination of Women, September, 1978 (5).

The paper examines the changing sexual division of labour in Tanzania - The sexual division includes control of the product of labour as well as the sex - specific allocation of productive activity. Discusses the process of primitive accumulation whereby agricultural producers are gradually separated from effective control of the means of production and become proletarianised. Periodicises the changing sexual division of labour. Throughout, the sexual division of labour is analysed

in relation to the production and reproduction of the social
formation and in respect to women's role in the family, lineage
organization, state and international capital. Special attention is given to Tanzanian women's developing consciousness
of their subordination, and the ways in which they struggle
against it.

29. BRYCESON, DEBORAH FAHY and MARJORIE MBILINYI (1980), "The
Changing Role of Tanzanian Women in Production". JIPEMOYO, 2,
edited by A.O. Anacleti, Scandinavian Institute of African
Studies, 85-116. Originally presented to the International
Political Science Association Congress, Moscow, 1979.

This is a condensed version of item 28. However, the conceptual
framework has been changed after the rejection of the concept
of the sexual division of labour as adopted earlier. Instead,
women are situated in the articulation of precapitalist and
capitalist relations of production, within which the sexual
division of labour is posed.

30. BRYCESON, DEBORAH FAHY and NAJMA SACHAK (1979), Proceedings of
the Workshop on Women's Studies and Development 24-29 September
1979. BRALUP Research Paper No. 60, University of Dar es Salaam,
85 pp. (The workshop has been referred to in all other annotations
as BW).

The main objective of the workshop was to provide a discussion
forum for researchers and those working directly on women's
issues. Participants therefore included researchers, people
working in a technical or policy-making capacity, and those
working in the mass media or others in a position to project a
progressive view of women's role in Tanzania's development.
The five themes of the workshop were women and rural development,
women and urban development, women and reproduction, women and
ideology and women's studies. "The proceedings" is in fact a
full report of the workshop: a description of the preparation
and organisation process, the full text of the Opening Speech by
the Minister of Justice, the Honourable Julie Manning, and the
two Action Documents, No. 1 "Suggested Research Priorities in
Tanzanian Women's Studies" and No. 2 "Final and Summarised
Suggestions on Research Dissemination Activities". There are
also summaries of each paper and the plenary and group
discussions.
     Based upon the participation of sixty people, nearly all of
whom were Tanzanian women, the workshop was a major step forward
in the development of women's studies in Tanzania. The report
represents a significant document not only as a summary of the
workshop itself and the papers presented, but also as a resource
for information on problems pertaining to different categories
of women today.

31. CHEM CHEM. A magazine published six times a year by the U.W.T.
University Branch and sold in aid of the U.W.T. Nursery School.

The authors were able to locate the following numbers only:
Vol. I no. 5 (Nov. - Dec. 1972); Vol. 4 no. 5 (Nov. - Dec. 1973);
issue No. 1 of 1974 and issue No. 1 of 1975. Articles are
written in both Kiswahili and English and cover a wide range of

topics of concern to women. Some like the series on "Women and
Education in Tanzania" (item published in issue No. 1 of 1975)
attempt to make a critical assessment of the politico-socio-
economic status of women in Tanzania. Others are practical
suggestions about domestic matters.

The University Branch of the UWT is somewhat unique because
of its situation in an environment that includes women engaged
in a variety of professional and non-professional occupations,
non-wage earning wives of teaching and other staff of the
University resident at the University and rural women of the
immediate hinterland of Mbezi (for the last see the article
"What is Happening On Mbezi" Vol. 1 no. 5). Though the articles
are "newsy" rather than a critical analysis of the situation,
they give an interesting insight into the membership, organisation and activities of this branch. An important article in
this context is the one entitled "Women Students on the Hill and
their concept of the U.W.T." in Vol. I No. 5.

32. HOKUHIRWA, HILDA (1975), "Towards Social and Economic Promotion
of Rural Women in Tanzania". Fikara, No. 1 (May): 1-16. An '
Institute of Adult Education publication, Dar es Salaam.

After a brief discussion of the changing role of women, analyses
the activities of different institutions and organisations which
affect women's lives. Much information is provided about U.W.T.
including a diagram attached showing its administrative
structure at that time. Women's cooperatives, literacy programmes,
day care centres and vocational education programmes are also
discussed.

33. IPPF (1980), "Women in Society: A People Wallchart". People,
7 (3).

Tanzania is one of the countries on which information is given
concerning presentation of data from the most recent surveys
carried out in the last 10 years on the current status of women.
Information is given on percentage of married women aged 15-19;
legal age of marriage; year in which women were given the vote;
the legal grounds for granting an abortion; government perception
of, and policies on fertility level; government policy on
contraceptive services; percentage of illiterate adults (female
and male); enrolment in schools of 12 to 17 year olds (female
and male); percentage of women and men in the total labour
force; female life expectancy and bodies responsible for
implementing the World Plan of Action in the country. (Taken
from Snell, XIV: 397).

34. KAMM, MARY (1976), "Women in Development". Paper presented to the
International Workshop on Education for Rural Women, Lushoto,
Tanzania (PMO/UNICEF), 12 pp.

The roles of women as mother, as wife, as producer, are
described, as well as the ways in which song and poems act to
socialise girls to fit their subordinated place in life. Women
must look to the future, and be fully involved in national
revolutionary struggles, and their participation must be
encouraged by leaders. Women "are docile, fatalistic and
passive and are resigned to their position", hence the need for

education to become aware of their oppression and the need for
liberation. Women are not struggling for "absolute equality",
it must be agreed that there is such a thing as being "equal
but different".

Many questions are raised by this paper. Contradictory
views on women's alleged resignation have been expressed by
others. The argument of "equal but different" can become an
apology for the continuation of subordination.

35. KJAERBY, FINN (1979),"The Dynamic History of the Subordination
of women in Classless African Societies" Paper No. 35, BW,
24 pp.

This provocative paper explores the origins of women subordination based on an analysis of production, control and
accumulation. The social organisation and sexual division of
labour of hunting bands was characterised by a complementary
balance of power between the sexes. The discontinous nature of
the labour process did not necessitate the control of labour,
and hence the control of women's reproductive capacity. The
transition to agriculture was necessitated by population
pressure, which led to struggles to control women's reproductive
capacity in order to ensure an adequate supply of potential
labour. This transition to agriculture was not an internal
development in Tanzania, according to the author, but rather
was the product of the importation of agriculture systems from
outside. Analyses tribal societies based in agriculture and
pastoralist systems in the temporal present in Tanzania. Women's
subordination rests on the necessary precondition of control of
labour for production, which conditions population growth as
well. Mechanisms of accumulation and control of women include
physical force and conquest; the development of kinship systems
where the exchange of women is institutionalised through the
control of marriage; the later development of bridewealth
whereby the exchange of women for bridewealth becomes a
mechanism for expanded material and social reproduction.

The analysis is a speculative one, resting on anthropological
and ahistorical abstractions without concrete analysis of
specific precapitalist formations and the dynamic process of
change within them. Explanations tend to rest on assumptions
of "natural" differences and on the determinancy of population
factors. However, the problems posed with respect to the
origins of women's subordination are significant ones, and the
lines of analysis adopted are suggestive for guiding future
concrete investigation.

36. KODA, BERTHA (1978),"Liberation of Women in Tanzania". Maji
Maji, No. 35, 54-61.

Argues that the exploitation of women began with the production
of surplus. In Tanzania, "Control over labour, which was a
necessary step to be taken after having control over land,
necessitated control over women". In the current social and
political context, there is a strong realisation of the
necessity to mobilise all the human resources of the country.
Some administrative and legislative measures have been taken

to effect this attitude, but traditional and religious customs militate against their effectiveness. The success of the liberation of women necessitates new structures and systems in order to give women equal opportunities in the productive sector.

37. KODA, BERTHA, n.d., "The Role of Women in Socialist Transformation in Tanzania". University of Dar es Salaam, Institute of Development Studies, mimeo, 28 pp.

The historical development of women's subordination in Tanzania is analysed, with emphasis on the colonial and post-colonial periods. Inequality in education is shown with statistics on primary school leavers and Form V student enrolment, and is related to inequality in occupational employment. Contradictions which beset women in the home, in the legal system and in politics are presented. Many specific and concrete recommendations are made to resolve these contradictions in all spheres, ranging from the need for labour-saving devices to relieve women of some of their arduous toil to sex education in the schools and the need for active participation of women in politics. The importance of using mass media of all kinds to struggle ideologically for women's liberation is included as another aspect of scientific and cultural education which enables people to develop a correct understanding of their oppression and exploitation.

38. MAKONI, B. (1977), "Modern Women in Developing Africa: Towards a New Identity". Studies in Adult Education, No. 30. Dar es Salaam, Institute of Adult Education.

Although the title seems to imply that it concerns the whole of Africa, the study is almost entirely based on the situation of women in Tanzania. Women in Tanzania have been and are still discriminated against in education, employment and access to modern technology. Tanzania has adopted several measures to end this discrimination, as for example, the Musoma Declaration, which facilities the entry of women into institutions of higher learning. Equality for women will take time and can only be achieved as the nation advances economically and technologically.

39. MANNING, JULIE (1979), "Opening Speech at the BRALUP Workshop on Women Studies and Development". BW, 7 pp.

"We must take stock ... of women's participation in Tanzanian development, in all spheres of the economy and society". The Minister of Justice challenged the participants at the BRALUP Workshop to go beyond research, to struggle in practice against sex inequalities and to disseminate research results in a form readily accessible to policy makers, implementers and women of all socio-economic groups. More attention is needed on in-depth explanatory research which clarifies the causes of women's inequalities. A great deal of research has already been done, as shown by the workshop papers themselves and the bibliography on women (XIV: 393). However, "... generation after generation of researchers read, analyse and write meanwhile:

(1) the policy makers and policy implementors working in the fields being researched know nothing about the research.

(2) the people who the researcher interviewed, who gave their time, who patiently answered probing questions of an often private nature, have no idea how the information they conveyed is used; wondering if it is being used for or against them; and

(3) the society at large that copes with the problems that have been researched remains unenlightened by the research findings and analysis.

We must make every effort to avoid this situation ... research findings and analysis must be transformed by re-writing, translation into Kiswahili and incorporation into booklets, professional manuals, literacy primers, primary and secondary school textbooks, as well as reforming nation's laws. The knowledge must be made available to the radio, newspapers and religious organizations. The knowledge should permeate the arts; it must appear in plays, novels and be sung in songs".

40. MASCARENHAS, OPHELIA C. (1979), "A Critical Overview of Women's Studies at the University of Dar es Salaam". Paper presented to BW. Paper No. 32, 21 pp.

Reviews women's studies done at the University of Dar es Salaam during the last ten years, with the aim of identifying the trends of such research and suggesting possible directions for future research.
    Points out that generally research and planning in Tanzania has tended to ignore the women's dominant role in development. It cites examples of extension services which are male oriented and Rural Integrated Development Plans which have totally ignored the productive and reproductive role of women.
    Even major works on rural development seldom consider the contribution of women. However, beginning with the mid-seventies quite a number of studies focusing on women have appeared in the form of theses, departmental series and articles in journals on peasant production, wage labour, demographic studies, legal rights, political organization, health and education.
    On methodology the paper emphasises the need for a conceptual framework that can show its applicability to local conditions. In the studies based on empirical data the paper cautions against the dangers of contradictory data and statements that are not supportable by the data offered. Concludes by observing the need for drawing up a strategy for research and ways and means to incorporate the findings into policies that will bring the necessary change.

41. MBILINYI, MARJORIE (1970), "Traditional Attitudes Towards Women: A Major Constraint on Rural Development". Paper presented to the Social Sciences Conference, University of Dar es Salaam.

Argues that the importance of agricultural production in the determination of status has now been offset by the effect of education. Women, however, are not highly educated as is shown by several tables, and traditional norms and attitudes prove a serious obstacle to the enrolment of girls in schools. The low standard of education among rural women is the chief drawback to their full participation in the development process.

42. MBILINYI, MARJORIE (1972),"The 'New Woman' and Traditional Norms in Tanzania". Journal of Modern African Studies, Vol. 10 No. 1, pp. 57-72. Reproduced in full in World Student Christian Federation, 1973, Women in the Struggle for Liberation 3 (2/3): 45-51. Shortened version in Marilee Karl (ed.), 1976, Ujamaa and Self-Reliance: Building Socialism in Tanzania. Rome, IDOC publications. 49-52.

Despite 'sub-ordination' to men, women traditionally had semi-autonomous roles as producers and distributors of goods. Modernization, urbanization and industrialisation have depressed this status. Among the factors now providing a hindrance to the full participation of women in the development of the country, the study identifies the following: family structure and socialisation, the ambiguities of the legal status of women in the matter of inheritance and rights to marriage property, and an attitude towards women and the education of girls that serves to keep women and girls ignorant of outside alternatives to their subservient and dependent status. Concludes that "the changes necessary for women's 'entry into history' are those necessary for Tanzania's full development as an autonomous socialist nation."

43. MBILINYI, MARJORIE J. (1972), "The State of Women in Tanzania". Canadian Journal of African Studies VI (2): 371-377. Reproduced in Third World File, File 7: Africa Speaks, Section IV: "African Responses" Development Education Centre, Toronto.

Women's function of biological reproduction is analysed and shown to hinder their full involvement in development. The role of women in biological reproduction is related to her role in production within peasant households, where women end up assuming responsibilities and tasks which were defined as male in the past. The positive or benefical aspects of the new Marriage Law are discussed, together with its limitations.

44. MBILINYI, MARJORIE J. (1974),"The Role of Women in the Socialist Transformation of Tanzania", in WFUNA/ISMUN 28th Summer School, The Role of Women in Society and in Development: 64-74, Kungälv, Sweden.

The struggle for women's liberation is situated in the context of the struggle for national liberation against imperialism and the struggle for socialism. The relationship between unequal access for women in education and in occupations is shown using contemporary data. The marriage law is examined to reveal the ways in which it actually inhibits the advancement of women. The role of UWT in the women's struggle and the contradictions between "traditional" male and female roles and women's involvement in national liberation and socialist struggles are discussed.

45. MBILINYI, MARJORIE (1975), "Tanzanian Women Confront the Past and the Future". Futures, VII (v): 400-413.

Underdevelopment of the national economy and the class formation where inherited from the pre-colonial and colonial periods and are perpetuated by dependence on external forces. These have

enhanced and continue to enhance restrictions for women. Full
scale capital accumulation in the hands of the people and a
programme of rural industrialization will provide the only kind
of institutional framework within which the emancipation of
women will be possible (Author's abstract).

46. MBILINYI, MARJORIE (1979), "Women's Liberation in the Context of
Tanzania". Papers in Education and Development, No. 4: 1-26.

Two basic questions are posed, with respect to the issue of
women's liberation: (1) liberation from what? (2) liberation
meaning what in the context of an African post-colonial state?
Through an analysis of primary and secondary contradictions in
the Tanzanian social formation, the contradictions specific to
women are situated. For example, property relationships which
dispossess women are in contradiction with incentives for
increased production. At the household level, the contradiction
between production and reproduction (work and home) is
fundamental. Some of the contradictions specific to women are
rooted in pre-colonial social relations such as patriarchy,
whereas others are rooted in the development of capitalist
relations and imperialist oppression. Hence, the liberation
talked about concerns the struggle against imperialism, racism,
feudalism and capitalism, and the struggle against old and new
sexist institutions. Socialist transformation is the
precondition for women's liberation. The necessary steps for
women's liberation are listed. The language used is straight-
forward and less technical and specialised than other papers
by the same author.

47. MBILINYI, MARJORIE J. (1981), "The Future of Women in Africa".
Paper presented to the International Seminar on Alternative
Futures for Africa, Continental and Regional Previews,
Dalhousie University, 1-5 May, 55 pp. and to IDS Seminar
Series. Revised version to be published in Taamuli, XII (1),
University of Dar es Salaam.

Some methodological arguments are made in the first section of
the paper: (1) that "analysis of the future of women in
Africa requires a thorough analysis of present tendencies of
capitalist and non-capitalist developments"; (2) that it is
impossible to generalise about the future of "Africa", with
the presumption of a homogeneous entity, and equally impossible
to generalise about the future of women in Africa; (3) rather
than posing the question of women as women, different classes
of women are situated within the changing social formation,
and the question is posed as to whether or not and how women
enter the labour force as peasants, workers and lumpen elements
differently than men and why?; (4) that a truly explanatory
theory capable of understanding the specificities of women's
oppression and exploitation in Africa is one which is rooted
in the practice of class and other social struggles situated
in Africa; reference is made to the work of Amilcar Cabral,
where theory is rooted in a party organisation engaged in
national liberation struggles, and to the development of
participatory research within historical materialism under

other conditions, which combines a set of research techniques
with a political strategy of democratic organisation among
peasantry and working class people.

The rest of the paper focuses on the changing conditions of
peasant and working class women in Tanzania, and the specific
ways they enter into the labour force and into relations with
capital, with comparative analysis of peasant and working class
women in other countries, particularly South Africa and Senegal.

48. MKESSO, S.H. (1977), "Mapendekezo ya Viji i na Kata za Mijini"
in Prime Minister's Office, Idara ya Maendeleo ya Ujamaa na
Ushirika, Mkutano wa Mwaka wa Maafisa Maendeleo ya Ujamaa na
Ushirika, wa Mikoa, Makao Makuu na Taasisi Mbalimbali
Zinazohusika na Idara, (see II:58).

49. REYNOLDS, D.R. "An Appraisal of Rural Women in Tanzania".
Paper prepared for USAID/REDSO, Nairobi, December 1975, 46 pp.

Discussed the situation of Tanzanian women and its implications
for agricultural development planning. Outlines the roles women
play in East Africa generally and notes certain effects of the'
colonial experience and the persistence of those effects in the
post-independence era. Also discussed are the influence of the
decision makers. The report covers Tanzania's legal system,
education, employment, extension services, technology,
agricultural loans, cooperative societies and marketing.
Presents useful recommendations for dealing with agricultural
development assistance.

50. SEMBAJWE, ISRAEL (1980), "A Note on Published National Data on
Economic Activities on Women's Studies and Development". Paper
No. 31, BW, 6 pp.

The paper critically evaluates the relevance of demographic
data available from sources like the population censuses and
the National Demographic Survey (NDS). It shows how women's
activities in the household are not considered in national
figures of economic activities. A full evaluation of women's
household activities is essential in order to understand the
constraints to women's full participation in economic activities
outside the sphere of the household.

51. SIDA (1973), Women in Developing Countries - Case Studies of
Six Countries. 98 pp. biblio.

The case studies concern India, North Vietnam, Rural Kenya and
Tanzania, Tunisia and Chile. Swedish aid as it relates to
women in Tanzania up until 1973 is listed in a final section of
the monograph, together with an extensive bibliography drawing
on international agencies and Swedish literature in particular,
but including other authors as well.

In the report on rural Kenya and Tanzania, obstacles to full
involvement of women in rural development are analysed in the
context of pre-colonial and present economies. Emphasis is
placed on the need to transform property relations concerning
ownership and control of land and other means of production.
Effects of land reform and other legal institutions are shown
to block membership of women in cooperative movements and to

hinder their access to credit and farm inputs. Two additional
conditions which must be fulfilled are noted, that "women be
given the opportunity to participate in productive work with
equal responsibility" and that women "have the opportunity of
acquiring new knowledge".

52. SIDA RESEARCH DIVISION (1975), "Rural Women in Kenya and
Tanzania". Development Digest, XIII, No. 3: 53-60.

In traditional societies in East Africa, men and women had
definite roles. The women were largely responsible for the
subsistence crop and had a great say in its consumption and
disposal by sale. Men were responsible for heavier work such
as land clearing, care of animals and provision of meat. Land
was communally owned by a clan of lineage. With the introduction
of cash crops and new agricultural techniques, two associated
changes affected women. Land became the property of the husband
and cash crops grown on this land became 'men's crops'. Secondly,
new techniques and tools became men's prerogatives. This
resulted in a shift in women's position from co-producers to
mere workers.
    The status of men and women was now based on economic
accumulation rather than female or male norms. As men took
over more of the economy, women lost their status as female
members of the society in which men and women had complementary
roles and mutual respect.

53. SINARE, HAWA (1979), "Women and the Struggle for National
Liberation in Tanzania". Dar es Salaam, Faculty of Law,
University of Dar es Salaam, 25 pp.

Discusses the structure of Tanzania's economy after the Arusha
Declaration and the role of women in this structure. Asserts
that the Arusha Declaration has not eliminated the dependency
structure. Concludes that the agricultural, industrial and
commercial sectors facilitate the exploitation of both men and
women.
    Women are further exploited through social systems in which
property rights and the proceeds of labour are dominated by men.
Using the Uru Society in Kilimanjaro Region, the study shows how
women perform an inordinate amount of work in the productive
and reproductive sectors but have very little control over the
proceeds of this work.
    The origin of the low status of women is based on the
evolution of the nuclear family unit and the development of the
concept of private property. This argument is not convincingly
presented because it does not show how the position of women was
better before these developments took place and how family and
private property eroded this position. There is also a similar
weakness in the argument that women's position became inferior
as societies changed from matrilineal to patrilineal. After
all, as the author points out, in matrilineal societies "The
property has to remain with the nearest blood relative of the
mother's side - uncles or nephews" - in other words, property
rights were still invested in males only and the women had no
rights to the proceeds of her property, and no authority to
dispose of such property.

54. TANZANIA BUREAU OF STATISTICS 1969-1973, <u>1967 Population Census</u>.
Dar es Salaam, Bureau of Statistics, Ministry of Economic
Affairs and Development Planning. 6 volumes.

The 1967 Census, the first of its kind in independent Tanzania
was held on the night of 26/27 August, 1967. Altogether
18,500 E.A.'s were delineated and plotted on maps. The unit of
enumeration was the person while the unit of inquiry was the
household. The main findings were published in 4 volumes, with
a fifth volume describing the census methodology and a sixth
volume published with BRALUP presenting an analysis of the
results:

Volume 1. <u>Statistics for Enumeration Areas</u>.
Volume 2. <u>Statistics for Urban Areas</u>.
Volume 3. <u>Demographic Statistics</u>, 217 pp.
Volume 4. <u>Economic Statistics</u>, 476 pp.
Volume 5. <u>Census Methodology</u>, 268 pp.
Volume 6. <u>An Analysis of the 1967 Population Census</u>, edited by
Bertil Egero and Roushdi A. Henin.

The volumes contain useful data on a wide range of topics,
from basic demographic charasteristics to socio-economic data.

55. TANZANIA. BUREAU OF STATISTICS (1979), <u>Agricultural Census of</u>
<u>Tanzania</u>, 1971/72. Dar es Salaam, Bureau of Statistics,
<u>Ministry of Finance and Planning</u>. Vol. 1: Peasant farming.
Vol. 2: Large-scale farming. Vol. 3: Peasant and large-scale
farming.

The importance of agriculture is evident from the fact that
90 % of the economically active population depends on agriculture.
The Census aimed at collecting "quantitative information on the
agricultural structure using as a unit of enumeration the
agricultural holding and covering the whole country within a
single agricultural year".
    Although the volumes are concerned basically with such
aspects as area under cultivation, crop and livestock production
statistics, and the use of fertilizers and agricultural equipment,
there is considerable data on the farming population e.g.

... Number of persons working in agricultural work on holdings,
    by age, sex and size of holding.

... Occupational distribution of those working on the holdings
    (paid workers, working proprietors, unpaid family workers,
    others) by sex and size of holding.

... Number of household members employed other than on holdings
    (agricultural occupation, non-agricultural occupation) by
    age, sex and size of holding.

... Farm population by age and sex (large-scale farming).

... Number of people employed by seasons (large-scale farming).

Data is presented at regional and national levels but is also
available at district level at the Bureau of Statistics.

56. TANZANIA. BUREAU OF STATISTICS (1980), <u>1978 Population Census</u>;
<u>Preliminary Report</u>. Dar es Salaam, Bureau of Statistics. 182 pp.

This is the first publication of the 1978 Census and includes the following information mainly in tabular form for mainland Tanzania and Zanzibar:

- Population in regions and districts by age and sex. District and ward population by sex.

- Number of households in districts and urban areas; percentage of households in villages, Tanzania citizens as percentage of total population; and sex ratio.

- Regional growth and density per region for 1967 and 1978.

- Population in regional headquarters by age and sex, number of households and average size of households.

- Urban areas other than regional and district headquarters - Tanzania Mainland - 1978.

- Urban areas in Zanzibar and Pemba.

There is also a map showing annual average population growth in percentages and another showing population densities by districts.

57. TANZANIA. Third Five Year Plan for Economic and Social Development. Vol. I. Part One: General Perspectives, Part Two: Regional Perspectives, Dar es Salaam, 127 pp.

Provides an overview of the economic and social policies of the government and about the implementation of earlier plans. A wealth of data is presented about the economy and about education and other social institutions. It is essential to read the plan in order to understand the basic conditions under which women work and live. At the same time, information about women in particular depends on the information provided by the different Ministries. Some ignore the question of women altogether, whereas others note the existence of women, for example, in their statistics. Very few actually pose the problem of women as a problem of social and national concern. A unique example of the latter is the emphasis given by the Ministry of National Education on the unequal access that girls have traditionally had to secondary and higher education, and the efforts being made by the Ministry to correct the situation. A contrary picture is provided by the Labour Division in the Ministry of Labour and Social Welfare, which consists of two brief paragraphs minus any self-criticism in general and no discussion of issues such as employment of youth and women in particular, labour productivity and so on.
    The overall tendency however is to ignore women, which is a problem in that understanding the role of women in production is crucial in order to achieve the specific objectives of the Third Plan. This is particularly so in the case of agriculture objectives such as increasing productivity in both cash and especially food crops. Implementation strategies such as price policies, promotion of better farm implements, agricultural research, storage programmes and so on are limited so long as the specific role of women in food production and storage, distribution and processing is ignored. There is a technicist bias to the analysis, recommendations and programmes

presented, which ignore the social relations that block the full
mobilisation of all peasants, men and women, toward increased
productivity. The research programmes reproduce this neglect
of the social issues surrounding peasant production and
productivity.

One way of correcting the general neglect of "the women's
question" would be to insert a specific section on women in the
next Five Year Plan and all Annual and Longer-range plans, This
could be the task of the Women's Section in the Prime Minister's
Office, and would involve monitoring the performance and plans
of all Ministries in order to ensure that the Party policy of
achieving full equality between men and women is achieved. At
the same time, the contribution that women are making side by
side with men as peasants and workers would be documented, and
problems hindering that contribution be studied and resolved.

58. TANZANIA. Prime Minister's Office, Idara ya Maendeleo ya Ujamaa
na Ushirika 1977 Mkutano wa Mwaka Maafisa Maendeleo ya Ujamaa
na Ushirika wa Mikoa, Makao Makuu na Taasisi Mbalimbali
Zinazohusika na Idara Uliofanyika Chuo cha Ushirika Moshi,
Dodoma.

Based on proceedings of the annual meeting of the officers of
the Department of Ujamaa na Ushirika, the report consists of
papers on the many aspects of that department's work: the village
managers training programme, the village management technicians,
cooperatives, financial institutions of relevance to villages,
crop marketing and the villagisation process. For example,
S.H. Mkesso's paper, "Mapendekezo ya Vijiju na Kata za Mijini",
analyses problems in the enforcement of the Village Law Act of
1975 and the City Authority Act of 1976; village size (too small
or too large), inadequate land; movement of villagers from good
locations with respect to land; soil fertility and water supply
to a non-satisfactory location; delays in setting up village
governments; ignorance about the responsibilities and authority
of the village government; the tendency to elect village leadership which is not in line with the Arusha Declaration or else
on the basis of age and "respect" or authority rather than
capacity to carry out leadership roles in line with socialist
policies, leading to the promotion of private business rather
than socialism; difficulty of getting credit or loans due to
complicated bureaucratic measures; the lack of adequate
expertise to service the villages; conflicts over marketing
procedures including weighing techniques between village/
cooperative society and the marketing boards or crop
authorities; the tendency of some district leaders to ignore or
dismiss village complaints without giving them serious
attention and investigation; the lack of adequate protection of
village property. This report is remarkably straight-forward
about problems in the villagisation policy.

There was only one woman participant in this annual meeting,
a UWT officer. This may reflect problems of recruitment and
promotion of women within the department itself, and the lack
of a deliberate policy to encourage the participation of women
officers in such meetings (such as providing child care
facilities during meetings and allowances to cover travel and

subsistence for younger children and infants).

59. TANZANIA. Prime Minister's Office, Idara ya Maendeleo ya Ujamaa na Ushirika, 1978 "Mpango wa Mafunzo kwa Halmashauri za Vijiji" Dodoma, 8 pp. + 27 pp. tables.

By 1978, 7,481 villages had been registered, and a total of 8,000 were expected. Village Councillor responsibilities include planning village development plans and managing their implementation; crop purchases and sale to relevant Crop Boards and Authorities; management of all cooperative activities in the village; allocation and management of the use of all natural resources including land within the village, and village property; keeping village statistics and accounts; and making small bye-laws of the village. Training on various aspects of the Village Act of 1975, bookkeeping, project planning and political education were necessary to enable village leadership to carry out their responsibilities. The timetable and syllabi for this training is provided, to be carried out between February 1978 and June 1979. A total of 89,772 village councillors were to be trained, 12 from each village, to include the Village Chairperson, Village Secretary, and the 5 Committee Chairpersons and Secretaries of each village. The Cooperative College and PMO were to cooperate in the preparation of teaching materials, the training of the teachers, and the administration of funds for running the VC training programme.

This large-scale training programme is a major development in adult education. However, its orientation solely to village councillors excludes all other village members, who will tend to be women and youth, and in many areas the poorer peasants as a whole. These categories of villagers are rarely elected as village councillors. One solution is to promote equal representation of women and men, youth and elders, rich and poor peasants in Village Councillor positions. Another more short-term measure is to include village members who are not Councillors in the training programme, in order to broaden the base of such skills and knowledge in the villages and thus ensure accountability of the councillors to their fellow villagers. An equal number of women and men villagers could then be selected to attend the course, including youth and elders.

With respect to the syllabus of the course for village councillors, it would have been more meaningful to include participatory research procedures to analyse the social relations within the village in relation to its productive forces, and how they relate to future village development. Abstract discussion about socialism, feudalism and capitalism already included in the syllabus would then be complemented by concrete analysis of real social relations at village and household, and national and international levels. The obstacles to full mobilization and development of the majority of peasants could then be more easily identified by the villagers themselves.

60. TANZANIA. Prime Minister's Office, VMTP 1976 Quarterly Progress Report No. 3 for period Ending 30th September 1976 VMTP 7611/R3 Dar es Salaam, 19 pp.

Women are usually selected for home economic courses at Buhare
and Ndamba, and are therefore unavailable for Village Managers
training. The policy adopted for posting VMT's is to allocate
them in wards which have already developed plans at district
and regional level, and have village cooperative economic
projects already established. This policy would seem to
contribute to further differentiation between villages and wards,
as the already more developed areas get the additional input of
village management cadres to further their development.

61. TANZANIA. Prime Minister's Office, VMTP 1979 <u>Evaluation of
Bookkeepers Training</u>, Dar es Salaam, 25 pp. + Appendices.

The village bookkeeping system was approved by the PMO for
nationwide use in 1977. The aim is to train a village bookkeeper for every village, who is selected by the villagers from
among their own members. The village bookkeeper is responsible
for keeping village account books and all other necessary records,
registers and stationery. The village bookkeeper works under
the supervision of the village manager and is answerable to the
village council. There is a three-phase programme of training
at Folk Development Colleges, with one to two years work
experience in between each phase. By June 1979, 1109 had been
trained in Phase I, and more were to be trained during 1979/80.
The evaluation report is based on personal interviews using a
detailed questionnaire (found in the appendix). However, it is
based on a very small sample of 32 village bookkeepers spread
around 5 regions, and therefore its findings cannot be
generalized. Nevertheless, they are suggestive for further
research.
     Ninety percent of the village bookkeepers were men. There
was a high dropout rate in the sense of not carrying out the
functions of the bookkeeper because of the lack of village funds
to pay the bookkeeper and/or to buy the cash books and other
materials necessary, and the lack of enough economic activities
warranting accounting, which led to low work load and low work
motivation; and inadequate supervision and assistance. Where
the village bookkeepers were functioning, cash and other books
were fairly up-to-date, and they were carrying out many other
responsibilities such as supervision of village projects. The
report recommends that married women should be deliberately
sought for training as village bookkeepers, because they are
usually tied to their villages because of family responsibilities:
"this makes it more easy to keep the bookkeeper stationed in the
Village as men more easily look for challenging jobs elsewhere".
It also calls for a minimum salary system, more supervision by
the responsible officers, and a revision of the training course.
In line with the above recommendations, we would pose again
the question of facilities at Folk Development Colleges needed
in order to ensure that married women can participate in the
training programme. A period of 7 weeks as recommended is a
relatively long time, and child care and other facilities are
necessary if women are to attend. Villages and husbands will
also have to commit themselves to providing for family needs
during the women's absence.

62. TANZANIA. Prime Minister's Office, VMTP 1979, <u>Evaluation of
    VMT's Training</u>, Dar es Salaam, 24 pp. + Instrumentation, mimeo.

    The second follow-up evaluation of 986 trained Village Management
    Technicians posted at the end of 1977, was based on a sample of
    only 19 VMT's (1.7 %) interviewed during a 6 week period in 5
    regions and 10 districts. As in the evaluation of Village book-
    keepers (item 61) there is a severe problem of sampling
    technique and size, and research technique, which relies
    completely on structured questionnaires and is not backed up
    by an in-depth investigation of village/ward political and
    economic conditions. If there are inadequate resources for
    such evaluation, it would be more meaningful to focus on VMT's
    in one district in a few carefully selected villages, where
    one could include the views of different groups among villagers
    including village leadership, other village-level government
    cadres, and other villagers such as youth and women.
        The evaluation found that VMT's are not performing as
    expected because of various problems such as the large number
    of villages allocated (up to 25 for one VMT, compared to the
    policy of 4 to 5); lack of transport; lack of adequate district
    and regional level supervision; the short training period.

63. TANZANIA. Prime Minister's Office, Mpango wa Mafunzo ya
    Msingi ya Mameneja wa Vijiji n.d. "Muwongozo wa Wakufunzi"
    Book No. 11, Dodoma, 20 pp.

    A detailed outline of the timetable for one-month training
    course for Village Managers, including a list of the subjects
    taught. As with the training of Village Councillors, the
    syllabus does not include concrete analysis of social relations
    at village and household level. Given the nature of the
    Village Manager's responsibilities, which include "mobilization"
    of villagers for development and higher productivity, such input
    into the training programme is essential, combined with procedures
    of investigation including participatory research.

64. UTAFITI (1978), "National Seminar on Science and Technology for
    Development Held in Dar es Salaam, Tanzania from 23-27 January
    1978". Dar es Salaam, 28 pp. and Annexes.

    The key issues and specific recommendations of the seminar are
    presented in the following broad problem areas: agricultural
    development; energy systems and development; industrial develop-
    ment; building and construction industry, science and
    technological education; manpower development, science and
    technology policy; research institutional development and
    strengthening. The significance of participatory research which
    is oriented towards the mobilisation of villagers and others to
    investigate problems and seek solutions with the assistance of
    multidisciplinary teams of scientists, technologists and social
    scientists was highlighted. Concrete conditions in rural and
    urban areas were taken into consideration in the deliberations.
    However, despite the central role of women in, for example
    agriculture production; food preservation and processing;
    village energy systems; and their historical lack of participation
    in science and technological education and relevant manpower

posts, no specific attention was given to such issues as the way the sexual division of labour hinders full mobilisation of all peasants and workers for development and social transformation when these respective topics were discussed. Recommendations, for example, on strengthening of the agricultural extension services, alternative energy sources etc. are not taking the position of women into account. These recommendations would have been strengthened if particular attention had been given to the objectively different role or impact of women and men in order to concretise the argument. As far as we can determine, about five women participated out of a total of 103 in attendance (i.e. less than 5 %).

65. UTAFITI (1978), "Science and Technology for Development, African Goals and Aspirations in the United Nations Conference". Report of a Symposium held in Arusha, Tanzania, January 30 - February 4, 1978, Dar es Salaam and SAREC, Stockholm, 48 pp.

The need for integrated national science and technology policies in the context of the struggle for a New International Economic Order is stressed, together with the development of adequate human resources and the infrastructure necessary, including mass participation at all levels and regional and international cooperation. Compared to the Dar es Salaam preliminary national seminar (item 64), the deliberation here was less concrete, and stressed very general objectives rather than specific, concrete measures to resolve specific problems. No attention was given to national and local level contradictions, including those related to the sexual division of labour in production and reproduction. So far as we can determine from the list of participants, there were no women out of 17 in attendance.

66. VITTA, PAUL B. (1981), "Dominance: The Influence of Circumstance on Science in Tanzania", University of Dar es Salaam, Professorial Inaugural Lecture as Professor of Physics, May 26th.

The major argument is that science and expertise are not valued in Tanzania. Scientific methods and attitudes towards problem solving have not been adopted by the policy makers and bureaucrats any more than by peasants and workers. This is revealed in the passive attitude towards nature, in helplessness for example to construct man-made solutions to drought, such as irrigation systems and dams, and the strong reliance on super-natural explanations for personal and national crises.

Whereas there has been a positive growth in numbers of children and adults exposed to schooling, the quality of schooling especially in scientific education has fallen. For example, most secondary schools lack adequate scientific equipment for practical sessions. Musoma Resolutions called for two years work experience prior to attendance at the University. There has been no planning however of how to post Form 6 leavers so that their work experience will reinforce subject specialisation, making a mockery of the aim of uniting theory and practice within specific disciplines.

Problems of productivity in industry and agriculture are partly due to the lack of scientific approaches, including constant investigation, and systematic planning. It is assumed that politics and political education alone promote economic development, leading to the substitution of words for action. The scarce resources which do exist in the country are not distributed in such a way as to promote both scientific experimentation and production. Policies are announced and directives issued without careful investigation and planning, like "the hunter who shoots first and aims later". Among the specific recommendations given, the development of extension and outreach programmes to popularise science so that peasants and workers become scientific in their work and life was noted.

This lecture has great relevance to the practices of programmes and organisations oriented to women, and research itself in women's studies. Politics has tended to be separated from scientific investigation and planning (and vice versa), and "rule by decree" by certain leaders has become the trend. Women with capacity for scientific investigation and planning are neither sought nor encouraged within such organisations, and are even chased out for being too "independent-minded". A scientific approach carries with it a critical attitude, which seeks to back up positions or programmes by relating them to analysis of concrete material reality and the different group or class positions reflected in them. Development of any movement, organisation or political programme, and of scientific knowledge itself, depends on a constantly high level of critique, not of persons but at the level of ideas and actions. This point was stressed, for example, during the debate held at Lumumba Hall during UWT week in 1980. Although Professor Vitta stresses scientific expertise at the expense of correct political practices, the problem concerns the lack of unity between the two.

67. VUORELA, ULLA (1981), "Participant Observation in Colonial Tanganyika: The Case of 'Anthropology in Action' in Iringa". Paper tabled at the IDS Regional Workshop on Research Methodology, Arusha, March 30th - April 11, 24 pp.

Analyses the "pilot project" in Iringa during the 1930's which focused on whether anthropological research could be fruitfully combined with colonial administration. The aims and methodologies of social sciences in the third world are problematised, and the contradiction between intentions and actual effects explored: "While anthropologists became sympathetic recorders of indigenous forms of life, they also contributed towards maintaining the power structure created by the colonial system". Phenomenological or pragmatic participatory research and participant observation embody similar contradictions today. The controversies and class struggles surrounding the extraction of the "Plural Wives Tax" are used to illustrate the contradictory nature of the research. The tax was meant to discourage polygamy by taxing men for each wife in excess of one, but it became in practice a tax on women, including widows and unmarried women. Native authorities and headmen rationalised this practice as a mechanism to discourage women from refusing to engage in a polygamous marriage. The different positions taken by the researchers and the colonial administrators on this issue are analysed.

III.   CASE STUDIES

Anthropological research has produced valuable information on certain
aspects of precapitalist social relations often called "traditional"
relations.   Detailed information about property relations and the
sexual division of labour is provided.   At the same time, the knowledge so produced must be critically reread.   The studies included
in this section are all within the anthropological problematic.
They were initially categorised because the object of analysis
tended to be "the tribe" or the "ethnic group" considered as a
separate entity.   Herein lies one of the problems with such
investigation, however, in that the way in which these groups were
related to the wider social formation defined by changing relations
of production and exchange and later by the colonial (and post-
colonial) state is not examined.
        Anthropologists working during the colonial period were employees
of the colonial state, or worked in alliance with its functionaries.
These conditions of work help to explain the emphasis on structural
analysis of political systems, lineage networks, property rights and
inheritance (e.g. in the work by Gulliver, III:75, 76).   Such
information was needed by the colonialists in order to subjugate
conquered groups and develop appropriate mechanisms of social
control.   An excellent critique of one "experiment" to development
policy-oriented anthropology in Iringa is that of Vuorela (II:67).
        Other anthropologists focused on analyses of economic activities,
but these were usually defined at the household and/or clan level
(e.g. III:70, 72, 82).   In neither case did the anthropologists
question to what extent the phenomena under observation were the
product of capitalist commoditisation and colonial rule, and not by
any means "traditional" society.   Moreover, the informants they
relied on were usually male elders, i.e. patriarchs, often members
of ruling clans or classes, with their own class or gender interests.
Methodological problems have persisted in contemporary anthropology.
Some of the more recent work has tried to situate a given "tribe"
within a wider context.   Feierman (III:73, 74) sought to move beyond
such a historical structuralism to an historical analysis, by
investigating the nature of a feudal state and the destructive
effect of dependency on long-distance trade linked to the worldwide
capitalist market.   However, the tension between structural
functionalism and historical analysis is revealed in the production
of two separate volumes, one emphasising the anthropological
approach, the other history.
        His analysis of kinship and clan becomes static and ahistorical,
and the "history" cannot cope adequately with the question of the
internal dynamics which led to the development and later destruction
of feudal relations.   Feierman's work illuminates the limitations
of anthropological analysis which is not guided by a materialist
framework.   Nevertheless, it remains "rich" in "raw materials" for
critical re-analysis.
        Huber (III:77) and Wembah Rashid (III:83) provide detailed
information about relations of sexuality and fertility situated
in each case within matrilineality.   Huber's analysis focuses on
the changes which occurred during the colonial and post-colonial

periods, and the constant tension between matrilineality and patriarchal relations.

We are left with the major question of how to reconstruct the past. How should researchers investigate pre-colonial pre capitalist relations which underwent substantial transformation long before colonial rule? Reliance on elders oral history is clearly not sufficient, given the fundamental changes which have occurred during the last century and more, as well as the issue of class and gender bias. Likewise, participant observation of contemporary society is problematic. Archaeological and linguistic research represent important methods to explore the past, combined with a materialist approach to history. Such research is extremely important to clarify the development of the sexual division of labour and pre-capitalist patriarchal relations, which contribute to our understanding of women's subordination today.

---

68. ABDURAHMAN, MUHAMMED (1939), "Anthropological Notes from the Zanzibar Protectorate". TNR, No. 8 (December): 59-84.

Various aspects of the life and work of the Wahadimu are presented, a group living in large villages on the East Coast and extreme North and South Coasts of Zanzibar. Detail about birth and childhood, circumcision, Quran school, marriage and daily life provide rich information about the life of women on the islands. Female initiation rites are described, where young girls are "taught the sexual relations of men and women and good manners towards their husbands when they are married". In general women do most of the cultivation and men control the trading of proceeds.

69. ABRAHAM, R.G. (1967), Peoples of Greater Unyamwezi, Tanzania. London, International African Institute. Ethnographic Survey of Africa, East Central Africa, Part XVII, 95 pp.

Summarises ethnographic material on the Nyamwezi, Sukuma, Sumbwa, Kimbu and Konongo tribes of West Central Tanzania. Social and economic activity was centred around the household. "A household was a distinct food production, food owning and child-rearing unit ... (It) was the basic economic unit with its well-defined division of labour". A table showing division of labour between sexes as followed in Unyamwezi in 1950 is included. Every woman had her own hearth, cooking equipment, fields, food and part of any cattle owned by her husband; but a woman's rights were more as a protection against other women than against her husband. The husband owned her hut, the fields on which she worked and most, if not all, of the households' food. Women were expected to work at cultivating cash crops on the husband's fields, but had no say in their disposal. At divorce, the woman was allowed to take her utensils, proceeds from crafts and any cattle she had inherited from her own family but she was not given any share of the food supplies.

70. BEIDELMAN, THOMAS O. (1960), "The Baraguyu". TNR, No. 55 (September): 245-278.

A detailed history of the origins of the Ilparakuyu (called Baraguyu in this article) begins this article, which must be balanced with other histories as in the case of all anthropologic material (see Ndagala 1978, for example). The political economy of the Ilparakuyu can be discerned, such as the tight balance between cattle and subsistence and the absolute necessity to include grains and vegetables as a part of the regular diet. Sex specificity of tasks and activities is outlined and patriarch relations underlying these are also detailed. The age group organisation is analysed and its relationship to the lineage.

71. BEIDELMAN, T.O. (1967), Tne Matrilineal Peoples of Eastern Tanzania. London, International African Institute, 94 pp.

Ethnographic surveys are provided of matrilineal groups: the Zaramo, Kwere, Luguru, Sagara, Vidunda, Ngulu and Zigula. Depending upon the sources available, which vary from group to group, the author describes demography, economy, lineage and clan systems, land and property rights, marriage and initiation, rituals and so on. Throughout there is a wealth of material related to sex specificity of tasks and activities, and patriarch relations in the context of matrilineality and matrilocal residence. The very nature of the task, a survey of a descriptive nature, limits its usefulness in that there is inadequate critical analysis. A bibliography is provided which is very useful, and includes much archival material. This remains a necessary resource for those interested in matrilineality, or in the women's question as it pertains to any of the groups cited. However it must be balanced with contemporary work of a more critical nature, some of which have been cited in this volume.

72. BRAIN, J.L. (1962), "The Kwere of the Eastern Province". TNR, Nos. 58-59: 231-241.

The effects of matrilineality on property inheritance, especially of land, and on the power and status of women are discussed. The analysis is basically ahistorical, posing the lineage and clan system to be fixed and static, with no periodisation in terms of changes resulting from penetration of merchant capital, the establishment of colonial rule, and later independence. Information is provided about cultivation and food production and consumption, and about sex, marriage and divorce. Female initiation rites are described, as well as the origins of infanticide in different manners of delivery or presentation of infants. The breakdown of the matrilineal system is shown to be related to commoditisation in agriculture.

73. FEIERMAN, STEVEN (1972), Concepts of Sovereignty among the Shambaa and Their Relationship to Political Action. Oxford University, unpublished D. Phil. dissertation.

This is the "anthropologic" analysis of the Shambaa, to be read in conjunction with the "historic" analysis in Feierman (III:74). Readers will find this one particularly rich in detail about the lineage and clan systems, the role of marriage and bridewealth in the reproduction of these systems and ultimately the society as a whole, descent groups and "Alliance, Domestic Groups and Territorial Integration". The technical division of

labour by age and sex is presented in chapter 3 and one can
interpret as well the way in which patriarch relations provided
a mechanism for surplus generation and appropriation. Litigation,
warfare and tribute are more clearly periodized than the others,
dealing with the period of the Kilindi state. The mechanisms
of appropriation and accumulation of surplus, including slave
relations themselves, are described here.

74. FEIERMAN, STEVEN (1974), The Shambaa Kingdom. A History.
Madison, University of Wisconsin Press, 235 pp.

Beginning with the period just prior to the establishment of the
Kilindi State, the author explores the origins of the state as
revealed in the famous "myth of Mbegha" (see Abdullah bin
Hemedi bin Ali Liajjemi 1936). The information contained in
the myth is compared to historical accounts of the development
of the feudal relations which led to the formation of the
Kilindi state. The emphasis is placed thereafter on the 19th
century and the development of contradictions inherent to the
mode of production dominating the state. Exaction of tribute
in the form of surplus product and surplus labour is juxtaposed
with the growing importance of international trade in the Shambaa
economy. The destruction of the kingdom partly results from the
developing slave trade, and is finalised by German conquest in
the 1890's. The author discussed the techniques of inquiry
he has relied upon, including oral history based on accounts
of elders, and re-analysis of the myths themselves.
      Although the problem of women is never posed as an issue in and of
itself, the reader can extract a great deal of information and
insight by a careful re-reading of the material. There is a
description of what we conceptualise to be patriarch relations,
and the sexual division of labour. The analysis of the economy
of the state provides material to analyse the interaction
between patriarch and feudal relations and where and how women's
position fits and is altered. The myths themselves presented
and discussed illustrate patriarch ideology of male dominance.
      Mbilinyi (IV:106) has developed a critique of this and the
other work cited by Feierman, which notes the richness of his
work but criticises the methodology used. The very existence of
two different works, one anthropological (1972) and one historical
(1974), is indicative of the problem at hand. The underlying
patriarch relations whose expression is found in the lineage
structure are never posed in the early work, and yet they remain
a fundamental mechanism for the generation and appropriation of
surplus (product and labour) in the feudal period. At the same
time, the history of the kingdom (1974) ignores the rich material
of the lineage, and cannot adequately explain the dynamics of
production relations which underlie the Kilindi state. The
crucial role of women as both surplus labour and producers,
through biological reproduction of surplus labour, is basically
ignored.

75. GULLIVER, P.H. (1961), "Structural Dichotomy and Jural Processes
Among the Arusha of Northern Tanganyika". Africa, 31 (1):
19-35.

Among the Arusha of Tanganyika, lineage groups and certain other
categories of people are divisible into two parts, which are
themselves divisible and re-divisible in a dichotomous manner.
The two parts comprising a whole is known as "olwashe"; the
prototype of the olwashe is within a family. A wife will recruit
another wife for her husband and bring her to her homestead in
order to gain adherence to her own olwashe. The relationship
is important in domestic and farming work as well as division
of property. Brothers of the same "olwashe" occupy adjacent
pieces of land. Incoming bridewealth is distributed among
sons of the same olwashe as the daughter who brought in the
bridewealth.

76. GULLIVER, PHILIP HUGH (1965), Social Control in an African
Society: A Study of the Arusha Agricultural Masai of Northern
Tanganyika. Edited by Philip High Gulliver, London, Routledge
and Kegan Paul. Relevant section: Women in the patrilineal
system (of the Arusha) pp. 141-44.

Presents the static, anthropoligic present with inadequate
attention to social change. According to author, an Arusha
female is automatically a member of her paternal lineages and
groups by virtue of her birth. However, women have no rights of
inheritance, cannot own land or livestock, cannot participate in
discussions, arrangements or contractual obligations concerning
property and cannot take part in rituals till they are married
and have children. Even when they have reached this last stage,
travel to the paternal areas is difficult and the right to
participate in rituals is therefore not exercised.
    She relinquishes most of her lesser membership commitments
in her natal group and yet remains a member there. Conversely,
while gradually increasing her interests in her husband's
groups, she never becomes a full member of them. It is this
ambiguity which contributes to the inferior status of women
among the Waarusha.

77. HUBER, HUGO (1973), Marriage and the Family in Rural Bukwaya
(Tanzania). The University Press, Freibourg, Switzerland,
266 pp.

One of the most detailed analyses thus far of a matrilineal
group, the work explores the historical development of the
Bukwaya and changes which occurred during the colonial and post-
colonial periods. Attention is given to the constant tension
between matrilineality and patriarch relations and how this
worked out over time. Based partly on archival sources, the
efforts of the church to impose bridewealth is related to the
colonial perception that patriarch relations are the correct
basis for family stability. Social relations at different
levels of sub-division, clan homestead and age groups are
examined, followed by a detailed analysis of marriage social
relations and finally "kinship ties and rituals". The rich
descriptive material provides the reader with insight about
many aspects of the society in question, its ideology of male
dominance and of matrilineality, its political structure of
patriarch and slave-owner rule combined, and the economic bases.
However, this is subject to the reader's own interpretation of

the material as shown below. The roots of lineage differentiation
are in the differential accumulation of cattle and women and
slaves. Slaves were taken as wives, they and their children
thereby subjected to patrilineal principles of lineage membership
(for offspring) and labour service. Alternatively, wealthy
patriarchs married women of north Mara with the same result of
patrilineality.

A careful reading provides us with indications of female
resistance against women's oppression, and the bases for
particular patriarchist sanctions and rules which then developed.
A dialectical view is needed in handling the author's discussion
of divorce, in that it is posed both as an anthropological and
moral problem. The ease with which women could secure divorce
and remarry under matrilineal conditions, and the persistence
of high divorce rates after the imposition of bridewealth and
limited patrilineality by the colonial state underlined the
relative power and independence of women in this society.

The study becomes an invitation to the reader to engage her/
himself in more investigation along similar though more critical
lines. The data is derived from elderly informants (three of
whom are women), archival sources, and participant observation.
Case histories are also provided as an appendix to the section
on marriage, which provide anecdotal information about wives and
their movements in and out of marriage (and back again).

78. JELLICOE, M.R. (1962), "An Experiment in Mass Education Among
Women: Singida District, Tanganyika". Occasional Papers in
Community Development, No. 1: 1-45.

Describes a survey done as a background to the UNICEF mass
education campaign consisting of a simple programme of improved
cookery, health and child care to 3,000 women in two years.
Specially relevant to this bibliography is the section entitled
"Position of Women".

Jellicoe writes that the very heavy emphasis on lineage in
the Turu society gives the woman considerable social status as
a mother, daughter and sister. "The excessive desire for human
fertility ... loads women with many heavy burdens, both practical
and ritual; but at the same time it ensures them the central
place, as mothers, in a society which at first glance appears to
be dominated by men". Economically, however, the Turu woman was
no better off than women in most other tribal groups. The husband
had to provide her with a house, land and cattle but he had the
complete right over her labour and consequently over the disposal
of any surplus from the fields or any of the livestock including
small livestock. Legally, the Turu woman was always considered
as a minor but women frequently spoke for themselves in court
and were elected to the Turu Council.

The author's acceptance of patriarchal ideologies about
women's "central place" in a male - dominated society exemplifies
"oppression by elevation" noted by Vuorela (XI:318). See also
Marguerite Jellicoe's The Long Path (Nairobi, East African
Publishing House, 1978) and Harold K. Schneider's The Wahi
Wanyaturu (New York, Viking Fund Publications in Anthropology
1970) for detailed research on women in Turu society.

79. NDAGALA, DANIEL KYARUZI (1974), <u>Social and Economic Change Among the Pastoral Wakwavi and its Impact on Rural Development</u>. University of Dar es Salaam, unpublished MA dissertation.

Although not specifically about women, scattered throughout the dissertation is information about the technical sexual division of labour, including the way women traders in Ilparakuyo (Wakwavi) and Wakwere communities relate to each other. The peripheral place of women in the age-set system is discernible, as well as the way the patrilineal lineage system structures their lives and work. This is among the few studies of pastoralist people in Tanzania (see also IV:99, 116 and 124).

80. POPPLEWELL, G.D. (1937), "Notes on the Fipa". <u>TNR</u>, No. 3 (April): 99-105.

The political economy of the Fipa situated near Lakes Tanganyika and Rukwa is described, especially the division of labour in cultivating and hunting, and the relations between chiefs and others. Much detail is provided on sex specificity of tasks and economic activities. The development of migrant labour in the area and its effect on the people is also discussed.

81. ROLLESTON, IAN H.O. (1939), "The Watumbatu of Zanzibar". <u>TNR</u>, No. 8 (December): 85-97.

A special section on the "Position of Women" provides limited information about sex specificity in tasks and activities. Women share cultivation with husbands, make pottery and fish for white bait and octupuses. This article is most notable for the statement that "Women are the drudges of the household and the slaves of their masters; they must keep well out of the way when he is entertaining guests".

82. SCHERER, J.H. (1959), "The Ha of Tanganyika". <u>Anthropos</u>, 54: 842-904.

This ethnographic survey of the Ha of Western Tanzania covers several aspects affecting the role of women in this society including their social status; division of labour; their contribution to food production; education; inheritance; marriage, and divorce. Claims that, though male dominance is emphasised and women enjoy less freedom than men, this does not necessarily involve a lowly status. A woman keeps a life-long right to her bridewealth cattle against her brother, and can refuse to be inherited when widowed. Women are not debarred from partaking or even officiating a magico-religious ceremonies. In certain circumstances they can inherit land and succeed to ruling offices, though in these cases they are considered as males.

83. WEMBAH-RASHID, J.A.R. (1978), <u>The Socio-Economic System of Wakwere An Ethnographic Study of a Matrilineal People of Central Eastern Tanzania</u>. University of Dar es Salaam, unpublished MA dissertation, 278 pp., biblio.

This is an extremely detailed ethnographic study of the Wakwere, providing rich information about the social relations of the homestead, sex specificity of tasks and activities, lineage and descent, inheritance and residence, marriage procedures, customs of pregnancy and birth, and the initiation of boys and girls. Relations of property and of different agents in the labour process itself can be worked out, as well as the ideology of male dominance underlying the initiation rites. The details about different forms of marriage provide a basis for theorising about precapitalist social relations such as slave relations. Although both husbands and wives cultivate, there is sex specificity in tasks of farming and gathering. At the same time, specifically matrilineal principles of property ownership and control of offspring provide women with power and independence vis-a-vis their husbands. This is so despite the control by the maternal uncle of the offspring (or because of it).

The analysis is of added interest given the position which the author takes towards matrilineality in general, and its expression among the Wakwere in particular. There is a tendency to impose patriarchist ideas of power and control in his interpretation of relationships. For example, in his discussion of casual marriages he notes that "The new 'husband' tends to put her (e.g. a divorced woman or young girl) on probation, and this 'probation', in some cases, becomes permanent". All the evidence he provides elsewhere in his work indicates it is the man who is on probation and not the woman! More to the point, he notes: "Most critics hold that these days they (matrilocal marriages) are a drawback economically, because by keeping the husband in a subservient position on the woman's family side they reduce his economic dynamism. This takes into consideration that men usually are at the vanguard of modern economics and general development ventures. A man sees no point in investing his time and labour in an area where he is not secure, and considering the insecurity or fluidity of modern marriages, a man is certainly not secure in his in-law's home-stead". Whereas we agree with the author that being put in a subservient position affects producers in a negative way, we reject patriarchist ideology that the wife should be so sub-ordinated. The problems of the husband and his lack of security and "strangeness" in his wife's homeplace could as well be the description of the majority of peasant women in Tanzania, situated in a patrilineal and patrilocal context.

84. WILSON, G. McL. (1953), "The Tatoga of Tanganyika". TNR, Nos. 33 and 34 (July and January): 34-47, 35-56.

The "Tatoga" include the Barabaig of Hanang and Mbulu, and this analysis centres on the historical development and changes of this group. The analysis is clear, critical and non-moralistic, showing great insight into such issues as the dispossession of young men and their need to find independent sources of cattle. Struggles between cultivators and the Barabaig pastoralists over access to land and water are delineated. Social relations of patrilineage provide the conditions which determine women's access to their means of production, whereas neighbourhood and generation groups effect relations between women and women, and women and men, across lineage lines. Sex specificity in tasks and activities is noted. The generation group of women have the power to sanction any individual (male or female) who has

infringed upon the rights of one of their members. Sanctions include
ridicule, confiscation of property, even death. Changes affected
by colonial rule and commoditisation of cattle are noted. The
article ends with recommendations on how to use the correct
understanding of the social relations of the Barabaig to detect
youthful murderers, thereby revealing how anthropology was used
to serve the interests of the colonial state.

85. WRIGHT, MARCIA (1977), "Family, Community and Women as Reflected
in 'Die Safwa' by Elise Kootz-Kretschmer", in Bengt Sundkler and
Per-Åke Wahlström (eds.), Vision and Service, Papers in Honour
of Barbro Johansson. Uppsala, The Scandinavian Institute of
African Studies, The Swedish Institute of Missionary Research,
pp. 108-116.

An analysis of precapitalist social relations of the Safwa
group in Mbeya area during 1880 to 1910, based on life stories
compiled by a German missionary. The relative independence of
Safwa women was related to women's inheritance of their mother's
cultivation rights and those of the mother's patrilineage, and'
the absence of men as migrant labourers. However, differentiation
among women existed; some were pawns (slaves), other were
commoners or royal clan members. Even the latter were subject
to patriarchal control over the exchange of women, however,
and to exceedingly high infant mortality rates.

94

IV. PEASANTS

The question of the subordination of women peasants centres around
these fundamental issues: land; labour; the labour product; "the
double burden" consisting in maintenance of the household and
production for the market; villagisation and class differentiation.
The development of more conceptual clarity in addressing these
issues has been accompanied by important developments in procedures
of empirical investigation. Although all of these issues relate
to each other, the works included in this section have tended to
emphasise or focus on particular questions.

Land

The question of "ownership" of land has been deepened to consider
the degree to which women peasants effectively "possess" the land.
Effective possession connotes the producers capacity to control
how the land (or livestock) is used and what is produced on the
land; and to put the land and other means of production to work.
In Bukoba and Kilimanjaro, for example, the fact that women do not
own the land on which they cultivate represents the material basis
for female subordination in several investigations (IV:86, 91 and
131). Research in matrilineal production systems indicate that
land ownership in itself does not constitute an adequate explanation
(IV:108-111, 114, 115). Women are not "free" to use their land as
they wish, so long as they are wives bound by the patriarchal
marriage contract. Wives are obligated to produce food on the
land for consumption needs for their households.

Labour

The question of control over allocation of labour therefore becomes
an essential problem to pose along with that of land. Labour time
studies have shown the major labour input of women peasants into
food production, as compared to production oriented solely to the
market which is dominated by men (IV:98, 117, 118, 121, 122, 126
and 136). Moreover, modernisation of cultivation has led to
intensification of the labour of peasant women in particular. The
absorption of most children between the ages of seven and fourteen
or more into schooling has also contributed to labour intensification, given the loss of child labour in cultivation and livestock
production. Central to the labour question is also the issue of
the tools of production at women's disposal. For example, Muro
(IV:114) found that women used short hoes, which were less
productive and more labour intensive than manufactured long hoes.
Ngalula (IV:117) notes that improved farm practices and machinery
substitutes for labour are oriented to cotton production, not
food production. Another "force" of production is knowledge.
Fortmann's (IV:92) research indicates women's unequal access to
knowledge about more productive farm practices provided by
agricultural extension officers.

Labour Product

Male heads of households control the cash proceeds of production on
their own land or with the livestock of the household, even when
wives and youth contribute their labour directly to their production
(see above items). Moreover, even where women produce export
crops on their separate plots of land, as in Mwanza and West
Bagamoyo, the household head effectively controls the cash proceeds
(IV:108-111, 114, 115, 117, 118).

Women's major source of cash income has historically been the
sale of food from small gardens, found by Ophelia Mascarenhas'
recent survey of three villages in Mufindi District or from the
separate plots women farm for household subsistence needs (e.g.
IV:90). Growing reliance on the market for basic subsistence needs
is forcing women to hire their labour/labour power on a seasonal
basis to more well-to-do peasants (often women); to brew beer, make
charcoal, or engage in other forms of non-agricultural economic
activity; or to migrate to towns in search of wage or other
employment.

The distribution of the labour product based on the various
economic activities of the household is changing in an oppressive
direction. Items like school costs, kerosene, medical expenditures
and clothing which were once entirely provided by the male household head are increasingly provided by wives. Cash controlled by
the household head is thereby "freed" for his personal consumption.
Research in Kilimanjaro notes this to be a major contribution to
malnutrition (XIII:378). Another is the distribution of food
itself within the household. Although women are the major
providers of food, the household head receives a greater than
equal share of whatever basic foodstuffs is available. Food
eating practices usually mean that children receive the smallest
share.

The Double Burden

Although women and men contribute nearly equal labour time inputs
into agricultural production, women contribute nearly all of the
labour time input into basic maintenance and child care (IV:97,
108-109, 114, 115, 117, 118, 119, 120, 126 and 136). Half of the
woman's working day is spent on cooking and water - toting, as
primary labour demands, as well as other tasks. Sachak notes the
"irrational use of female labour" in peasant production, and we
would broaden her assessment to include "non-economic" activities
as well. Studies have shown that labour represents a major
constraint on production output, a point emphasised in Mary
Kirimbai's research in Dodoma (1981, also items cites below).
Women have refused to contribute labour to village production
activities on the grounds that they are already "over - burdened".
Oomen-Myin found that the labour demands on women limited their
participation in village political activities (IV:119, 120).

Villagisation

Nearly all of the studies which focus on the villagisation process
as a problem of analysis have argued that villagisation not only
has not contributed to the liberation of women, but indeed has

heightened women's oppression. Both Storgaard (IV:128) and Oomen Myin (IV:119) explain this tendency as due to the failure of the villagisation programme to openly confront oppressive sexual relations (rooted in the patriarchal relations). Although the Village Act demands that each village member be allocated separate plots of land, for example, in practice land is allocated to household heads in many places. Moreover, no attention in governmental analysis or action concerning villagisation has yet been placed on such issues as the distribution of labour burdens in maintenance and child care by all village members, male or female.

Class Differentiation

There have been very few studies of class differentiation among women peasants and its impact on the above issues. Bader (IV:86) argues that the degree of women's oppression depends in part on class position, based on her research in Bukoba. Mary Kirimbai's research in Dodoma indicates different kinds of sexual divisions of labour depending on class position. Whereas in poor peasant households, both women and men engage in food production for subsistence, in kulak households only women and hired labourers do so. The male kulak devotes his time to livestock and other forms of commodity production and trade. Much more research is needed which attempts to explore all of these issues, using a mix of participatory research and quantitative household budget and labour time surveys.

REFERENCES

Mary Kirimbai (1981), "The Impact of Water Supply Projects on Rural Population and their Role in Production and Reproduction in Dodoma Rural District". University of Dar es Salaam, unpublished M.A. Dissertation.

---

86. BADER, ZINNAT K. (1975), Women, Private Property and Production in Bukoba District. University of Dar es Salaam, unpublished M.A. Dissertation, 229 pp.

The focus of the study is the role of the peasant woman in economic production as effected by class differentiation. In the two villages surveyed in Bukoba District, women play a dominant role in production but this dominance lies not so much in the control of production but rather in the oppressive division of labour. Although a dominant producer, the woman receives far less than her male counterpart at the family level thus suffering appropriation at both the market level and the household level. The degree of oppression depends on the forces of class differentiation. Three classes are identified: rich peasant women; smallholder peasant women; and the poor peasant women. Each class is further subdivided into dependent and independent women. Women could not inherit land

unless there were no male heirs. The degree of independence is
closely related to ownership of land. Independent women are
those who had broken away from married lives, those who were
widowed, those who inherited land and stayed out of marriage
or those who had purchased land through prostitution. The
independent rich peasant woman was the best off. She could
hire labourers and enjoyed a status that entitled her to join
men's work parties. The worst off was the dependent peasant
woman.

Other topics considered include the question of land ownership, communal production, women in politics and the effect of
ujamaa villagization. On the question of political participation,
she knows that the level of participation is rather low due to
the disproportionate time spent on production and the divisive
nature of the various classes. Politicization through adult
literacy also fails to reach women for similar reasons. Ujamaa
villagization has done little to radicalise the position of
Haya women in agricultural production.

87. BADER, ZINNAT (1979), "Social Conditions of the Peasant Woman
in Zanzibar and Pemba". Paper No. 18, BW, 5 pp.

A brief historical analysis of the development of plantation agriculture side by side with landless squatters. Poor peasants have
historically increased production of subsistence crops through
accumulation of wives, whereas rich peasants have relied on the
exploitation of hired migrant labour. Focusing on the effects
of land reform on women, it was found that after the Zanzibar
Revolution land was distributed in principle to the family, but
in practice to the family patriarch. Women have not been
involved in either the decision-making or the implementation of
land distribution. As elsewhere in Tanzania, peasant men and
women prefer to produce subsistence food crops rather than cash
crops, including cloves. Clove production has declined, partly
due to delay in planting new trees, a change in the credit
system which no longer operates as before, and relatively low
prices and wages for picking. There is a sexual division of
labour in the agriculture labour process, which is also found in
rice schemes and state farms. Women are delegated to seasonal,
low paying, unskilled work. Whatever cash women earn is used
for family reproductive needs.

88. BRAIN, JAMES L. (1975), "The Position of Women on Rural
Settlement Schemes in Tanzania". Ufahamu, VI (1): 40-59.

The village settlement schemes were the first attempt of the
government of independent Tanzania to persuade people to live
in villages rather than in scattered homesteads. The study
argues that the women in the settlements were worse off than
in the traditional society, using as a case study, the village
settlement scheme at Bwakiri Chini. Here the settlers were
mainly from the Luguru and Kutu tribes. Both the Luguru and
Kutu are matrilineal and the women in these societies possess
similar land rights as men. Women choose the leader of their
sub-clan and get custody of children in the event of divorce.
In the village settlement scheme women who accompanied their
husbands had no right to land. All rights rested in the

husband so that if divorced of widowed, they would have to leave
the settlement. By joining the scheme, the women also ran the
risk of forfeiting their clan traditional lands through
absenteeism. Traditional rights of inheritance and respect for
women's domestic duties were also ignored.

89. BRAIN, JAMES L. (1976), "Less than Second-Class: Women in Rural
Settlement Schemes in Tanzania". Women in Africa, edited by
Nancy J. Hafkin and Edna G. Bay, pp. 263-282. Stanford, Stanford
University Press.

Compares the status of women in two villages forming part of the
government sponsored village settlement schemes and one village
in the Ruvuma Development Association where the initiative to
live and work together was entirely local and spontaneous.
In the government sponsored villages the women were worse off
than in their traditional societies. All rights in land were
vested in the husband and all proceeds handed to him, although
the wife was expected to do a full load of 8 hours work in the
fields in addition to her domestic chores. If widowed or
divorced she could well be destitute. In the Ruvuma Development
Association Village, on the other hand, all profits were equally
divided between all settlers regardless of sex or age. Women
were expected to work less hours in the field than men because
of domestic chores and every effort was made to involve women
in decision-making. The study argues that the contrast is due
to the bureaucrats in the government sponsored villages who are
quite insensitive to the need to involve the women more fully
in the new development projects.

90. BRYCESON, D. and KIRIMBAI, M. (eds.) (1980), Subsistence or
Beyond? Money-Earning Activities of Women in Rural Tanzania.
BRALUP Research Report No. 45, Dar es Salaam, BRALUP and UWT:
165 pp.

A survey of the cash earning activities of rural women in Tanzania
was carried out in the following four regions in Mainland Tanzania:
Arusha, Kigoma, Dodoma and Coast. A similar survey was carried
out in Zanzibar and Pemba Islands. The introduction discusses
the importance of cash to the rural women, UWT's policy on rural
women's money earning activities and the research project. The
region by region survey gives a brief regional profile; 4
village profiles; the extent of UWT activities in the region and
the state of cooperative projects in the region. The village
profiles describe the village infrastructure; village productive
base; women's role in production and maintenance of the family
including their cash earning activities; forms of women's
organisations and constraints to their development. The information is variable both quantitatively and qualitatively,
nevertheless the study has a wealth of information on women in
the rural sector. Shows that the primary role of women is
provisioning the family's daily requirements of food, water
and firewood. These activities alone can occupy a women from
pre-dawn to 10:00 p.m. Child care and associated morbidity
and mortality including miscarriages, stillbirths and infant
deaths add a further burden.

Women's money earning activities can be divided into: (a) commoditised agricultural production, meaning predominantly the sale of food crops; (b) petty trade, and here beer selling seems to be the most profitable and; (c) sale of labour as permanent or casual labourers. Agricultural production for sale appears to be predominant except for Zanzibar and Dodoma where other activities dominated. Average earnings ranged from 300/= per annum to 400/= except for Arusha Region where the annual average earnings were really outstanding. Participation of women in cash earning activities varied considerably and showed no correlation to the general socio-economic conditions of the regions. In all regions almost all the earnings were used for purchasing food, clothing, and household items. Cooperative efforts had a high rate of failure and UWT activities were faced with many problems.

Some of the data was found to be faulty even by the editors and the general conclusion was that more research was required. Nevertheless the main conclusions about the participation and role of women in cash earning activities are confirmed by other research reported on in this section and in section VI.

91. CHUWA, P.A.A. (1977), The Role of Women in the Rural Economy of 12 Villages of Uru: Pre-Colonial Era to 1976. University of Dar es Salaam, undergraduate History dissertation, 35 pp.

The paper is a comprehensive account of how the Chagga women in Kilimanjaro District have been exploited both in the pre-colonial era and more so in the modern era. Women are the backbone of subsistence and cash economy but they are not considered as producers of wealth because they do not own land. The practice of bridewealth also contributed to reducing the women to the status of "being the property of the man and his family". Capitalism, the introduction of the cash economy and wage-labour heightened the inequality by strengthening male dominance although the labour of women, both in cash crop production and food production, was vital. The introduction of the cash economy did away with the traditional division of labour between men and women. Even agricultural labour, previously the domain of men, is now being dominated by women. However, inspite of their dominant role in production, women still have very little say in the proceeds of their labour, cannot inherit the wealth they have earned in case of widowhood and are socially treated as inferior to men.

92. FORTMANN, L. (1979), "Women and Tanzania Agricultural Development". Papers on the Political Economy of Tanzania, edited by K.S. Kim; R.B. Mabele; and M.J. Schultheis. Nairobi, Heinemann, pp. 278 - 287.

The current role and status of women in both food and cash crop production in Tanzania is examined and factors which effect their participation in agricultural development are identified. In Tanzania 97.8 % of the economically active women are involved in agriculture but only 5 % of the agricultural employees are women. Women are the backbone of both food and cash crop production, but the prevailing image is that women are "ignorant, passive and traditional" cultivators. Extension service is geared towards men.

There were neither "statistically nor substantially significant differences" between the good maize practices scores of male and female farmers with the ability to purchase modern inputs. The wives of male purchasers were also aware of improved technology since it was the women who did the bulk of the jobs in certain activities such as weeding, planting, applying insecticides, etc. Nevertheless their participation was hampered by their lack of access to the resources of production, land and information, and the proceeds of their labour. They were thus deprived of any power to effect changes and influence decisions about the use of inputs, expansion of acreage, etc. Their unduly heavy load of work both in the fields and at home also made them reluctant to use technology that would increase their work load.

The recommendations include greater availability of agricultural extension services directly to women, women extension officers and greater participation of women in cash crop production in their own right as independent producers or cooperatively in communal agriculture.

93. GIBLIN, MARIE J. (1980), "Women Peasants and the Transition of Socialism in Tanzania", Columbia University, unpublished paper for POL SCI G9492y, Problems in Modern Africa, April 14th, 39 pp.

Situates the analysis of Tanzanian women peasants within a critical examination of the literature on peasantry and capital penetration and the subordination of subsistence production and unpaid domestic labour to capital. The question of the sexual division of labour and differential control of cash returns in peasant household production within the context of villagisation is probed through secondary analysis of empirical research in Bukoba and Geita. The contradictory consequences of technical innovations in cash crop (or food crop: OM/MM) production are presented, including heightened labour demands and lowered status for women. The tendency towards technocratic methods and solutions characteristic of programmes oriented to peasants and women peasants in particular helps to maintain the present production relations or power relations. Tanzanian programmes exemplify the failure to identify and unleash the "force towards socialism" embodied in women.

It is necessary to examine the relationship between production and reproduction, family and society. Patriarchy is the mechanism of social control and the reproduction of the sexual hierarchy. The argument that increasing awareness of male domination among women will act as a divisive force in the struggle for socialism is firmly rejected. "Heightening women's consciousness of their oppression by both factors (capitalism and patriarchy) will serve to produce critical consciousness which is absolutely essential in combatting both fronts".

94. CONDWE, F. (1977), "Division of Labour in Mwenge Village and if it Does Liberate Women". Dar es Salaam, Dept. of Sociology, University of Dar es Salaam, Mss. B.A. dissertation. 36 pp.

Unlike most ujamaa villages, Mwenge Village consists of a mix of people with different backgrounds and originating from

different tribal areas. In addition almost all its people have
a post-primary educational level; some have even reached
university level. On the whole, the spirit of working together
is lacking in Mwenge and both men and women resort to employing
paid labour as substitutes for their work share. There are some
cooperative efforts but participation by women is minimal. The
cooperative shop is run by men only. Men dominate all
committees except those of UWT and the committee for cultural
affairs. Women are significantly absent in the committee for
economy and planning and the committee for elders. Women
appear to be tied to domestic chores and this conflicts with
their participation in the activities and management of the
village. The study is yet another example to illustrate how
the mere living in ujamaa villages cannot liberate women and
enable them to become full members of the productive sector
of society. It appears that the nature of differentiation by
education and income also militates against cooperating among
women.

95. GULLETH, MOHAMMED; LUNDEEN, ALISA and DEPPE, ROSE MARIE (1979),
Arusha Women's Participation in Development; Project Paper
621-0162. Dar es Salaam, USAID. 73 pp.

USAID financed a pilot project in 2 villages of Arusha Region
to assist in identifying and testing methodologies which might
help women recognise the importance and viability of their role
in development. This paper outlines a proposal for a follow
up project to cover 16 villages over a period of 3 years and
to involve 120 women per village. The aims of the project are:
(1) to increase awareness among women of their potential to
improve the quality of their lives by involving women in
development projects; (2) to have women play an active role in
initiating some self-determined action plan to solve perceived
needs; (3) develop a process of communication that is
dependent on dialogue and group action; (4) evaluate the
cost/effectiveness of audio-cassette technology for rural
education in Tanzania; (5) develop a handbook for participatory
development approaches.
    The techniques to be used are worth mentioning. The
proposal hopes to use audio-cassettes in an attempt "to combine
mass media with interpersonal and group communication". Among
the benefits described as resulting from this technology are
the following: adaptability and flexibility; easily produced
locally; easily operated; reusable, literacy free, is a two-
way system of input and output and one can listen at convenience.

96. HAMDANI, SALHA (1979), "Peasantry and the Peasant Women in
Tanzania". Paper No. 8, BW, 9 pp.

The historical development of human society and its consequences
for women is briefly presented, followed by a general analysis
of peasant women in villages found along the road from Morogoro
town to Mlali. Wives do most of the tasks in food production,
whereas the male household heads work on cash crop production
with their wives. Husbands market cash crops, even if wives
have grown them on land allocated to them by their own maternal
matrilineal group. The basis for male dominance is the bride-

wealth whereby the husband purchases the labour of the wife.
Beerbrewing has become a means of independent support resorted
to by divorced women in some of the villages.

97. JORGENSEN, KIRSTEN (1980), "Water Supply Problems in Rural
    Africa: the Implications for Women". Interregional Seminar on
    Rural Water Supply - A Contribution to the Preparation of the
    Water Decade, Oct. 5-16, 1980, Uppsala, Sweden, (CDR 80.4)
    28 pp.

Shows that water potage puts a very heavy burden on the rural
women. On an average it uses about 12 % to 25 % of their
energy but in some cases there is a depletion of as much as
50 % of their energy. Besides being exhausting it is also an
uneconomic activity. Suggests that the seriousness of the
implications of fetching water is not realised because women
on the whole have very little say in decision making. It
recommends, therefore, that women should use grass-root
organizations to voice their problems. Also emphasises that
"the benefits of water projects in rural areas should be
evaluated in relation to its multisectoral interdependence".
Water improvements should be seen in the context of improvements
to health and nutrition. Above all, water projects should aim
at increasing the scope of women to be included into technological
training and employment.

98. KAMUZORA, C. LWECHUNGURA (1978), "Constraints to Labour Time
    Availability in African Smallholder Agriculture: The Case of
    Bukoba District in Tanzania". University of Dar es Salaam,
    ERB seminar Paper, 15 pp.

A time-budget survey was conducted in 1976 on 105 male-headed
farm households, covering every member of the household for the
14 hour period, from 6 a.m. to 8 p.m. People reported on all
of their activities for the previous day, and this was done on
two alternate days of the week for sample days of the four main
seasons. Activities were classified as economic, domestic,
social and others, and aggregate figures were averaged for all
household members, male and female. On the average it was found
that 36.4 % of time was spent on economic activities, 14.7 %
on domestic, 12.1 % on social, 30.1 % on leisure. The low
proportion of time devoted to economic activities is explained
by problems of "morbidity and mortality", i.e. high rates of
disease and death.
    There are significant problems with this analysis, which
can be summarised by noting that crucial social and production
relations at the level of the household are ignored, which would
provide more powerful explanations for differential labour time
inputs in different activities. By lumping together the
activities of household head (patriarch), wife (wives), children
of all ages, it is next to impossible to analyse who does what.
The description of household head activities confirms the
arguments presented elsewhere that the head uses his time to
manage and supervise, whereas the wives do the actual work on
the farm; in addition to work of a maintenance nature (domestic
labour). For example, "from 6 to 8 o'clock in the morning it
is breakfast time: while the wife would prepare breakfast, the

husband would go around part of the banana-coffee farm to see how the plants are doing". Moreover, all of the 30 % leisure time is actually spent by the head, which means in fact approximately 60 % of his time is spent "taking meals and rest, visiting neighbours, bars and time unaccounted for (!)".

The conceptualisations underlying the distinctions between economic, domestic and social are also problematic, although it is important to underline the advances made by this paper over those which simply ignore work put into domestic labour. For example, tending the sick is a part of domestic labour. The concept of economic as opposed to domestic needs tightening up. For example, some tasks of food crops production are included under economic and others under domestic, such as the wife going to the farm to pick and carry back a banana bunch or dig up sweet potatoes and carry them home: this is classified as food preparation and domestic, when it is a part of food production itself (harvest, transport and so on).

99. KJAERBY, FINN (1978), "Introduction to History" and "Cattle and Conflict". Draft chapters of work on the Barabaig, University of Dar es Salaam, BRALUP.

A critical analysis of the historical development of the Barabaig. Explores the exploitative relations underlying the age set system, whereby women and youth provided labour service to male elders in exchange for means of subsistence. Special attention is given to sexual division of labour, and to the "dispossessed youth" who must hunt lions and enemies and steal in order to acquire cattle of their own. The issue of property relations is dealt with here very differently from Rigby (IV:124). One of the few studies of pastoralism which includes the problem of women in production and reproduction as a central object of analysis.

100. KOKUHIRWA, H, (1975), "Towards the Social and Economic Promotion of Rural Women in Tanzania". The Design of Educational Programmes for the Social and Economic Promotion of Rural Women. International Institute for Adult Literacy Methods. Teheran, Iran, pp. 239-254.

Agriculture is the basis of the economy in Tanzania and it is the women who do most of the work in this field. The aim of this work is to relate the changing image of women in rural Tanzania in an endeavour to increase the understanding that progress in development can come about more rapidly only by the increased participation of women. The Union of Women of Tanganyika (UWT) is discussed, relating projects and programmes designed to aid women to assume their proper role in society as equal partners in the development of Tanzania.

101. LANDBERG, P.L.W. (1969), "The Economic Roles of Women in a Tanzania Coastal Community". Proceedings of the Social Sciences Council Conference, 1968/69, Sociology Papers. Vol. 1 pp. 221-232.

Gives a general description of the types of economic activities undertaken by women in a coastal community of Kigombe, Tanga Region, and relates them to the economy of the village as a whole. Individual cases are discussed to illustrate the situation.

The main focus of the village in terms of male occupation is fishing. Agriculture is also carried out by both men and women but this is mainly for subsistence. The women are therefore engaged in other activities such as cooking and selling of food, the production of handicrafts, retailing farm produce and even small-scale fishing for cash. The amount of time spent on these activities depends on the extent to which the women are able to engage themselves in agriculture. Crucial factors are health, age, availability of assistance during agricultural activities, marriage status and time available after agricultural and domestic duties. In most cases the business is small and the profit margin low, but the activities are highly valued as the only source of cash income.

102. LEWIN, ROGER (1969), "Matetereka". Mbioni, Vol. 5, No. 3, pp. 13-34.

Describes the importance of the contribution of women to the success of the productive activities of the Ujamaa Village. "It is the women who make Matetereka possible. The work they do and the spirit in which they do it compel deep respect. At Materereka it is not uncommon for many women to work ten to twelve hours a day in the fields in addition to managing their homes and caring for their children". However, their work load leaves them very little time or emergy to consider innovations in tools and techniques "While the men debate enthusiastically, women fall asleep during ajamaa meetings. They have worked so hard in the course of the day to make ujamaa living a reality that they are too exhausted to stay awake". The process of change is complicated and risky but necessary. To be effective it must come from the people themselves. The women have made some effort towards lightening their work load. They have organized themselves into a women's group and set up a communal nursery school and child care centre for all their children. Radical change is seen as a possibility for the next generation, resulting from exposure to socialist education and evolving as and when people see that the circumstances are changing and that therefore the traditional roles assigned to women are no longer valid. Based on the Ruvuma Development Association programme of development, which was later banned by the government.

103. MAPOLU, HENRY. The Social and Economic Organization of Ujamaa Villages. Thesis (MA.A) University of Dar es Salaam, 191 pp. (relevant section is "The Role of Women", pp. 161-168).

Membership in ujamaa villages is based on the individual rather than the family and remuneration is given according to each individual's merits. Theoretically, therefore, women should receive a fair return for their work. Social attitudes are such that women are not able to keep all their wages for themselves. In addition, women are still expected to do all the household chores on individual family basis, in addition to communal labour. Their participation in village politics and leadership is severely handicapped. For instance although the ratio of women to men was 2:3 in 55 per cent of the villages

surveyed, women constitute less than 10 per cent of the membership
of all the committees. Several tables are included to illustrate
the point.

104. MBILINYI, M.J. (1973), "Education, Stratification and Sexism
in Tanzania: Policy Implications". The African Review, 3 (2):
327-340.

Two basic arguments are, (1) peasant attitudes and expectations
towards children, and girls specifically, act to keep them out
of school in poor peasant homes, but these attitudes and
expectations have an economic and social basis which must be
changed first, in order to "free" children to go to school and
otherwise to fully engage in development; (2) socialist
transformation is essential in order for conditions to develop
which allow for the emancipation of women and the transformation
of the education system itself. The shortcomings of current
Ujamaa village policy are noted, as well as problems arising from
urban-rural differences. Specific policy recommendations
arising from these arguments are made concerning ujamaa village
service centres and an alternative structure of the schooling
system which incorporates out-of-school village-level learning
systems. Industrialisation at village level and collectivisation of at least some aspects of work would create conditions
leading to individualisation of the work of men, women and
children, thus freeing them from the bonds of patriarch
relations. Security systems such as provision for old age, food,
fuel, housing and burial which are incorporated within the
village structure would make patriarch relations and other
vestiges of precapitalist relations obsolete. Those most
immediately effected by such changes will be youth (male and
female) and women. The need for ideological struggles against
sexist ideologies and sex-stereotyping at school, at home and
in the government at all levels down to the village is stressed.

105. MBILINYI, MARJORIE (1977), Women: Producers and Reproducers in
Peasant Production. University of Dar es Salaam, ERB Occasional
Paper 77.3, biblio. 39 pp.

Analyses the nature of the labour process in which women are
engaged, taking into account both production and the reproduction
of the labour force. The first section traces changes which
took place in the family and women's place in production and
reproduction as capitalism developed in advanced capitalist
countries. Recent debates on the nature of domestic labour are
included. The changing but still contradictory role of women
in socialist countries is analysed. Briefly analyses the
penetration of smallholder peasant production systems by capital
and the development of the periphery industrial sector.
Meillassoux's analysis of women's role in production and reproduction is critiqued, and the implications for women of
imperialist penetration explored. Ideological struggles to
keep women in their place, and women's resistances, are discussed
in the final section. The problem of sexuality is posed, i.e.
the need not to take for granted stereotyped, socially-defined
behaviours which are labeled as masculine and feminine, including
heterogeneous sexual relations themselves.

106. MBILINYI, MARJORIE (1979), "The Changing Position of Women in
Peasant Commodity Production: The Case of the Shambaa Kingdom".
Paper presented to the Symposium on Women and Work in Africa,
April 29 - May 1, 1979, University of Illinois at Urbana-
Campaign, 28 pp.

The position of women is theorised in relation to the development
of a feudal state and its later destruction during the 19th
century. The concept of the "sexual division of labour"
employed in earlier work (II:28) is dropped and instead women
are situated in terms of precapitalist and capitalist relations
of production. Women were dispossessed and exploited through
the mechanism of patriarch relations at the homestead level
during the feudal era in Shambaa. With the growing dominance
of capitalism commoditisation in agriculture production during
the colonial period, patriarch relations became the basis for
the generation and appropriation of surplus labour of wives and
children of patriarchs for the ultimate profit of capitalists.
Ideological struggles and the different forms of resistance of
women during the different periods are explored. Throughout
there is a critique of the anthropologic colonial method as
adopted in the work of Feierman (III:73, 74). The final version
of this paper "Wife, Slave and Subject of the King" is to be
published in TNR, No. 88/89.

107. MBILINYI, MARJORIE (1979), "Patriarch Relations in the Peasant
Household". Paper No. 20, BW, 12 pp.

Analyses the ensemble of social relations in the peasant
household, including property relations and differential
ownership and control over the labour product, as well as
distribution relations. The material basis of the generation
and appropriation of surplus in peasant production at household
level has historically been the patriarch relations. The male
head of the clan and/or extended family controls the means of
production and the allocation of the labour force at his
disposal (wives, youths and others), and the product of their
labour. Patriarchal relations are found in both patrilineal
and matrilineal groups. Although effected by destruction of
feudal and other precapitalist relations and subjugation to
capital, they persist as the basis of peasant women's oppression
today. This concept of patriarchal relations has since been
refuted by the author (see Part One).

108. MBILINYI, MARJORIE (1980), "The Unit of 'Struggles' and
'Research': The Case of Peasant Women in West Bagamoyo,
Tanzania". Paper presented to the Institute of Social Studies
Workshop on "Women's Struggles and Research", The Hague. June
9-20, 70 pp. Shortened version to be published in proceedings
edited by Maria Mies, published by the Institute of Social
Studies.

Presents the researcher's development towards a participatory
research approach, and the day-to-day research activities
conducted in one village in Tanzania. Analyses the results of
the empirical investigation at village and household levels.
Labour time studies based on observation indicate that women

work double the hours that men do, due to their labour input in
basic maintenance of the household. Although wives have separate
fields for cultivation, they are not free to allocate their
labour as they wish, in that they are responsible for providing
food supplies for the household. Household consumption studies
indicate that peasant households depend on the market for their
basic subsistence, including food during drought periods. The
impact of famine on peasant economic activities and the sexual
division of labour is investigated, as women, men and children
struggle to survive. Gender struggles are related to class
struggles between the poor peasants in the village, the state
and capital, sited in the struggle over allocation of land and
labour of cotton production according to state demands.
Accounts of a village baraza/assembly and a women's meeting
reveal the forms of resistance adopted by peasant women. Poses
the questions: (1) capital and the state, or patriarchs?
(i.e. as "enemies" of peasant women); (2) persistence of with-
drawal to subsistence production, or the commoditisation of peasant
production and reproduction; (3) women's subordination: a land
question or a labour question?

109. MBILINYI, MARJORIE (1980), "Peasant Women Struggles in Production
and Reproduction". Paper presented to the K.U.L.U. Women's
Research Conference in Copenhagen, July 10-13, 57 pp.

Based on the same research as IV:108, this paper focuses on a
reformulation of the theoretical analysis of the exploitation
of poor peasants, and peasant women in particular. There is a
critique of the articulation of modes of production analysis
followed by a summary of recent work by Bennhold - Thomsen and
Werlhof which analyses the non-wage form of the capital-labour
relationship, and focuses attention on the question of
reproduction.

110. MBILINYI, MARJORIE (1981), "Participatory Research among
Peasant Women in West Bagamoyo, Tanzania". Paper presented to
IDS Regional Workshop on Research Methodology, Arusha, March
30th to April 11th, 45 pp., to be published in Jipemoyo forth-
coming, ed. by Ulla Vuorela, Scandinavian Institute of African
Studies.

Brings out the problems and contradictions underlying this
research approach. The basic conceptualisations underlying the
research are briefly presented, with concrete analysis of the
changing nature of the Tanzanian social formation and the
relationship between patriarchal and capitalist relations
explored. The major part of the paper presents findings about
the place of peasant women in peasant production and reproduction
systems situated within the class struggle between poor peasants
on the one hand, and the state and capital on the other, as
revealed in the village context. Labour-time and budget figures
are presented, as well as analyses of women's place in village
politics. Develops basic theoretical issues arising from the
empirical investigation concerning the relationship between class
and sexual struggles among poor peasant women. (The final
reworking of material presented in 108).

111. MBILINYI, MARJORIE (forthcoming), "Participatory Research on the
Problem of Women in Agricultural Production in West Bagamoyo" in
Janice Jiggins (ed.), <u>Women in Agricultural Production in Eastern
and Southern Africa</u>. Nairobi, proceedings of the workshop
sponsored by the Ford Foundation, Nairobi, April 9-11, 1980.

This is an earlier report on the research analysed in IV:108-110,
with a less developed conceptual framework but a similar analysis
of the participatory research process.

112. MBILINYI, SIMON M. (1976), <u>The Economics of Peasant Coffee
Production: The Case of Tanzania</u>. Nairobi, Kenya Literature
Bureau, 224 pp.

A detailed examination of the organisation of coffee production
in the peasant sector based on survey research in five regions
(Arusha, Kilimanjaro, Mbeya, Bukoba and Ruvuma). In the early
1970s, coffee accounted for 20 % of total value of agricultural
exports and was the major source of cash income for the coffee
producers. The problems of reliance on an export crop due to
the nature of the capitalist market are noted. Analyses age and
sex composition of labour; the phenomenon of labour loss due to
poor health, looking for wage employment, attending school, etc.;
the extent of reliance on hired labour; and the male-female
breakdown in hired labour. More women are hired than men during
the peak seasons of the year in all areas except Mbeya and Bukoba,
but generally for only short periods. Children are also hired
during these seasons. Unfortunately the same detail on labour
inputs was not provided for "family labour" except children,
given the assumption that all contribute labour.

Although the technical sexual division of labour is changing,
it remains as a fundamental aspect of the organisation of the
labour process. New crops or new techniques of farming have
been rejected if they did not "match" the sexual division of
labour, thus clarifying the way the latter limits the development
of productive forces and provides a basis for the reproduction
of the peasant production system itself. Detailed tables on the
sexual division of labour for all labour (family and hired)
broken down by region, crop and farm activity is an extremely
useful basis for secondary analysis.

113. MOSHA, A.C. (1975), "Training Extension Staff for Ujamaa
Villages". Paper presented to the Workshop on Agricultural
Extension in Ujamaa Villages, University of Dar es Salaam at
Morogoro, 22-27 September, 11, TFNC.

Provides a brief but informative analysis of the villagisation
policy in Tanzania and the historical role of agriculture
extension work in peasant production. The tendency in the past
to rely on coercion rather than persuasion is criticised. The
problem of stagnancy in agricultural production is related to
weaknesses in the agriculture extension services. However,
there is no mention of such issues as the lack of adequate women
in the services, the neglect of attention to women's role in
agriculture production, etc. The description of "the present
Ujamaa village farmer" completely ignores the fact that village
agriculture production is based on households rather than

individual farmers, and that it is impossible to generalise
about male and female peasants.

114. MURO, ASSENY (1979), The Study of Women's Position in Peasant
Production and their Education and Training: A Case Study of
Diozile I Village in Bagamoyo District. University of Dar es
Salaam, unpublished M.A. dissertation, 179 pp.

Concrete analysis of a specific group of women peasants in West
Bagamoyo is related to the literature on the women's question
as posed nationally and internationally. A critical review of
the relevant literature is found in chapter 2, which serves as a
useful introduction. Basing her field work on participant
observation in one village, Muro analyses women's role in
village production, their status in the village and household,
domestic labour and women's access to adult education. Dialogues
with four women are provided as illustrative material. Specific
short and long-term recommendations are provided which are
rooted in the concrete reality of the case village and yet have
relevance to other areas. The nine-page bibliography covers
national and international work on the women's question.

115. MURO, ASSENY (1979), "Women in Agricultural Production and
their Education and Training: A Case Study of Diozile I Village
in Bagamoyo District". Paper No. 11, BW, 42 pp.

Drawn from the author's MA dissertation, the research findings
are concretised by "dialogues" with two peasant women. The
conclusions and recommendations focus on the impact and
implications of villagisation for women as producers and reproducers. The specific recommendations are refreshingly
concrete and practical.

116. MUSTAFA, KEMAL, MELKIORI MATWI and JONAS REUBEN (1980),
Participatory Research and Pastoralist Development: The
Experience of the Jipemoyo Project in Western Bagamoyo District.
Dar es Salaam, Ministry of National Culture, mimeo bound, 494 pp.

An exhaustive analysis of the pastoralist question, which
includes survey data based on a household livestock census, as
well as verbatim reports of several meetings. The analysis is
based on a materialist participatory research approach, in
which pastoralists became participants in the research process
and the ministry researchers participants in the political
process. Struggles at the local level over such issues as
registration of the pastoralist village of Mindu Tulieni;
pastoralist curriculum in primary schools and destocking are
related to the process of subjugation of peasant production
systems to capital and the state. The research findings
reported here were first presented in various ways to the
pastoralists, and incorporated into their planning and
organisational practices. The account of the Lugoba Seminar
provides a great deal of information on economic, political
and ideological practises related to women. The sexual
division of labour in production, the nature of patriarchal
production relations and their ideological expressions, and
sexual practices are presented by pastoralist women and men.

117. NGALULA, THERESIA K.F. (1977), Women as Productive Force in the
Tanzanian Rural Society: A Case Study of Buhongwa Village in
Mwanza District. University of Dar es Salaam, unpublished M.A.
dissertation. The findings chapter is to be published in
Marjorie Mbilinyi and Cuthbert Omari (eds.) Peasant Production in
Tanzania, forthcoming.

Examines the roles of women and men in the rural economy of
Tanzania by studying 90 households in a typical village in Mwanza
Region, Tanzania. Agricultural and non-agricultural production,
domestic work and child care activities were examined. Appropriation and distribution of returns and participation in village
policies were also considered.
  Shows that food production is predominantly female farming
whereas men spend slightly more time on cash crop production
when they had more access to better tools such as ploughs and
tractors. 90 % of the households used the hoe in food production.
In non-agricultural activities, women had less time than men
owing to domestic chores. Women, therefore, engaged themselves
in making pottery, weaving and beer brewing whereas the men
could take part in activities that brought better dividends, for
example running a shop, tailoring and charcoal making. Domestic
work and children were entirely the work of women although single
men admitted to doing domestic work. Men were the sole owners of
land as well as livestock purchased from the sale of crops or
obtained as bride-price for daughters. Most items bought from
the sale of crops, e.g. cattle and bicycles were men's things.
Women had to beg for money to buy soap, salt, bus fares etc.,
and depend on the good will of their husbands for these things.
Participation in village politics was also limited, partly due
to the undue distribution of workload and partly through
traditional attitudes towards politics. In some cases women
were actively prevented from being party members. Their
attendance at adult education classes was similarly affected.
Some suggestions are made to correct the situation including
changing the current attitudes of both men and women to the role
of women; giving women more access to better tools and
techniques; improving the infrastructure in villages and
establishing laws to secure equality of status.

118. NGALULA, THERESIA K.F. (1979), "Domestic Labour and Property
Ownership: A Case Study of Buhongwa Village in Mwanza
District". Paper No. 13, BW, 10 pp.

Summarises the major findings of the M.A. dissertation (IV:117).
Relates women's role in domestic labour (including child care)
to differential sex ownership of the means of production, land
and livestock, and the appropriation of income by men.

119. OOMEN-MYIN, MARIE ANTOINETTE (1981), Involvement of Rural Women
in Village Development in Tanzania: A Case Study in Morogoro
District. University of Dar es Salaam, Department of Agricultural Education and Extension, Morogoro, Research Monograph,
136 pp.

The research reported on here is a part of a more general
research project concerning the constraints to the development

of small-scale village projects. This particular research
focuses on the question of women's participation in decision-
making processes at village level, the constraints on involvement of women, and factors which could stimulate women's
participation. A combination of survey and participant
observation research approaches were adopted in eight villages
in Morogoro District for an initial period of two weeks, with
a later follow-up period of feedback of research results to
the villagers. A statistical model of correlation was adopted
to test the hypotheses of the researcher, using women's
participation in decision-making as the dependent variable, and
as independent variables: level of formal education, husband's
position for married women, proportion of women in village
leadership positions, type of village agricultural projects
(cash/food), level of internalisation by women of their
devaluation, membership in UWT, women's marital status
(married/heads of household). Basic findings were that women
did participate less than men in decision-making processes,
though they worked the same number of hours as men in village
agricultural projects. The main constraint was men's negative
attitude towards women, confirmed by the fact that female heads
of household participated more than married women in decision-
making, and where the village chairperson was a woman (two out
of eight villages!), there was more female participation at
village level. Level of formal education and UWT membership had
no relationship to women's participation. The amount of daily
work women had to perform, the numerous pregnancies and large
number of children, and the negative opinion women have of
themselves acted as significant constraints. Argues that
villagisation has not had favourable effects for women, and if
anything, has worsened their situation: village projects
increase their work load without their participation in deciding
about the projects themselves; village government is controlled
by men; villagisation procedures have not confronted oppressive
traditional structures such as land tenure which act to
dispossess women, and the political pratices in the name of
villagisation policy tend to subordinate women.

Useful summaries of literature on extension services,
innovation and decision-making and on women's roles and status.
The findings are presented along with information about the
socio-economic conditions of each village, so that it is possible
to relate the question of women's participation to a wider set
of issues, as well as to generalise about the geographical area
as a whole. A major strength of this research is the attention
given to ideological aspects of the problem, such as differential
perceptions of married women and female heads of households and
men about the sexual division of labour and women in village
politics. When asked their views on the three most important
problems rural women face, an overwhelming number mentioned
having to bear too many children as highly significant, and family
planning was the most frequently mentioned solution to their
problems. In further discussions during the feedback period, the
women noted that "all women with 2 to 3 children would be eager
to use contraceptives if there were any", whereas men would be in
opposition so that the women would have to hide the contraceptives.

The point they stressed was that the contraceptives don't get distributed to villages, and that urban women and men were revealing their ignorance about peasant women when they said that the latter did not want or did not know about them.

Although the author states she has adopted a participatory research approach, in fact the approach used is mainly participant observation and questionnaire survey. The important innovation however is that of reporting back to the villagers about research findings, and the use of visual aids in the form of posters to codify results (some of which are reproduced in the report). The researcher has also written a simplified research report in Kiswahili, (IV:120), to be distributed to villages concerned and elsewhere.

120. OOMEN-MYIN, MARIE ANTOINETTE (1980), "Wanawake Vanavyoshiriki Katika Shughuli za Kijiji, Utafiti uliofanyika katika Vijiji Vinane vya Wilayani Morogoro". Chuo Kikuu cha Dar es Salaam, Idara ya Elimu na Ushauri wa Kilimo, Morogoro, AEE Working Paper 80.18, 11 pp.

A research report based on an eight-village study in Morogoro District about women's involvement in village-level decision-making processes, constraints and possible means of overcoming them. The objectives of the research, the research design, and the major findings are presented in a straight-forward manner. The posters used to codify results during the feed-back sessions are also reproduced.

This version is not bound as the English version was (IV:119). The Department of Agricultural Education and Extension would better achieve its objective of reporting back research results to peasants if a more permanent written product was produced, using larger typeface which new or semi-literates could more easily read. Nevertheless, it is rare for any department of the University to undertake such a reporting-back procedure, and should serve as a positive example to others (see also IV:116).

121. RALD, A. (1969), Land Use in Bihaya Villages, A Case Study from Bukoba District, West Lake Region. Dar es Salaam, Bureau of Resource Assessment and Land Use Planning (BRALUP) Research Paper No. 5, 63 pp.

Describes a farm economic survey in two divisions in Bukoba District. Particularly relevant to the present study is the section on "The Division of Labour". Modern methods of cultivation appear to have increased the workload of women much more than that of men. The author illustrates that women do an average of 3,067 hours a year as compared to 1829 hours by men. Includes a table showing division of labour and labour inputs on an average farm.

122. RALD, JORGEN and KAREN RALD (1975), Rural Organization in Bukoba District, Tanzania. Uppsala, Scandinavian Institute of African Studies, 122 pp.

The study is mainly concerned with how the people of Bukoba organise their life in society with regard to productive time and spare time. Detailed land use maps are used to investigate allocation of

family labour, sexual division of labor and cultivation techniques. It
is also useful for the detailed labour time budget and household
incomes and expenditures provided for a people living in a high
density area where land is scarce and expansion has to be
carefully planned and organised. Labour time budgets show
significant differences between farmers as well as between men
and women. For men agricultural work occupies 45 percent of the
daylight hours, social activities, 11 per cent and leisure 44
per cent. The corresponding figures for women are 59 per cent,
12 per cent and 29 per cent respectively. The conceptualisation
of leisure includes attending the sick, helping with funerals
and other social obligations, all of which entail work to some
extent and in particular for women. Also provides findings of a
household budget survey.

123. REINING, PRISCILLA (1970), "Social Factors and Food Production
in an East African Peasant Society: The Haya". African Food
Production Systems, edited by Peter F. McLoughlin, Baltimore,
John's Hopkins Press, pp. 41-89.

Describes the activities of men and women in the daily and annual
labour schedules. Variation in the distribution of the major
components of crop husbandry among the households, and
consequently labour inputs, are strongly influenced by the
developmental phase of the family living on the farm. Generally
the division of labour is based on sex. "A clear cut dichotomy
exists in the division of labour between men who are responsible
for and have the right to the tree crops and women whose
gardening activities centre on the annual crops grown on the
farms and on the open land". Women are also responsible for
household duties and the care of children. However, these
divisions are considerably affected by the wealth and status
of the family. Chores like carrying water, cooking, weeding
and harvesting are done by paid labourers in rich households.
In addition to agriculture, the Haya also engage themselves in
a wide variety of occupations. Most of these "specialities"
are slated for men.

124. RIGBY, PETER (forthcoming), "Pastoralist Production and Socialist
Transformation in Tanzania", in Marjorie Mbilinyi and Cuthbert
K. Omari (eds.) Peasant Production in Tanzania. Earlier mimeo
version.

The women's question is situated in the context of a detailed
and original analysis of pastoralism among the Ilparakuyu, the
Barabaig and the Maasai. The exploitation and subjugation of
women in patrilineal pastoralist studies is assumed and not
examined in most studies. Women are situated in terms of
lineage and age set relationships. Bridewealth and marriage
ceremonies are analysed in relation to the question of control
over property and labour. The basic assertions are (1) that
men own the primary means of production but women have an
essential role in the transfer of and control over property,
due to the mediation of matrifiliation (the wife/children
segment of the homestead); and (2) in the production-
consumption process, women virtually have full control over the
major objects of the production process, i.e. milk, fat, hides,

skins. The technical sexual division of labour is described
the social relations within the homestead.

In a critique of Rigby's position (II: 28, 29) it is argued
that in fact women do not have control over the means of
production nor over their own labour. The conditions based on
patriarch relations necessitate female labour to be spent on
maintenance functions, and define how the product of female
labour will be distributed.

125. SACHAK, NAJMA (1979), "Creating Employment Opportunities for
Rural Women: Some Issues Affecting Attitudes and Policy". Paper
presented at International Political Science Association
Congress, Moscow, August 12-18, 19 pp. and paper No. 6, BW.

The need to redefine definitions of "employment" in order to fit
the situation especially in rural areas is noted. Self-help
schemes and famine relief activities are considered employment
in this research, as well as casual hired labour and other more
formal types of work. Based on a survey of six villages in
Dodoma rural District, employment opportunities for women were
related to the history of famine and poverty in the different
villages. For example, in an earlier pilot study 55 % of the
people in one village tried to get employment during famine
periods. The most common work women can find is that of farming
for larger, richer farmers on a seasonal basis. Others are
forced to go to nearby towns in search of work as domestics,
or carrying water and making and selling charcoal. The women's
responsibility to maintain the family on the one hand drives
her to seek sources of income off the farm, and on the other
hand acts as an obstacle to completely free her from the family
and its needs. Hence, women are not always able to migrate to
town, in spite of the lack of adequate employment opportunities
in many villages. Information was acquired which actually shows
the growing importance of wives in providing cash needs in
the household (meat, women's and children's clothes, and so
on). Male ownership of cattle, the most basic commodity in
the area, provides men with easier access to cash than women,
and yet, women are increasingly providing cash needs
"traditionally" the responsibility of men. Women's perceptions
of village needs and their own needs and capabilities were
highly related to the economic conditions of their respective
villages. The major demand was for labour-saving devices such
as provision of flour milling facilities where these did not
exist or were inadequate. Villages noted that married women
were the largest number of migrants from the villages, who
leave their children behind while they go to seek work. The
women migrate because of the failure of the domestic economy
to provide for basic needs such as food and clothes. The
irrational use of human labour in peasant agriculture, and the
particular waste of female labour, is stressed as one of the
conditions which push women to leave the villages and also acts
as a major constraint on rural development.

126. SHAPIRO, KENNETH H. (1978), "Water, Women and Development in
Tanzania". Paper presented at the Third Annual Conference of the
International Water Resources Association, Sao Paulo, Brazil, 10 pp.

Quantifies the relationship between greater convenience of water
supplies and increased productivity, and provides data based on
labour-time studies of women's non-farming tasks. Based on a
survey of 75 peasant households in Geita District, calculations
of opportunity costs indicate that up to shs. 13/= per year in
equivalent labour time is spent on fetching water, compared to
average total cotton earnings of shs. 500 per household. A
comparison of male and female labour time allocations to
different non-farm tasks and activities showed that women spend
much of their time maintaining the household (39 %) whereas men
spend at most 8 % of their time doing so, even if house repair
is included. Much more of men's time is spent drinking beer
and otherwise resting or being sick, than is true of women.
Hence, new farm inputs like water spraying of insecticide which
demand more labour time of women to fetch more water are
unlikely to be adopted, due to female resistance. Moreover, men
resist fetching the water themselves. It has been necessary to
seek alternative oil bases for insecticide sprays as a result (!).
The data is useful and representative of the kind of labour-time
surveys needed.

127. STANLEY, JOYCE and ALISA LUNDEEN (1979), Audio-Cassettes
Listening Forums: a Participatory Women's Development Project.
Washington D.C., 108 pp.

The Audio-Cassette listening Forum Project (ACLF) was an attempt
to provide women with the opportunity to assess their problems
and implement self-determined action plans primarily related to
nutrition and health. In addition, the project was designed
to evaluate participatory research which involved the
participants in planning, implementation and evaluation and of
using audio-cassettes in a development education programme. The
project involved two rural villages in Arusha Region namely
Majengo and Kimundo villages. The women participants of the
project were involved in a village needs/resource survey,
locally produced problem posing and information tapes,
discussions and action planning, and implementation of activities
to solve identified priorities. Concludes that the method
"works" but it is significant to note that the project affected
the women in these two villages quite differently. Significant
factors appear to be the level of basic needs, the existence
of group activity and the number of development projects in the
village. The study is quite enthusiastic about the feasibility
and cost/effectiveness of the technique but cautions that
transferability to other areas may well depend on socio-political
factors such as good local leadership, receptability of the
participants, etc.

128. STORGAARD, BIRGIT (1976), "Women in Ujamaa Villages". Rural
Africana, No. 29, pp. 135-155.

Using Bukoba District as a case study, the author describes
the traditionally inferior status of Haya women and analyses
the impact of the policy of Ujamaa in changing this position.
Argues that the potential for fundamental change in the position
of women was missed during the implementation of the ujamaa
policy. The traditional division of labour and the unit of

production – the family – were transferred to the ujamaa villages, thus carrying over the concept of the inferior status of women. The dual models of production prevalent in ujamaa villages also discriminated against women. The communal plot might have given women some control over the basic means of production but it was found that most women were wives and were expected to work on their husbands' private plots where the traditional division of labour and allocation of the proceeds of production were strongly entrenched. Social amenities such as piped water, village wells, day care centres did not radically alter the status of women in ujamaa villages. Includes tables on labour inputs in hours by sex, educational attainment, attendance at cooperatives meetings, etc.

129. SWANTZ, MARJA-LIISA (1974), "Youth and Development in the Coast Region of Tanzania". Research Report (New Series), Dar es Salaam, BRALUP, University of Dar es Salaam. 47 pp.

Conducted in five villages in the Coast Region, it focuses on the problem of migrating of youth from rural areas to the cities. Aims at evaluating the existing potential for youth in the villages and their opportunities for personal development as well as for participation in village development. Shows that youth migration in Coast Region was so high that in some villages there was an "almost total dearth of male youth between the ages of 15-25 except for those enrolled in schools". The number of migrants was not affected by education alone. The youth left the villages primarily because of the lack of opportunities to participate effectively in the productive activities of the village. Shortage of land, dearth of cash and markets for crafts or simply harsh traditional authority combined to "push" youth out of the villages.

130. SWANTZ, MARJA-LIISA (1977), "Free Women of Bukoba" in Bengt Sundkler and Per-Åke Wahlström (eds.) Vision and Service, Papers in Honour of Barbro Johansson. Uppsala, The Scandinavian Institute of African Studies, The Swedish Institute of Missionary Research, pp. 99-107.

Provides brief life-stories of Bukoba women, including prostitutes who have returned to the area. They bring out the oppressive nature of production, distribution and consumption relations in the patriarchal organisation of the peasant family. Verbatim accounts of women's views concretise the analysis and clarify the significance of biological reproduction. For example, many prostitutes left their marriages as a result of bearing no children or only female children. The way that the christian church has contributed to the construction of bourgeois morality is also apparent, though not posed in this way by the author.

131. SWANTZ, MARJA-LIISA (1977), Strain and Strength Among Peasant Women in Tanzania. University of Dar es Salaam, BRALUP Research Paper No. 49. 81 pp.

Small-scale peasants in two regions, Bukoba and Kilimanjaro, are studied in order to analyse the poorer peasant women's position in present day Tanzania, highlight obstacles to

equality among sexes and identify unutilised potentialities
within the ranks of women. The basic cause of the lower status
of women is that in both societies women do not have the same
rights to land as men. Since 97.8 % of the economically active
women are engaged in small-scale farming on land which is not
theirs by right, they work under conditions where they have
no control over their labour input nor over income emanating
from their labour. The study shows how the women in each
region have responded variously towards attaining some measure
of independence. Considerable equality was seen to be achieved
by single women, divorcees and widows even with children to
care for. They were economically and socially better off than
married women and contributed more towards development and
communal activities.

132. TANNER, R.E.S. (1962), "Relationship Between the Sexes in A
Coastal Islamic Society: Pangani District, Tanganyika".
African Studies, Vol. 21, No. 2, pp. 70-82.

In the peri-urban areas of Pangani District in the 1950s, women
were questioning the tribal and Moslem patterns of female
subordination. The change was reflected in the growing number
of divorces and the fact that one third of the adult population
preferred to remain unmarried.

    The author described the change to the influence of western
ideas obtained through the cinema or contact with European
women. Here the error of using common-sense, surface-level
perceptions as explanation is clear. As other items show, the
material basis of existence of the coastal belt had radically
changed by this time.

133. TANZANIA. Ministry of Agriculture (1977), "Demonstrations of
an Interdisciplinary Approach to Planning Adaptive Agricultural
Research Programmes". Report No. 3, December 1977. The Drier
Areas of Morogoro and Kilosa Districts, Tanzania. Research
Division, Ministry of Agriculture and Faculty of Agriculture,
University of Dar es Salaam in association with CIMMYT, Nairobi.

Adaptive agricultural research which combined crop husbandry
with agricultural economies was used to explore solutions to
the priority problem of adequate food supply in dry areas of
Morogoro and Kilosa Districts. A short term maize variety
which would allow for later planting and earlier harvesting was
selected as the most advisable solution, given the major
constraint of labour supply in the context of uncertain rainfall.
The "farming system" is described, as well as marketing and
price structures. However, the particular role of women in
crop production, preparation, processing, storage and marketing
is completely ignored. Throughout the focus is on "the farmer"
as farm manager, and his supply of "family labour". Women only
enter the research programme as tasters of different varieties
of maize. That this oversight may invalidate the conclusions
reached is hinted at in the final evaluation. A decision was
made to leave household plots out of the survey work. With
hindsight it is possible to see that, though the volume of
produce from these plots is small, the timing of the production

means it plays an important part in household food supplies.
Such household plots are frequently worked on exclusively or
mainly by women. Moreover, the manipulation of planting and
harvesting schedules in order to release labour and/or land
for increased cash crop production ignores the question of
differential control over resources and crop proceeds. If
women do not have access to cash proceeds, they are unlikely
to increase their production of cash crops. The assumption of
an undifferentiated and quiescent family labour force is
incorrect. Although "no specialisation of work between men and
women was observed in the area", this is more likely to be due
to research methodology. Moreover given differential benefits
and therefore incentives to produce of household heads and
dependent wives, it is highly unlikely that "all labour can be
considered as available for all operations".

134. TOBISSON, E. (1980), Women, Food and Nutrition in Nyamurigura
Village, Mara Region, Tanzania. A report presented to Tanzania
Food and Nutrition Centre, 127 pp.

Focuses on implications of shifting from a diversified
subsistence production to a specialised one in order to
participate in cash crop production, with particular emphasis
on the conditions of women and children. Shows that both
colonial policies and post-independence strategies for rural
development have reinforced the subordination of women relative
to men in the productive sector. At the same time these
policies have increased the work load of women, negatively
effecting not only their participation in decision making
activities and communal work, but also the nutritional status
of the family.

A great deal of data is presented on the diet and health
status of Nyamurigura Village; particular diets of pregnant and
lactating mothers; the relations of production between men and
women at household level and the problem of the direct and
indirect exclusion from political discussions, decision making
and communal work.

135. VUORELA, ULLA (1978), "Research Proposal: Women's Role in
Food Production", Dar es Salaam, Ministry of National Culture
and Youth, Directorate of Research and Planning, Jipemoyo
Project, typescript, 6 pp.

The objective of the research is to use the anthropologic
approach to explore the importance of food on nutrition and
the complexity of the socio-economic factors affecting nutrition.
Nutrition is therefore viewed as a social and economic problem,
not to be separated from issues of food production. What is
eaten is dependent on what is produced and people's access to
this production. Food consumption is also culturally
conditioned. The research will try to clarify which aspects
of traditional nutrition behavior hinder food and nutrition
and which could be promoted to improve the diet with local
resources. Another related problem is to analyse how the
material conditions combine with cultural traditions to "bind"
the women to food production and food handling activities. A
participatory research approach is used, based on in-depth

village-level work, in West Bagamoyo villages of Lugoba, Msoga
and Msata. Preliminary findings based on earlier work are
presented in the form of problem-areas for further study. The
research links up with the work of research associates to the
West Bagamoyo Project (as Jipemoyo Project is now called) and
other Utamaduni staff. This is the first research project of
the overall Project in West Bagamoyo to specifically focus on
peasant women, the second being that of Asseny Muro and the
third that of Marjorie Mbilinyi.

136. VUORELA, ULLA, assisted by JONAS REUBEN (1981), "Women's Role
in Post-Harvest Food Conservation, Tanzania Case Study".
Research report presented to UNU, mimeo, 87 pp.

This research is Phase I of the Post-Harvest Food Conservation
Project sponsored by the United Nations University World Hunger
Programme. Notes that participatory research cannot be an
individual effort. It needs to be multidisciplinary, where
knowledge and action are integrated. If economic or education
projects are included, they must be planned and carried out
within existing structures of the community. Nutrition is
broadly defined as a total process consisting of production,
processing and distribution and consumption of food. The major
concern of nutrition research is "nutritional opportunities".
     Analysis of different diets and cultural practices in general
of the pastoralist and cultivating groups in Lugoba Ward confirms
the dialectical relationship between material resources of food
production and culturally shaped ideas about food. The two
groups share the same natural resources but have developed
totally different diets. Comparative demographic statistics
are given and details concerning the sexual division of labour,
the nature of a woman's working day, property relations, diet,
relations of sexuality and fertility and ideologies concerning
female-male relations. The section on Mindu Tulieni is a rare
detailed analysis of such issues as they relate to a pastoralist
society. Women are perceived to be children, and according to
customary law they are objectively put into the position of
dependent children. In the words of one elder, "Women don't
need property of their own," because "we take good care of her,
like we take good care of our cows". The author argues that
women are reified as objects comparable to commodities, and
often rated secondary to cows. Women have exchange value for
fathers in the form of bridewealth, and use value for husbands
as a means of production and reproduction. The minor status,
almost non-existent existence of women was exemplified most
starkly in the failure to count all adult women in the households as among the adults. Counted as adults were men and old
women past the age of child-bearing, usually mothers of the
household head. In addition, sexuality and fertility are
discussed, including clitorectomy which is still a mandatory
practice for all young girls.
     The significance of mwali or coming out ceremonies of
young girls in matrilineal society is analysed in relation to
Msoga village, where the equivalent of 7 months maize meal
consumption of a family is consumed in the preparation of beer
for the mwali ritual in one household. The situation of women

in the village is related to struggles of the villagers to be registered as a village.

The Lunga case study revealed the lack of independent income-earning activities of the wives of the local merchants, who lead a very confined existence compared to women peasants, beer brewers and traders. A market survey provides unusual information on the sexual division of labour in petty or local trade, rarely a problem of analysis in Tanzania.

V.   WORKERS

Participation of Women in the Wage Sector

Tanzania is a predominantly agricultural country and has neither
extensive large scale farming nor a well developed industrial sector.
Wage labour therefore forms a small proportion of the economically
active population, but of this small number, women constitute less
than 15 % (V:137-140, 146, 148, 150, 158, 161). The lack of fuller
participation of women in the employment sector is traced back to
the position of women in the pre-capitalist and capitalist modes
of production (see IV:138, 148-151). Colonialism and the capitalist
mode of production reinforced the pre-capitalist sexual division of
labour and patriarchal family relations emphasising the women's
role as reproducers. Whereas men were exposed to new ideas,
participated in migratory labour and had access to the limited
educational facilities and new technologies, women were expected
to reproduce labour and maintain the household and the family land.
In this way capital was relieved of the burden of paying high wages,
family allowances and terminal benefits.

     In areas where smallholder cash cropping led to a proletarisation
of the poor peasants, women were often forced to sell their labour,
the earliest such labour being associated naturally with agriculture
(IV:138, 148). The numbers were small because of the dual role of
women and the often seasonal nature of the job. The 1951 Labour
Census revealed that women composed 5 % of the total labour force.
More studies are required for an analysis of the situations that
forced women into wage labour. Was this true of only those areas
where smallholder cash cropping was dominant? Was it only the need
for money that made women seek employment? When, for example, did
women of some tribes conceive of the idea of prostitution as a form
of employment to enable them to obtain land which under traditional
patriarch relations they would seldom be allowed to inherit from
parents, relatives of husbands. More research is also needed to
find out about the effects of migration on family relations, kinship
ties and marriage stability and the alternatives that were available
to women to obtain cash to pay taxes and purchase necessities when
economically active males were away in plantations and mines and
women had to assume the roles of heads of households. This will
contribute to a better understanding of the process of female
wage labour during the colonial period.

Female Urban Migration

Further analysis of the factors leading to female migration to
towns is needed. One author argues that the institution of the
family allowance after independence stimulated increased female
migration. Evidence is provided in the form of a rise in the
average annual growth of towns between 1967 and 1970 (IV:138, 139).
This evidence will have to be supported by breakdowns of households
to show that family allowances contributed towards a greater number
of females, wives and others, in the households during 1967 and
1970. Several other studies have also analysed the issue of urban
migration (137, 153, 154, 157-159). The most comprehensive data

was that collected by the National Urban Mobility Employment and
Income Survey of Tanzania (NUMEIST). It shows that in the more
recent years female migration rates were higher than those for men,
although unemployment rates for women were also higher. Women were
no longer coming as wives. While only 13 per cent of those who
came to town in 1952 were unmarried, the proportion had increased
to over 30 per cent by 1970 and is probably higher now (IV:158).
The NUMEIST data also found that most of the migrants were young
people.

Migration is perceived by some as a product of two factors,
the relationship of education and employment and the disparities in
development and wage earning opportunities between rural and urban
areas (V:137, 153, 157). Barnum, however, lays greater stress on
education and argues that many rural residents with formal
education will migrate independently of income differentials. The
role of education in migration cannot be denied, but if income
differentials are not the reason why the educated youth are
migrating, it raises many questions. The youthfulness of the
migrants and the increasing rate of female migration poses the
question as to whether migration is not a form of protest against
the patriarchal family relations which persist even in ujamaa and
new developmental villages - a deliberate and voluntary
proletarisation (V:138). The lack of opportunities in the rural
areas may be due as much to lack of employment opportunities but
also as to who owns the means of production in the patriarchal
family structure, of who controls the income earned by various
family members.

However, the theory of protest against the patriarchal relations
must be seen in the context of several other factors: the mismatch
of school curriculum and small scale agriculture (V:157). It must
also be seen in the context of parents' expectations of educated
children and the socio-economic structure of the national economy
that has still not achieved a socialist orientation to urbanisation
and the distribution of industries, services and utilities to the
rural areas.

Situation of Women in Urban Areas

The situation of women in urban areas is the subject of analyses
of nearly all the studies in this section. Unemployment rates
among women are higher than among men. Women are discriminated
against not only in obtaining jobs but also in maintaining or
improving them. They are usually given the most labour intensive
and boring jobs while the more supervisory and scientific and
technical jobs are reserved for men (V:148-151). In job redundancies
women suffer the most because of their position in wage labour.
The chief reasons for this discrimination are identified as the
sexual division of labour, the sexist concepts about women and their
role in the home and society and the lack of scientific and technical
education. The studies clearly show the conflict between the women's
dual role as worker and maintainer of the family household - a role
that affects her opportunities for employment, training and ability
to work odd hours or to go to distant places outside her place of
work. This role is made doubly difficult particularly for the low
and medium wage earners by the lack of adequate housing, transportation,

shopping and child care facilities so that these workers suffer both
from their position in society as workers as well as from their sex
specific roles. The sexual division of labour is also reflected
in the attitude of employers towards women. Women are considered
as poor workers compared to men because of their obligations to
take care of children and frequent pregnancies (V:138, 140, 148-
151, 162), even though men are the most vocal against family
planning programmes. The idea that women are less reliable than
men has been clearly shown to be false by Virju and Mgaya.

Have women in wage labour achieved better control over their
income and their lives? This clearly depends on the class of women
we are discussing (V:141, 143, 147, 154). In the case of the
lesser educated and lesser skilled women, the poor wage received
may have to be supplemented by other activities such as prostitution
or agricultural activities. Moreover, women in manual jobs are
usually the least secure in terms of employment. At the same time,
women workers have the "least to lose", in comparison to petty
bourgeois women. Their income is usually equal to that of husbands,
and wage employment provides them with an alternative to
"dependence" on a husband for subsistence. In contrast, the majority
of wives of the petty bourgeois lack the educational and other
resources to maintain their class position independently of their
husbands, and therefore "depend" more on the marriage relation.

Prostitution brings its own problems in the form of unwanted
pregnancies and children, forced abortions often leading to
serious medical problems and baby-dumping (V:147). Single women
failing to find employment may also resort to prostitution if
other means of earning incomes fail (V:154). On the other hand, the
women with more education and better jobs find that employment gives
them freedom, economic independence and higher standards of living
(V:143). This differentiation between various women workers is
significant and more work needs to be done with specific reference
to their position in the social hierarchy. Generalisations are too
often made about women workers, married women versus women heads
of households and discrimination against women that may distort
meaningful analyses.

Measures to Alleviate Women's Conditions

Several studies see education as the key to increasing the
participation of women in the employment sector (V:148-151, 158).
This is true to a certain extent. The relationship between education
and income earning cannot be denied. However, the ability of women
to join wage labour will depend on their education and skills but
also, and perhaps even more importantly, on the extent to which the
country can economically absorb such potential labour. Urban labour
surplus is a reality of the present system and conditions of economic
development, dependent as it is on the international economic system.
Access to education will also depend on the present social structure.
One study cautions that the children of the poor classes of women
may not do better because the educational facilities and job
opportunities are controlled by the bureaucratic bourgeosie
(V:150). On a more general level a great deal remains to be done
about the concepts of the role of women in the home and society and
the division of labour at home, the socialisation of child care and
other domestic activities (V:148, 150).

Some attempts have been made to provide women with security of
employment and assistance in the care of their own health and that
of their children. However, legislation like maternity leave can
have negative effects on women's employment (V:138, 146, 148, 159).
Perhaps a more effective way for women to bring about fairness
and sex equality is to effect radical social changes through the
worker's organisation JUWATA, the women's organisation (UWT) and
the nation's political party.

REFERENCES

H.N. Barnum and R.H. Sabot (1976), Migration, Education and Urban
    Surplus Labour: the Case of Tanzania. Paris OECD 115 pp.

———————

137. BIENEFELD, M.A. and SABOT, R.H. (1972), The National Urban
     Mobility Employment and Income Survey of Tanzania. (NUMEIST)
     Dar es Salaam Economic Research Bureau. 4 Volumes. (Only
     volumes II and III were available for annotation).

     Volume II: Urban Migration in Tanzania
     Describes the number of People that have been involved in the
     migration process during the post-war era; the age, sex and
     educational characteristics of more recent arrivals, their
     place of origins, the economic background and experience of
     migrants before leaving their home area, the adjustment to
     their new home and place of work, length of stay and ties with
     the rural villages from which they came.
         Volume III: Wage employment
     Describes the demographic characteristics, occupational struc-
     ture, industrial distribution, status of employer, wage incomes,
     time spent at work, stability of employment. Many of the
     sections deal with differences between male and female workers,
     the most significant being in the actual numbers of wage
     employed, 87 % of the males were found to be in the labour
     force compared to 29 % of females, of whom one in three found
     it difficult to secure a job.

138. BRYCESON, DEBORAH FAHY (1979), "The Proletarisation of Women in
     Tanzania". Paper No. 2, BW, 45 pp. published in Political
     Economy.

     Explores the development of women's participation in the urban
     labour force and posits a theoretical argument as to why women
     were not given opportunities for wage employment during the
     colonial period, nor found in great numbers in the urban areas.
     After national independence, minimum wage legislation
     established the "family wage", making it possible for women to
     migrate to the urban areas with their husbands. As time passed,
     divorced and single woman began to migrate in significant
     numbers as well. The gradual expansion of female wage
     employment is associated with the growing presence of women in
     the urban areas. It has in fact, gathered its own momentum as

as one of the more positive alternatives to female subjugation
in the traditional patriarchal family. Based on reanalysis of
data presented in V:159.

139. BRYCESON, D.F. (1980), "Social, Political and Economic Factors
Affecting Women's Material Conditions in Tanzania". Infant
Feeding in Dar es Salaam, edited by O. Mgaza and H. Bantje.
TFNC Report no. 484 and BRALUP Research Paper No. 66, Dar es
Salaam, TFNC and BRALUP, pp. 115-167.

Examines women's position in the social organization of
production and reproduction. Women in the rural areas shoulder
the main responsibility for providing the family's food, water
and firewood. In addition, the patriarchal concept of the
importance of many children keeps the woman busy in child
bearing and child-rearing so that women have very little
opportunity to participate in the national cash economy through
commodity production or wage employment. In the urban areas
too, a very small percentage of women participate in the national
cash economy. Here the greatest stumbling block is their lack
of education. Most national programmes for the improvement of
the conditions of women are centred around their role as human
reproducers. The paper suggests that ultimate change can only
be brought about through "women's defiance of the traditional
patriarchal value system which points their role first and
foremost as 'mothers' bearing children for the sake of
perpetuating and proliferating the patrilineal family". It
would also solve the national decline in productivity coupled
with high fertility which "erodes the material well being and
standard of living of the Tanzania population".

 This argument appears to fall in the best tradition of the
Malthusian and neo-Malthusian theories about population being
the root of poverty! It ignores contradictions in the national
economy and social organization that concern increase in
production not only by women but also by men - aspects such as
the price structure both at national and international level;
the high rate of inflation; the marketing infrastructure; and
control of family income. If women produced more who would
ultimately benefit? The petty trader, the bar owners, the men
who own large herds of cattle? The bureaucrats? It also
ignores the objective dependency of peasants on offspring for
labour and future security.

140. BRYCESON, D.F. (1980), "A Review of Statistical Information on
Women in the Work Force and Seeking Employment in Dar es
Salaam and Their Families' Economic Welfare with Special
Reference to Areas Surveyed in Oyster Bay, Upanga, Temeke and
Manzese". Infant Feeding in Dar es Salaam, edited by Olivia
Mgaza and Han Bantje, TFNC and BRALUP.

Presents a numerical and structural analysis of women's
employment in Tanzania based on the NUMEIST (see item 160) and
government statistics. Generally women were found to have
fewer opportunities for work than men although since the 1970's
more women than men were migrating to towns. The age and
marital status of migrants as well as distribution by income is
also discussed. Describes female employment: high income;

professional wage employment; medium income skilled wage
employment; low income unskilled wage employment; high income
informal self-employment; low income informal self-employment;
and non-money income earning. Also discusses the prospects
for future employment of women. The argument appears to be
that increasing insistence on material benefits and child care
facilities at places of work will lower women's chances for work
in the middle and low income groups.

The article is useful as a review of women's data on
employment in the urban sector as gathered by NUMEIST and
analysed by Sabot and Shields (V:157, 158). The data is not
specific to Dar es Salaam nor to the few areas mentioned in
the title.

141. BUJRA, JANET (1973), "Peri-Urban Settlement: Dar es Salaam".
The Young Child in Tanzania, Dar es Salaam, Tanzania National
Scientific Research Council: 398-448.

In order to obtain a correct perspective of child care in peri-
urban areas in Dar es Salaam, the author describes aspects of
the socio-economic variables that influence child care in Dar es
Salaam: (1) family income, both wage and subsidiary, as well as
income of mothers; (2) income in kind i.e. food cultivated on
farms owned by the family or relatives; (3) expenditure pattern
including which parent buys the food, and the problem of money
spent on non-essentials; (4) fertility, and family planning;
(5) ethnic background of mothers, tribal and religious beliefs
and their effect on family life; (6) knowledge and ability of
mothers including level of formal education; (7) access to help
from kin; (8) housing and environmental sanitation; (9) medical,
educational and child care facilities in the area.

Provides useful insights into the problems faced by women in
raising a family. Also shows that the socio-economic status of
the chief income earners, mostly the men, determines the level
of hardships a woman faces, but that the overall dependent and
precarious status remains if she herself does not contribute to
the family income.

142. GREEN, ALLEN JOHNSON (1979), A Socio-Economic History of Moshi
Town: A Case Study of Urbanization. University of Dar es
Salaam, unpublished MA dissertation, Department of History,
162 pp.

Argues that the primitive accumulation process, the process of
separation of the producers from the means of production, is a
precondition for capitalist development, which continues during
the present epoch of monopoly capital. Capital accumulation and
primitive accumulation are concurrent economic processes. This
is revealed in the way capital moves into formerly non-capitalist
sectors such as family production of use values in goods and
services, or the way smaller capitalist enterprises are destroyed
in competition with big capitalist firms. It is necessary to
analyse the dynamic development of precapitalist social formations
during the pre-colonial period in order to clarify the processes
of capital accumulation and primitive accumulation which
developed during the colonial and post-colonial periods. This
is done in an analysis of Moshi Chiefdom during 1860-1920, and

the breakdown of precapitalist relations of production (as a process) during the colonial and post-colonial periods. Unfortunately, the author does not relate his analysis of feudal relations to patriarchal relations at the level of clan and household.

One of the most visible signs of the destruction of precapitalist relations was the growing significance of child labour in settler and kulak coffee production. There was an intense struggle over child labour between settlers, kulak farmers, estates, the state and the chiefs and elders. This struggle reveals more than just the breakdown of precapitalist relations. It also indicates the process of commoditization in production and reproduction and the growth of a surplus population, in latent form within peasant families, and a growing floating form of landless rural people and unemployed urban dwellers. As Green notes, urban-rural relations are not relations between different geographical areas, but rather "social relations between different classes".

Explores the dynamics of peasant differentiation, which developed partially on the basis of precapitalist feudal relations. Chiefs transformed the way they approached production. Moreover, coffee production on whatever scale necessitated, and still necessitates, the exploitation of hired labour in the absence of a truly communal form of property ownership and organisation of production. A source of cheap hired labour has increasingly been available among the landless and impoverished peasants in the area.

The workers in town were dependent on their wages for their reproduction, and farmed gardens to supplement the wage. The alternative point of view is rejected, that is, that wage labourers are in fact migrant labourers, a non-proletariat group ultimately tied to the soil. The low wages African workers received were simply not adequate to cover family consumption costs (a range of 27/= to 60/= per month wage, to cover monthly total expenditures per family of 127/=) which forced the working class family to supplement the wage with farming and other activities, as proletariat have done historically in Europe, America and so on.

Green engages in self-criticism of his neglect to analyse the sexual division of labour and the women's question in general. This would have strengthened the analysis, given the different place of women in the labour force in precapitalist social formations, as well as in wage labour and peasant commodity production today. Nevertheless, the research represents a very careful analysis of the changes in family relations as capital penetrated and destroyed certain aspects of precapitalism, and transformed others. The methodology adopted is exemplary, and the author has contributed through this work to major debates on such issues as proletarisation and peasantisation. These issues are of particular importance in women's studies in Africa today. The appendix also provides archival material which illustrates the efforts of the colonial state and its Native Authority functionaries to regulate marriage in a desparate move to

counteract the breakdown in patriarchal marriage relations
accompanying the subjugation of precapitalist relations to
capitalism.

143. HATTON, MICHELE F. (1979), "The Economic and Social Position
of Women in the Development of Tanzania: Case Study on Urban
Wage-Earning Women". University of Minnesota, unpublished
student report, 138 pp.

Provides insights into the problems of work at home and in the
office, based on interviews with 33 women employees at one
branch of the National Bank of Commerce, as well as personal
experiences of the researcher while living in Dar es Salaam.
Heads of personnel, both women and men, agreed that women
tended to be steadier workers since they lacked alternative
job opportunities. There was a much higher turnover rate for
men. Problems management faced in hiring women reflected
their role in sexuality and fertility relations: absence due
to maternity leave or the responsibility of caring for sick
children, attendance in maternity clinics or other domestic
responsibilities; and leaving employment because of husband
transfers. The first set of complaints have been found out in
studies of women workers in factories as well.
     Most of the women (85 %) said there was no overt sexual
discrimination, although older women complained of the difficulty
to get employment. Ninety percent shared their earnings with
parents. Economic independence and higher standards of living
were the major advantages given for wage employment, as well
as broadened horizons and greater respect from husbands. The
personal power derived from employment helps to stabilise
marriage, although men were also threatened by their working
status. "Because you are working, you are free". "You have
the power to talk in front of these men with your own opinion."
Unemployed women were dependent on their spouses. Nearly all
of the single women said they would continue to work after
marriage. Conflict between work on the job and at home was a
major problem, due partly to minimal assistance from husbands.
Sunday was "cleaning day" for the wives, whereas it was a day
of leisure for the husbands. Half of the mothers in the group
were unmarried, female heads of household.
     Husbands made all the big decisions in the married households.
Wives ask their husband's permission to visit family and friends,
to leave the house for any reason after returning from work,
and to travel during their leave from work. There was a
tendency to complain but also to accept the situation as
inevitable. "I must do what he says and have to accept it
because he's a man". In the evenings, most husbands visited
bars while women stayed at home alone with the children. The
greatest cause of divorce was "other women", as well as mis-
understanding and "higher consciousness among women". In the
words of one, "If you are a woman and want to be equal you
can't stay with your husband anymore". Another said, "Many city
women know that, after all, it isn't necessary to live with a
man, why live together if you're always disappointed. It may
end up that you live only on a little salary but you can
manage". And as a third said "Women won't sacrifice anymore".

Several also criticised UWT for being "old and conservative", and not active in backing up women in legal struggles.

144. KASULAMEMBA, S.P., "Problems of Working Women: the Case of Dar es Salaam City Council". Paper No. 9, BW, 4 pp.

Highlights the problems of working women in Dar es Salaam based on the experiences of women working at the Dar es Salaam City Council. The problems include the difficulty of maintaining jobs during husbands' inter-regional transfers, the dilemma of obtaining reliable child-care facilities, marital problems affecting work performance and opportunities for study and training and sex discrimination.

145. KHERRY, A.S. (1979), "Extra-Marital Pregnancies and the Position of Women". Dar es Salaam, Sociology Department, University of Dar es Salaam. 50 pp.

Extra-marital pregnancies are considered as a serious social crime resulting in discountinuance in schools and inability to do national service or join the armed forces. 146 cases dealt with by the Tanga Magistrates Court were examined in order to identify possible socio-economic reasons leading to these pregnancies. It was found that girls engaged in sexual relations as a result of social problems such as financial deprivation, poor housing and breakdowns in families. In many cases women were unaware of modern contraceptives and ended up by having children whose paternity could not be established so that neither marriage nor maintenance assistance resulted. In order to maintain the child, the young woman was forced into further illegitimate unions. Nearly a half of the cases were girls below 20.

   Some interesting findings were obtained from interviews with 50 of these cases. Results showed that the number of Muslims exceeded the number of Christians; the level of education was significant but even so, it did not exclude those with primary and secondary education from engaging themselves in extra-marital unions; the unskilled and unemployed were more prone to such unions and among the employed, the salary level was a decisive element; that the number of rooms in a house had a considerable impact on extra-marital pregnancies.

146. MASCARENHAS, OPHELIA (1979), Promotion of Equality of Opportunity and Treatment by Reinforcing the Social Structure. Mimeo. Forthcoming as BRALUP Service Paper, 67 pp.

Using primary and secondary sources, describes various conditions of women in the wage labour sector under the following sections: the right to work; women wage-earners in the modern sector; non-wage-earning women in the rural sector; measures taken to lighten family and domestic responsibilities; problems of rural and urban women and recommendations. Tables are provided to illustrate the arguments.

147. MBAH, F.U., "Prostitution in Tanzania (A case study of Dar es Salaam City)". Dar es Salaam, Dept. of Sociology, University of Dar es Salaam, 1979. Ms. B.A. Dissertation. 55 pp.

Argues that prostitution, mainly an urban phenomenon, is a
direct result of the forces of colonialism and the capitalist
mode of production in Tanzania which led men and women to
migrate to towns for economic support. Women also migrated to
towns in order to circumvent social customs regarding land
ownership and inheritance rights that make women totally
dependent on males and which render them landless if divorced
or widowed. The case studies show that prostitution can be a
full-time lucrative employment or part-time occupation to
supplement meagre income from full-time employment.

    The study also has a lengthy discussion on the implications
of prostitution. On the negative side it shows how prostitution
leads to increases in venereal diseases, abortions, baby
dumping and divorce. Nearly half of the out-patients in
hospitals and health centres are related to gonorrhea;
abortion is the single most frequent cause of admission in
gynecological wards. On the relationship of prostitution and
divorce the evidence presented is less convincing, and no
figures are given for baby dumping. On the positive side, the
author argues that prostitution is a safety valve for men's
tensions in a class society such as present day Tanzania. If
it were not for these prostitutes, the author argues, rape
would be rampant. It is also a means of earning a living,
very much like a clerk. Taken to its logical conclusion one
would therefore assume that it should not only be tolerated
but actively encouraged to protect one class of women in society.

148. MEGHJI, ZAKIA MOHAMMED HAMDANI (1977), The Development of
Women Wage Labour: The Case of Industries in Moshi District.
University of Dar es Salaam, unpublished M.A. dissertation,
126 pp.

Traces the development of women labourers in Moshi District,
Kilimanjaro Region, and describes the present status of women
employees in the district by examining three industrial set-
ups: Kibo Match Corporation; Moshi Textile Mills Limited; and
African Flower Industries Limited. The first women wage
labourers in Moshi District were poor peasant women working on
the farms of richer peasants and on plantations. They worked
as seasonal labour since they also had to maintain family and
coffee trees. With the establishment of industries the number
of women wage labourers increased, but even in the most
favourable circumstances their number did not exceed 30 per cent
of the total wage labour.

    An examination of the three industries revealed that women
were generally given unskilled jobs or jobs related to domestic
activities. Most of the women were employed on temporary terms
and generally considered as less productive than men. Wherever
new machines and techniques were used to improve efficiency,
the number of women employees was reduced so that, given this
trend, the author feels that less women will be employed in
industries in the future. Part of the problem lies in the historica
discrimination against women in the matter of education. With
a rethinking of girls' education and the number of girls
attaining science and technical education, there is a likelihood
that, though the number of women doing unskilled jobs will not

decrease, the number of women in key technical positions will
increase.

Includes statistics of women in manufacturing industries for
1963 to 1972; development of women wage labour in Tanzania,
1947-1963, and educational data showing enrolment of girls and
boys at primary, secondary and university level for the years
1961, 1971, 1975.

149. MEGHJI, ZAKIA (1979), "Nature of Female Urban Employment".
Paper No. 37, BW 5 p. Summary of V:148.

Using industries in Moshi District, the paper shows that women
in industries are mostly employed in labour intensive and
unskilled jobs and are easily redundant when automation is
introduced, while men predominate in the automated sections even
without the necessary technical education. The chief drawback
to women getting more technical jobs is the prejudicial attitude
of management reflective of the societal attitude that a woman's
place is at home.

150. MGAYA, MARY HANS (1976), A Study of Workers in a Factory.
University of Dar es Salaam, unpublished M.A. dissertation,
174 pp.

Examines the conditions of women workers of the middle and lower
grades in the employment pyramid in Friendship Textile Mill, Dar
es Salaam. Women's dual roles of homemaker and factory worker
which are based on the traditional sexist division of labour
seriously affect their training opportunities. Traditional
attitudes towards women also contribute to discrimination
against women, preventing them from appointment to managerial
positions. Even in sections where the majority of workers are
women, the supervisor or head of section is a man.

However, the lack of adequate education is one of the major
causes for discrimination against women. Traditional education
contributed a great deal towards the present attitudes of men
and women towards education and their roles in life. Colonial
education catered mainly to young men. The few girls who went
to school learnt subjects that would make them better wives and
mothers. Even after independence girls are trained" for services
and not for productive labour. ... There is no technical school
for girls, even in Dar es Salaam". The study also shows how in
the capitalist social system, education is a means to a white-
collar job in towns. Here the opportunities are few and the
dominant class, men, use traditional sexist attitudes towards
women to keep the women out of jobs or use sexual relations as
a method of employing or promoting women. The author feels
that future generations of the lower and middle groups will not
fare better in education since these opportunities are controlled
by the petty and bureaucratic bourgeoisie.

151. MGAYA, M.H. (1979), "Women Workers in a Factory in Tanzania".
Paper No. 1, BW, 14 pp. A summary of V:150.

Shows that women workers are discriminated against in job
allocation and training opportunities. Their problems are
rooted in their lower level of education, their dual role as
mothers and workers and the male chauvinistic attitude of the
management about women's work performance in technical jobs.

152. MIHYO, N.Z. (1981), "The Involvement of Women in Small-Scale Industries in Tanzania (Case Study: Dar es Salaam City)". Paper presented at the Institute of Development Studies Seminar, November 7th, 26 pp.

After an historical analysis of women's education and employment in Tanzania, analyses the situation of women employees in six workplaces, four of which are factories. Statistics are provided on sex composition of the labour force, education levels and job allocation in each situation. A sexual division of labour is found such that women are relegated to the lowest paying jobs, with limited access to on-the-job training necessary to move from unskilled or semi-skilled work to semi-skilled and skilled work.

153. MLAY, W.F. (1976), "Checking the Drift to Towns". Journal of the Geographic Association of Tanzania. No. 14, 182-203.

Despite the inability of the urban sector to absorb all the job seekers coming into towns, the movement to towns to secure wage employment continues. The author relates this to expansion in education and disparities in development and wage earning opportunities between rural and urban areas. Official attempts to stop the drift to towns are discussed. The author emphasises greater economic incentives in the migration to towns in search of jobs.
   Although there is no sex breakdown of the migrants and there is no discussion of the special problems facing female migrants, the study is nevertheless useful in understanding why the rural women migrate to towns in search of employment.

154. MWAKALINGA, SIMON JIM (1979), "Problems Facing Single Unemployed Urban Women in Tanzania: A Case Study of Mwanjelwa Area in Mbeya Town". Dar es Salaam, Dept., of Sociology, University of Dar es Salaam. Ms. B.A. Dissertation. 41 pp.

The study is based on a questionnaire and interviews involving a total of 312 respondents in 2 wards. It found that single women came to towns to seek for education and economic opportunities. Many had economic problems due to marriage instability. The setbacks to employment were found to be lack of education, physical prowess, training and sheer prejudice. In the absence of regular employment, the single women engaged themselves in 3 main occupations: selling foodstuffs; selling local beer; working as barmaids. About 60 % had unspecified jobs. In most cases the income earned was below the statutory minimum wage. About a third of the women supplemented their income by prostitution. Most of these women had less than 3 meals a day and lived in housing with poor sanitation. About 44 % had children to support and their plight was worse. Attempts to help the women by giving them a piece of land to cultivate to supplement their income were not successful due to land shortage.

155. ORDE BROWNE, G. St. J. (1967) (1933), The African Labourer. London, Frank Cass and Co. Ltd., 240 pp.

The author was head of the Labour Department of Tanganyika for many years, and drew on his colonial experience to analyse the

employment of African wage-labourers. Of central concern was
"detribalisation" of landlessness, which rendered the individual
Africans "a danger to the state" in the words of Lord Lugard in
the Foreword. There are two basic themes running through the
analysis. First, the significance of the fact that the majority
of African workers retained land and other means of production
in their home villages. Their wives and relatives continued to
work in the land and provided for their own support, and the wage
only covered the costs of maintaining the individual migrant
worker. Social security benefits of various kinds were not
provided. These conditions made the African a source of cheap
labour. Second, and contrary to the above, the very same
circumstances established the conditions for a shortage of
labour, in that "producing themselves almost all that their
simple needs required, they lived a self-sufficing existence that
rendered them slow to see any sort of advantage in going to work
for strangers in order to obtain goods for which they had no
particular use when gained". Hence the need for taxes, direct
force and legal enforcement of contracts in order to ensure an
adequate labour supply.

Despite the basically correct assessment of the significance
of the land to which the labourer may always return, the author
ignores such questions as who actually produces on the land, and
is therefore left to maintain the family in the absence of the
labourer. Indeed, in the author's conception the loss of "young
men and youth" does not alter the labour process of the peasant
household at all, and their return is beneficial in that they
will have become more healthy and more critical of unsanitary
conditions at home! Moreover, "their absence will leave a
larger share of the available food constituents to be consumed
by those remaining at home". There is no conception here of the
nature of the labour process in the peasant household, and the
different roles of men and women in maintaining the family.
Concern is only shown about the effects of migrant labour on
the stability of the African family and the possibility of
prostitution becoming prevalent in urban and rural areas. The
subject of women is dispersed throughout, though scantily, and
usually in terms of the women peasants left behind. There is
some discussion of women and child workers, and the kind of work
women usually receive in wage labour and the legal provisions
accompanying that work. There is also a summary of colonial
laws concerning wage labour in Tanganyika as of 1933.

156. PAN, LYNN (1975), Alcohol in Colonial Africa. Helsinki, Finnish
Foundation for Alcohol Studies, Volume 22, Uppsala, Scandinavian
Institute of African Studies, 121 pp.

Provides "an historical review of the liquor trade", "an account
of the international conference convened to devise its control"
and case studies of alcohol control in three African territories.
Manufactured alcohol ranked with guns, ammunition and cotton
goods as the most significant trade goods bartered by European
traders for slaves, palm oil and other commodities. Manufactured
alcohol also was used as a form of currency in international trade
in Africa, as a form of wage, and as payment, for land and trading
rights. Efforts to control and/or restrict importation of alcohol

were mainly expressions of the different interests of different national capitals. European and American, and the different ways in which labour was exploited in Africa.

Manufactured alcohol (imported and later manufactured locally) has always had to compete with "homebrew", which is mainly consumed by low income workers and peasants. Home brewing is a "cottage industry" especially for elderly, single or widowed women with no other means of livelihood; or else is used to supplement incomes from wage or crop proceeds which are inadequate to subsist. In the 1936 report to the Permanent Mandates Commission of the League of Nations, the British Government noted that Tanganyika Breweries Ltd., could not compete with homebrew in Dar es Salaam towns and had it withdrawn. Instead, the colonial state granted licenses on a monthly basis to twelve African brewers, usually women, who were each provided with "a stall, a kitchen for brewing, and a lock-up-store".

157. SABOT, T.H. (1979), Economic Development and Urban Migration, Tanzania, 1900-1971. London, Oxford. 279 pp.

An intensive analysis of the micro- and macro-determinants and consequences of migration in the economic development of Tanzania is presented, based on the National Urban Mobility Employment and Income Survey of Tanzania (NUMEIST) covering 7 towns in Tanzania. Determinants of migration, demographic characteristics and socio-economic background of migrants, occupational opportunities, the social costs of urban surplus labour and the options available to deal with the problem are discussed. Migration was found to be caused by the decline in wage employment in the rural sector and the rise of wage employment opportunities in the towns. Two other factors also played a key role in migration: the relationship between employment and education and the "mismatch" of school curriculum with vocation in small scale agriculture. The migrants who were mostly located in Dar es Salaam, were found to be young people; the average age for males and females was 22.2 years and 25.1 years, respectively. In the past migrants were predominantly men but in more recent years females had more than doubled their rates of migration and they were no longer coming in as wives. In the urban areas fully 80 per cent of the women had no income compared to 13 per cent of the men. The low participation rate was due not to a less desire for employment but to a disadvantaged position in the labour market which was worst for those with very little or no education. The higher rates of participation of educated women supported this hypothesis. Evidence is also given to show that the lower educational level the greater was the difference in earnings between women and men.

158. SHIELDS, NWANGANGA (1978), Women in the Urban Labour Market: The Case of Tanzania. Washington D.C., World Bank Staff Working Paper No. 380, 141 pp., with tables.

Based on secondary analysis of the 1971 National Urban, Mobility, Employment and Income Survey (NUMEIST), the report illustrates the amount of information and understanding which can be derived from already-generated statistics. The analysis covers characteristics of women in the urban labour market, determinants

of female employment, the effects of differential education
attainment on earnings, and policy implications. One of the
major questions posed is why an increasing number of women have
migrated to towns between 1950 and 1971, and what job
opportunities they actually find. Women who come independently
(i.e. not as dependent housewives) form a growing proportion
of the total migrants, seeking some form of employment in town.
Women have unequal access to jobs, and to incomes, reflected
in higher wages for men even after education and other factors
are controlled for. This is explained by "cumulative
discrimination", beginning at home with decisions over education
resources, at school where sex bias is found, and at work where
employers favour men for training and promotion, and women are
relegated to lower positions and less secure work. It is
worthwhile citing the policy suggestions in full:

"(1) Providing girls with more access to education by making all
schools coeducational and ensuring that the school intake
reflects the ratio of the sexes in the population and ensuring
that girls are not automatically put into the inferior educational
stream which would not give them a chance of competing in high
status and high income jobs.

(2) Adult education system which would provide the current
illiterate, underemployed and poor urban women and opportunity
of upgrading their skills and ability to increase their income.

(3) Restructuring the educational system so that provision is
made for the school dropout and older people to re-enter the
system to obtain education which would improve their earning
potentiality".

159. SWANTZ, MARJA-LIISA and BRYCESON, D.B. (1976), Women Workers in
Dar es Salaam: 1973/74 Survey of Female Minimum Wage Earners
and Self-Employed. University of Dar es Salaam; BRALUP Research
Paper No. 43, 35 pp.

A survey of low income female workers in Dar es Salaam was
conducted at two factories in the city, at the Ministry of
Education, the Prime Minister's Office and at the University in
1973. A sample of women sellers at Msasani and Kijitonyama
areas, Dar es Salaam, were also surveyed during April-July, 1974.
The survey examined the age, origin, educational and religious
background, family patterns, urban living arrangement and
conditions of work of these workers. The aim was to determine
why women migrated and sought employment in urban areas and how
their lives were affected by it, including the degree of economic
independence attained by working women, their attitudes in the
urban setting, the awakening of consciousness and awareness of
social inequalities. Economic independence depended on marital
status in conjunction with ability to earn a steady income
through wage or self-employment. The survey revealed a
growing consciousness among women of the economic and social
advantages of employment.

160. TANGANYIKA (1955), A Report on the Migration of African
Workers to the South from the Southern Highlands Province with
Special Reference to the Nyakyusa of Rungwe District, by

P. Gulliver. Tukuyu, Government Sociologist, Tukuyu, 1955.

Discusses the numbers and characteristics of the migrants, the
reasons for migration and the effects of migration with special
reference to the Nyamwanga and Nyiha of Mbeya District and
Nyakyusa of Rungwe District during the early 1950s'. The latter
went mostly to the mines south of the border while the former
went chiefly to Tanganyika agricultural enterprises. The study
shows that migrants were chiefly young men. The prime cause
for migration was economic pressure particularly among the
Nyakyusa where land was fertile but scarce. Young men had less
access to land then the old. As they grew older they inherited
land and the need for migratory labour declined. Although the
study attempts to make light of it, labour migration affected
agricultural production, caused tribal disunity and increased
the divorce rate. Many of the migrants were unmarried but of
those who were married, only a third were accompanied by their
wives.

This study is important to understand how labour migration
and capital reinforced the inferior position of women by
relegating them to the house while the men went abroad and
controlled the cash thus earned.

161. TANZANIA BUREAU OF STATISTICS (1975), Survey of Employment and
Earnings, 1973-74. Dar es Salaam, Bureau of Statistics.

Consists of commentaries and tables regarding employment and
earnings by sectors, industries, regions, age and sex. The
labour economy covered includes both enterprise (private,
parastatal, non-profit, cooperative) as well as the public
sector. An important omission is the wage-earners employed in
small-holder agriculture and the self-employed in rural and
urban areas. Industrial divisions include agriculture, mining
and quarrying, manufacturing, public utilities, construction,
commerce, transport finance, and services. Several tables include
statistics about the employment and earnings of women workers.

162. VIRJI, PARIN J., "Summary of Labour Turnover at Friendship
Textile Mill - 1978 with Specific Reference to Women Workers".
Paper No. 3, BW, 8 p.

The policy of the Management at the Friendship Textile Mill, Dar
es Salaam, is to employ less women because women workers are
considered to be less reliable. The author uses the figures
for labour turnover at the Mill to refute this argument and to
show that it is based on prejudice rather than on fact. Women
constitute 10 % of the labour force at the Friendship Textile
Mill, yet their turnover was found to be only 7 %. Of those
dismissed for absenteeism men constituted 3.3 % of the turnover
while women constituted only 2.2 %. Of the 190 dismissed on the
grounds of insubordination not one was a female worker, while
of the 15 who left to look after their aged parents, only 1 was
a woman. It was found that most female workers were single
women with children to support. They therefore tended to be
steady at their jobs. Also provides statistics on the
distribution of the labour force of the Mill by department and
sex. Considers the problems experienced by women workers at the
Mill. In addition to problems associated with the working class:

low wages, inadequate transport, food and medical services, women
also suffer from specific problems arising from their sex and
their role as mothers and domestic labourers.

163. WESTERGAARD, MARGARETA (1970), Women and Work in Dar es Salaam.
University of Dar es Salaam, Sociology Department, mimeo, 32 pp.

The research explored the proportion of "idle" wives in Dar es
Salaam, the employment situation in Dar es Salaam, factors
influencing job activity among wives, male attitudes towards
married women taking wage employment and alternatives to wage
employment in Dar es Salaam for women. The scarcity of wage
employment for women is documented, as well as the resistance
of some men to allow their wives to work. Only 22 of the 191
women in the sample were female heads of households, and 41 %
of these were wage earners, as compared to 9 % of the 169 wives
of male heads of households. This finding is consistent with
findings cited in II:28, 29 that female wage-earners tend to be
heads of households. The report does not explain clearly enough
the techniques used to acquire the information: for example,
were both husbands and wives interviewed in all cases? In one
place or separately? How were the households selected for the
sample? This is important because the sample was based on
residence, not place of work.

VI. WOMEN'S PROJECTS AND COOPERATIVES

The importance of cooperatives for development and as protection
against exploitation was recognised by many cash crop producers and
traders early during the colonial period in Tanzania. Marketing
cooperatives were set up to protect smallholder coffee and cotton
growers in the 1920's and 1930's. After independence the movement
spread to cover other agricultural crops and non-agricultural
activities, finally culminating in the policy of ujamaa cooperative
village unions for rural development.

The membership of women in cooperatives has generally been
small (VI:167, 173-175). The reasons for this are rooted in the
origins of the cooperative movement in Tanzania and in the woman's
role in the productive and reproductive sector in the capitalist
mode of production. As stated above, earliest cooperative societies
were agricultural marketing societies involving cooperative marketing
of cash crops. The role of women in the productive and reproductive
sector is already discussed at length in the sections above. At the
household level, any surplus obtained from the productive sector
through sale of crops tended to be appropriated by the male head of
household. It is therefore not surprising that women considered
cooperatives as "men's shops" (VI:167). Secondly, marketing
societies specified that membership was limited to bona fide
farmers who occupied land. Occupation of land was interpreted to
mean ownership of land (e.g. VI:167, 174). This interpretation was
possibly necessitated by the need for security of loans and other
obligations of the members. Nevertheless, as most women in Tanzania
did not own land, the majority of them were excluded from membership
of the early cooperative societies. In addition restrictions on
women's movements and responsibilities ensured that she did not
participate in activities outside the house and farms of the male
head of household.

These factors are still prevailing in most of Tanzania. It is
therefore not surprising that the number of women in cooperatives
remains small. Several organisations are involved in setting up
women's cooperative projects as a means of improving the conditions
of women and their families. These projects range from income
generating activities like vegetable farming, brick-making, tailoring;
to educational projects in health and nutrition; as well as
cooperative child care facilities. These have experienced various
levels of failure (VI:164, 165, 170, 178, 179) and rare success.
The chief causes of failure have been identified. They can again
be related to historical factors as well as prevailing social and
economic relations. The most frequently mentioned causes are:
women's lack of education and skills, particularly in technical,
managerial and commercial fields; excessive burdens of domestic
work and child care aggravated by conditions in the rural areas
where women have to spend long hours collecting water and fuel-wood;
lack of capital and personnel; lack of training facilities, and
deficiences in equipment (VI:164, 174). In areas with large migrant
population, as for instance in large urban centres, there is also the
problem of lack of cohesiveness (VI:178).

Three questions have been raised regarding these projects.
Kiyenze questions whether small-scale projects like pottery production
can effect any meaningful change (VI:169). This trend of thought is
worth researching further in evaluating the contribution of women's
projects to the development of women in Tanzania. Chale and Ngonyani,
on the other hand, are very optimistic but clearly show that improvements depend on both the success of the project and the extent of
the success (VI:165). However, here one must question the concept
of "improvements" as used by these two authors for sometimes it is
interpreted as meaning even the ability to buy a khanga or earn
20/=. This issue is closely related to the question of the
advisability of exclusively promoting women's cooperatives (VI:173,
175). Opondo sees women's cooperatives as an initial step, to give
women skills that will help them get over the historical and
traditional reluctance to join cooperatives. A third issue that
has been raised rather implicitly is the exploitation of the poorest
women by the richer members in women's cooperatives. This issue is
not specific to sex and is experienced even in cooperatives where
the members are predominantly men or where the membership is mixed
as in consumer societies. It illustrates, yet again, that the
struggle of women cannot be reduced simply to gender.

Not much analysis has been presented on the membership of the
women's projects so as to evaluate the possible relationship between
cooperative membership and class position. Chale and Ngoyani
generalise that urban projects were more successful than rural
projects (VI:165) yet Sijaona's description of urban projects
involving low income women shows how they were generally unsuccessful
(VI:178). This issue is important in understanding why women do
not participate in women's projects even when their household
duties are alleviated through house-help or are not very strenuous.

It cannot be emphasized enough that although women's projects
can contribute towards an improvement in the conditions of women,
the final success of these projects will ultimately depend on the
extent to which women participate fully in all the productive
sectors of the national economy and are accepted as full members of
the society both socially and politically (VI:174).

---

164. CHALE, FREDA U. (1976), "Quarterly Report of the Visits to Eight
    Regions on Women's Activities and Children's Programmes". UNICEF,
    Dar es Salaam, 47 pp.

    Freda Chale, Assistant Regional Officer for UNICEF, reports on
    her visits to view the impact of efforts by the Tanzanian
    Government and UNICEF in eight regions of Tanzania where UNICEF
    projects for women and children have been launched. Projects
    include food preservation and storage workshops, child spacing
    and nutrition, home economics, day care, poultry, and vegetable
    farming, brick-making, pottery, sewing, and textile weaving. The
    document reviews projects by region. Discussions of women's
    activities in the region, problems in projects, suggestions and
    recommendations are brief and to the point. The reader gets an
    overview of each project, its constraints and suggestions for
    overcoming these constraints. The main problems are equipment

deficiencies and breakdowns especially in transportation and the lack of training for day care teachers and for women heading projects - for whom management and accounts training might lessen the attrition rate.

165. CHALE, FREDA U. and GENEROSE H. NGONYANI (1979), "Report on a Survey of Cooperative Income Generation Projects for Women and its Impact on the Welfare of Children and the Family". Paper No. 24, BW, 41 pp.

Starting with self-criticism of the research adopted, the authors argue that it is necessary to investigate the problem at two levels, at the level of "root causes" rooted in under-development within an unjust international economic order, and at the level of everyday problems of production, management and administration. Participatory research is necessary where "women can do research on their problems, analyse them objectively and plan for remedial action". Their own research was based on a more standard survey approach, based on interviews with leader-ship and regular mambers of cooperative projects. Among the "everyday" problems were the lack of adequate capital, materials, credit, and qualified staff. Recommendations include having feasibility studies before beginning a project, having minimum fixed capital of shs. 10,000/=, raw materials which are locally available and where marketing outlets exist for the products, and the education of women leaders. The analysis tends to identify women's interests with the well-being of the family, and not with the well-being of the women themselves, thus reproducing the concept of women as mother and not as human beings seeking liberation. For example, the objectives of income generating projects include: increasing income earning capacities in order to improve family living standards; increasing women's involvement "in more productive activities directly beneficial to the family members" and the provision of "skills and knowledge necessary for the care and maintenance of the family". Whereas it is certainly important to increase the welfare of the family, family welfare is the responsibility of both men and women, and women are not reducible only to family.
    A big difference was found between the number and viability of cooperative projects in urban and rural areas in the four regions surveyed. Two major explanations presented refer to the heavy workload of rural peasant women, including child care as a major element, which do not allow them to participate; and the low purchasing power in villages, a result of national dependency and underdevelopment. Other problems were shared by urban and rural projects: the tendency for the poorest women to be exploited by the richer members; the workload of domestic work which is heightened by the lack of basic services like water facilities and day care centres; the lack of adequate skills and competition from the private business sector. The paper is notable for the amount of detailed information provided about individual projects and for the critical analysis of major issues.

166. COOPERATIVE COLLEGE, PMO & UNIVERSITY OF DAR ES SALAAM (1975), "Cooperative Retailing in Tanzania Mainland". Moshi, Research Report - Draft Copy.

Based on a thorough survey of cooperative retailing, the study
found three common types of cooperative counsumer shops: those
attached to marketing societies, consumer societies and ujamaa
villages. The most prevalent is the latter found in more and
more villages. The village shops tend to be small, with poor
layout, poor security from burglary, dirty, and staffed by
managers with standard VII education and one or two years of
experience. The majority of staff lacked any special training,
but at least one fourth had some cooperative training. The
accounting was poor in all shops, however, which meant villages
could not control or supervise. One half of the assistants
received no pay, and others received a nominal payment of around
50/= monthly. In terms of turnover of goods, these shops are
over-staffed. They carry basic foodstuffs like sembe, rice,
sugar, salt, milk products, cooking oil, soap and kerosene.

Few of the local village leaders interviewed were women and
only 14 % of the cooperative shop managers. Nearly half of the
shop assistants were women.

167. I.C.A. Regional Office for East and Central Africa (1980),
Report on the Evaluation of the ICA Women Cooperative Education
and Other Activities Project. Moshi, ICA, 69 pp.

Reviews the women's cooperative project of the ICA. The project
started in recognition of the need to incorporate women into the
cooperatives. It identifies 3 factors that prevented women from
joining cooperatives: traditional role accorded to women as home
makers; existing legislation about membership that was interpreted
to mean that only those who owned land were eligible to be
members and educational programmes that were aimed at members
only. The women's project was set up to inform women about work
and responsibilities of existing cooperatives; organise cooperatives using traditional crafts and provide education in the
management of cooperatives. This was to be done through grass-
root and national seminars. Although the national seminars
showed a high degree of participation by women, 80 % of the
participants were employees of cooperatives or members in their
own rights. ICA had not yet succeeded in mobilising women
peasants or wives of cooperators.

168. I.C.A. REGIONAL OFFICE for East and Central Africa, The Women
Cooperator Newsletter 1979. Moshi.

The Newsletter, newly revived, is oriented towards women
involved in cooperative movements in East and Central Africa.
Reports are published on ICA Seminars and other activities, and
also on women's cooperative groups and sources of financial
funding. The language is English. As stated by the editor,
Zakia Meghji, who is the Education Officer (women), "Finally I
would like to make a request to all cooperators to bring to us
any news, articles, pamphlets and different items, which could
be used to educate others in the region".

169. KIYENZE, BERNAD K. SHIJA (1978), The Establishment of Small-
Scale Industries out of Traditional Handicrafts Based on a
Development Study of Socio-Economic Change in Western Bagamoyo
District. University of Dar es Salaam, unpublished MA
dissertation.

The problem posed in this thesis is whether traditional handicrafts can be the foundation of viable small-scale industries
today. Among the crafts dealt with is pottery production by
women in this particular locality. Crafts production is set in
the context of the historical development of the Bagamoyo Region.
Limited attention is given to the division of labour by sex.
However there is a detailed description of pottery production
itself as well as plaiting and weaving done both by men and
women. The impact of commoditisation during colonial rule on
pottery production and other crafts is also dealt with.

170. KODA, BERTHA (1980), "The Involvement of Women in Small-Scale
Industries in Tanzania (Case Study: Dar es Salaam City)".
Paper presented to IDS Seminar Series, 49 pp.

Combines a general historical analysis of transformation of
relations of petty commodity production and the development of
capital-wage labour relationships in Tanzania with concrete
case studies of four women's small-scale industrial cooperatives
in Dar es Salaam. Detailed information on resources and problems
of each group are presented. The problem shared by all groups
included the lack of financial resources, market opportunities,
technical knowledge, child care and other basic services, and
the competitive nature of the capitalist market. Recommendations
of a practical nature are included.

171. MEGHJI, ZAKIA (1978), "Report on First Year 1977/78 on Women
Cooperators Education and other Activities Projects". Moshi,
ICA, mimeo.

The importance of an integrated approach to women cooperative
education is pointed out, where experts are drawn from the
fields of cooperatives, health, nutrition, family planning and
so on. Education is primarily in the form of seminars of
cooperatives leaders, often at their own request. Basic
principles for the ICA women's section are noted, which emphasise
direct assistance to particular women cooperatives, seminars based
on particular needs of such groups and taking place in different
consecutive stages, the expansion and linkage of women projects
and the focus on youth and school leavers.

172. MEGHJI, ZAKIA (1979), "Report on the trip to Morogoro,
Tanzania to Attend a Women Grassroots Seminar Organized by
Union of Cooperative Societies (UCS) 21st to 26th May, 1979".
Report to Ag. Regional Director ICA, Moshi, ICA.

Eighteen urban and rural women of Morogoro town and rural
districts and Kilosa District participated in this grassroots
seminar. The topics covered included the significance of
Cooperative group officers, the basic principles of consumer
cooperatives, family planning and basic book-keeping. Thirteen
of the 18 women registered themselves to participate in two of
the Cooperative College correspondence courses, "How to Run a
Consumer Shop" and "Basic Book keeping". Appendix to the
report is a summary of discussions held with the District
Ujamaa and Cooperative Officer and the Women Committee of the
TUKE Consumer Cooperative Society of Morogoro. TUKE has a
membership of 655 Women and annual turnover of T.shs. 2 million.

They operate one main consumer shop, two branches, two milk
kiosks, and are expanding into the hotel business. Access to
goods is sometimes frustrated by Regional Trading Corporation
authorities who tend to distribute last to women cooperatives.

173. MEGHJI, ZAKIA (1980), "Women Involvement in Cooperatives in
Developing Countries. The Case for East and Central Africa".
Paper presented to the ICA Women's Conference in Moscow,
October, 9 pp.

In Kenya and Tanzania, women rarely became members of agricultural marketing cooperatives during the colonial period and
even after independence. The absence of men due to the migrant
labour system in Southern Africa meant that women in Zambia and
Botswana did become active members from the outset, and held
leadership positions. Since independence, the women's
organisations in each country have actively promoted and even
operated small-scale women's production and commercial
cooperatives.
        ICA Regional Office (Moshi) began to run training seminars
for women cooperative and other leaders in the early 1970's.
In nearly all countries within the Region, women's sections
(like that of the Moshi Cooperative College) or women training
officers are active in training and mobilising women in the
cooperative movement. The question of promoting exclusively
women's projects and cooperatives as opposed to women's
participation in larger cooperative societies is posed, with
concrete examples of the issues involved. Where women can
participate effectively in the larger cooperatives, their
activities tend to be more viable economically. Before further
promotion of small scale industries, the marketing infrastructure needs to be investigated in order to ensure outlets
on an international scale. In Tanzania, for example,
"HANDICOOP" markets handicrafts nationally and internationally.
There is also a need to systematise production output and
quality control. Future development will depend on the creation
of large-scale, multipurpose cooperatives involving women and
men. Special activities oriented to youth are necessary, as
well as child care and other facilities to relieve some of
women's "double" labour demands.

174. NAALI, S. (1979), "Legal Provisions for Women Participation
in Cooperatives". Paper No. 15, BW, 10 pp.

The advantages of registering a group as a cooperative society
are given, which includes having power to own property and to
enter into contracts. Cooperatives can be tools through which
women can unit together and fight against poverty, ignorance
and oppression. The different kinds of societies and their
relevance to women are presented, including the constraints of
female participation. For example, members of marketing
societies are expected to own land in their own right. In
these societies the male heads of household become the actual
members, although the women produce much of what is marketed
through them. Other obstacles besides legal ones to full
participation of women in cooperatives include lack of
education, the burdens of domestic work, the need for basic

technical and management skills, and continual pregnancies.
Specific recommendations are given to counteract some of these
problems.

175. OPONDO, DIANA (1977), "The Integration of Women in Development
Through Cooperatives". Paper presented to the UN Regional
Conference on the Implementation of National, Regional and World
Plans of Action for the Integration of Women in Development,
Mauritania, 27 September - 2 October 1977. ICA.

Women cultivate, store and deliver produce to village
cooperatives, and yet do not participate nor lead them. In
order to expand and improve the quality of production, it is
essential that they be organised through the different forms of
cooperatives. Special women's cooperatives are needed initially
but the aim is for women to join with men in running the
mainstream cooperatives. The failure of women cooperative
groups is partly due to lack of managerial know how, and hence
the ICA emphasises cooperative education and training for women
cooperators. The Regional Office of ICA concentrates on
"Training the trainers" (CEPO'S - Cooperative Education and
Publicity Officers) whereas the national organisation (Union of
Cooperative Societies - UCS) handles the actual movement at the
national and grassroots level.

176. SHAYO, F.C. (1978), "Field Assignment on the Role of Women
Cooperative Activities at Moshi Vijijini District". Moshi,
Cooperative College, unpublished coursework field report in
Management and Administration Course.

The histories of five different women cooperative groups in one
district are provided as well as the membership composition and
education backgrounds of officers. The group had differential
access to accounting and other skills relevant to the activities
engaged in. In general all face problems of conflict over
control of proceeds, revealed in cases of corruption and in
dropouts, similar to men's groups. (See VI:169).

177. SIDA (1979), Tanzanian Women Activities and Development
Cooperation. Dar es Salaam. 16 pp.

The programmes of governmental and non-governmental organisations,
including donor agencies, concerned with development of women
in Tanzania, are briefly surveyed. A description of the
administrative structure of the U.W.T., is included. The report
is useful as an inventory of "women's programmes" in Tanzania.
The report concludes that women's programmes must be coordinated
through the UWT and the women's unit in the PMO's office but
that this will not be possible unless the UWT is restructured
and the size of the women's unit in the PMO's office is
expanded to enable it to assist in concrete programmes.

178. SIJAONA, S.T. (1979), "Women's Projects in Urban Areas - Dar
es Salaam City". Paper No. 10, BW, 9 pp.

Describes projects sponsored by the Dar es Salaam City Council
to improve the socio-economic conditions of women in the lower
economic strata. The women in this category have very little
education and therefore very few opportunities for viable

employment to improve the family income and life. The projects
described are of three types: educational, mainly in the fields
of nutrition and home economics; economic ventures and service.
The most successful of these are the service projects such as
the maternal and the child health care centres and the nursery
schools. The educational projects are less successful because
of lack of trained personnel needed to run these projects. The
cooperative economic ventures such as poultry keeping,
tailoring and handicrafts usually started out well but have
not been successful due to lack of funds, raw materials, scarce
managerial and financial skills and the low quality of goods
produced which seriously affect the marketability of these
goods. The differences in educational and tribal background
also affects the cohesiveness of cooperative ventures.

179. TESHA, NANCY (1979), "Women's Projects - Dodoma Region".
Report submitted to SIDA. Dar es Salaam, 70 pp.

Primarily a compilation of data on general development projects
and specific women's projects in Dodoma Region. For the former
category the report specifies the aims, costs and implementation
status whereas information for ongoing "women's" projects is
restricted to types of projects, the number of such projects,
income and expenditure. A large part of the report is devoted
to projects planned, giving detailed description of the
materials needed and the costs of such materials. The
report is disappointing because there is no analysis of the
membership of the women involved in these projects. One would
have liked to know the socio-economic background of these
women, how and why they got involved in the projects, whether
the activities contributed positively towards improving the
conditions of the women, their families and the village as a
whole etc.

180. YWCA - Tanzania, n.d. YWCA Review 1969-1976. Dar es Salaam,
20 pp.

The YWCA began in 1959 and is affiliated with the World YWCA
and with the Christian Council of Tanzania. By 1976 there were
six branches in major city centres, running cottage industries,
and in Dar es Salaam a nursery school, hostel and canteen and
catering service. The programmes are described in detail, and
are oriented towards the needs of young working women and
unemployed women in towns. Future plans include the development
of village level projects (reported in interviews with YWCA
staff).

VII. IDEOLOGY

The relationship between folklore, traditional education and rituals as a process of assigning sex specific roles to men and women in various patrilineal and matrilineal societies in Tanzania has been discussed in many studies in this section (VII:181, 185, 193) as well as in other sections. They show how these customs were used to establish the ideology of male dominance and female submission. They do not, however, discuss how this ideology was linked to social and economic relations both at the household level and the society at large.

Patriarchal Ideology in the Arts

It is in this context that the studies on the art, theatre and literature presented at the BRALUP workshop are specially significant. They emphasise the ideological nature of such work and its inter-relationship with the role of women in production and reproduction. Lihamba argues that the position of women and thus their image is constantly changing. "The image of women in the theatre today is the result of the co-existence of modern and traditional economies, the breakdown of tribal organization and the changing role of female labour as the result of the growth and development of commodity and money relations" (VII:188). Mlama argues that the transition from pre-colonial to colonial and post-colonial societies has not only affected the form and content of culture but has also led to the loss of women's traditional role as transmitters of art and literature. This in turn affects ideological content and has led to commoditisation of art (VII:193).

Matteru sees oral literature as a concretisation of the socio-economic relations which subordinate women. Her analysis of the image of women as depicted by oral literature is very illuminating. Women are depicted as mothers; objects of men's pleasure; and as property, reflecting women's role as biological reproducers; their subordinate position vis a vis men and the fact that they are considered to belong to men. As such, men have full control over their labour and produce (VII:191). As objects of men's pleasure they must be beautiful, but also hard-working to satisfy men's needs both in production and reproduction. Lihamba, analysing the way women are depicted in theatre, shows that women are either not "visible" or they represent a conflict between "traditional" and "modern" women. In most cases the women's struggle is proved futile and she returns to the village subdued and penitent (VII:188). Mbughuni identifies two roles assigned to women in Kiswahili literature: one is women as the embodiment of evil and social disorder, who ensnare men and whose salvation lies in being domesticated. Paradoxically, the other is that of a submissive, ideal housewife (VII:192). These two roles are also depicted by the newspapers and the radio (VII:182).

Commoditisation of Art

At least two studies discuss the effect of commoditisation of art production (VII:182, 193). The distortion and sensationalism so

common of cheap "western" novels seems to have changed the primary
role of art and literature to symbolise and reinforce the social
framework. The popular novels written in Kiswahili degrade and
humiliate women. The implications of this development are quite
serious to the workers' struggle for full participation in national
development, since women are portrayed as mere lovers of luxuries
or submissive non-entities.

Women's Protest as Seen in Art, Literature and Rituals

The theme of a rebellious woman appears from time to time in the
studies in this section. In literature and drama it has been dealt
with directly by Lihambe (VII:188, 189) and implicitly by Mbughuni
(VII:192) and Matteru (VII:191). In the case of the former, two
examples, are given of a successful rebellion by women against the
domineering male, although even here, the success was ultimately
possible because of the support of the rebellion by other men.
Since these two plays were written by male authors, it´is not
surprising that the plays could not make the transition to recognise
women as being able to effectively organise to struggle against
their oppression; nevertheless it represents a recognition that
women are not always submissive and resigned to their fate. In the
case of Mbughuni and Matteru, the fact that women are depicted as
needing "a strong hand", implies a recognition of the potential
ability of women to protest. They obviously are not submissive,
hence they need to be tamed by rituals, as for instance, the Mwali
ritual or by sanctioning physical punishment. Further examples of
protest are described in VII:187 and 194 and range from suicide,
breaking the cooking pots, to the threat of ancestral curses and
witchcraft.

Women's Own Contribution to Ideology

The portrayal of women in literature, the performing arts and the
mass media is due to the social and economic relations in which
they find themselves, as well as two other factors: the contribution
of women towards protesting against sex stereotyping, and the role
of women themselves in reinforcing male superiority. The number
of women contributing to the literary and theatre arts is very
small compared to men and is a reflection of the historical processes
that gave women less access to education and educational facilities.
Women are also few in the fields of broadcasting and journalism,
again partly related to the small number of women trained in these
fields but also because of enduring prejudices against them. These
prejudices affect women obtaining top grades in the mass media
organs and demoralise others from entering the fields (VII:186,
195). Careers in these fields are also affected by sex-specific
problems arising from the women's dual role as worker and mother/
wife. For example, husband resistance to night duty and travel
blocks women from reaching the top grades, unless they choose to
ignore their husbands' demands.

Women also contribute towards a perpetuation of the image of
themselves as portrayed by men (VII:184, 186, 195). It has already
been pointed out that in pre-colonial societies women played a
dominant role in communicating social norms of behaviour through
dance, songs, folktales, figurines and ritual (VII:183). In this

148

way women contributed a great deal to maintaining male dominance, to
the extent of upholding false myths. The way in which women as
mothers reinforce sexist stereotypes in child rearing practices
indicates another dimension in ideological practices. Concrete
investigation of sexist child rearing practices in different classes
is necessary to find out what changes have take place, if any, in
the context of commoditisation and proletarisation. At work,
some women still use discriminatory practices toward colleagues,
are not supportive of women's programmes and refuse to cooperate
in assisting towards these programmes (VII:186, 195). Art,
theatre, literature and the mass media are very important in
critically exposing the problems of female oppression and
exploitation at all levels. It is essential that women in Tanzania
both understand and utilize this form of communication to protest
against their oppressive conditions and promote future changes in
their interest.

181. ABDALLAH BIN HEMEDI BIN ALI LIAJJEMI (1936), "The Story of
Mbega", trans. Roland Allen. TNR No. 1 (April): 38-51, No. 2
(October): 80-91, No. 3 (April 1937): 87-98.

This legend is said to represent the origins of the Kilindi
state in Ushambaa (Shambaa Mountains), and in another form as
oral history it has been relied on heavily by Feierman (1972,
1974) and others to trace the history of the Shambaa. It is
of particular interest to women because of the ideology of
male dominance which permeates the legend. A great deal of
insight is also provided about pre-colonial social relations
such as the way in which the labour process was organised and
the product of labour distributed between the rulers of a group
and their followers, including women.

182. BESHA, RUTH (1979), "The Mass Media and Entertainment". Paper
No. 34, BW, 15 pp.

Newspapers and the radio in Tanzania have a powerful impact on
societal attitudes because of their accessibility and entertainment value to a fairly large proportion of the general public.
Newspaper feature stories and songs played on the radio
generally depict women as evil, greedy temptresses leading
innocent men astray. Paradoxically in another theme men are
depicted as superior beings mastering women into submission
mainly through marriage. Argues that the general situation of
women in the rural and urban areas has been deliberately
distorted in order to achieve sensationalism as depicted by
cheap western novels. Recommends that artists, producers and
editors who are involved in the projection of the women's image
should exercise the same judgement in entertainment features as
they use in publishing or broadcasting current issues. Listeners
and readers are also advised to question what they hear and
read.

183. BRYCESON, DEBORAH FAHY (1979), "Notes on the Educational
Potential of Mass Media Vis-a-Vis Women's Roles in Tanzanian
Society". Paper No. 23, BW, 10 pp.

The mass media such as newspapers and radio should be used much more extensively to highlight contradictions in women's traditional position in changing society, thereby increasing awareness of these contradictions and the need for change. A survey of two English language newspapers, Daily News and Sunday News showed that women have been excluded from reports on "newsmaking", partly because they are excluded from positions of political and economic power. Four basic questions are posed, with an attempt to answer each: (1) How are women's social roles reflected in the news? (1) To what degree are women instrumental in generating the news as newsmakers or writers? (3) To what degree are women affected by news coverage? (4) To what degree are they influenced by news coverage? A list of topics relevant to women which were presented in the newspapers during 1973-1978 reflect the contradictory place of women in Tanzanian society. Beginning in 1976 coverage of women increased. Recommendations include a women's daily page in Kiswahili and English press, same as the sports page, and daily half-hour radio programmes in both languages.

184. KHONJE, MARGARET (1979), "Some Notes on the Role of Women in Maintenance of Women Oppression by Men". Paper No. 40, BW, 9 pp.

Women contribute to the oppression of women in various ways. Within the family, they socialise children to accept: differential sex roles; the power of the husband as head over all other family members, expressed most visibly in wife-beating; and the role of being decorative flowers rather than independent productive workers, expressed in purchases of fine clothes to the neglect of food and children. Within the community women sanction inappropriate "female behaviour" and encourage fellow women to sell themselves rather than to be productive and serious at the workplace. At the level of overall society, women are not valued as human beings first, and hence are not considered for responsible positions.

185. KORITSCHONER, HANS (1937), "Some East African Native Songs". TNR, No. 4 (October): 51-64.

The songs are mainly drawn from Sukuma and Nyamwezi contemporary songs and concern the experience of workers, the impact of colonial rule on village life, and so on. Many are also expressions of the ideology of male dominance and threats to that dominance.

186. KYARUZI, AGNES (1979), "Women's Image in the Mass Media: Newspapers". Paper No. 45, BW, 4 pp.

Women are involved in mass media in two ways; as a source of news and as writers of news items. In the first case, women rarely make news except if associated with important personages. The special women's page is generally ignored by men and on the face of it discriminatory, nevertheless, it should be retained so as to retain some venue for discussing women's issues. Female journalists are rarely given the top career posts thus

demoralising potential female journalists from joining the newspaper media. The study offers no analysis of the situations
described nor empirical data to substantiate the statements.

187. LANDBERG, PAMELA WEAVER (1971), Women's Roles and Spirit
Possession Cults: Witchcraft or a Question of Options? Paper
presented to the Annual Meeting of the American Anthropological
Association. 9 pp.

Begins with a brief summary of the theory propounded by I.M.
Lewin (1966) in his article "Spirit Possession and Deprivation
Cults". Lewin argues that the exclusion of women from important
matters gave rise to mystical forms of redress on the part of
women. Spirit possession for exerting pressure on their
socially defined superiors – the men and particularly their
husbands". Using Kigombe village on the northern coast of
Tanzania, the author argues that spirit possession in Tanzania
is somewhat more complex. The dominance of men in Kigombe
village is strongly centred around Islam and activities
associated with the mosque to which women are barred. Women
have certain legal rights under Islamic and civil law but most
matters are settled outside courts by leaders who are elected
on the basis of their mosque going. Unlike Islam, the main
authority in spirit possession cults is not barred to women.
Yet the women are in the minority in leadership positions in
spirit possession. They are, however, very dominant in the
associated rituals where all the women in the village can be
involved. These rituals are popular because they give women
an escape from daily lives. Claims that the predominance of
women in spirit cults is the result of the allocation of roles
based on rigidly defined sex lines: ceremonial activities to
men; ritual to women, and is yet another example of the
inferior status of women.

188. LIHAMBA, AMANDINA (1979), "The Image of Women in the Performing
Arts". Paper No. 46, BW, 28 pp.

An exceptionally clear and well-written critical analysis of
the role of women in production and reproduction, as expressed
in a few carefully chosen plays written by Tanzanian women and
men, with focus on the work of Ebrahim Hussein, Godwin Kaduma
and Penina Mlama. Analysis of drama as ideology provides the
framework in which the specific problem of the image of women
is posed. Women are either "invisible" or else express the
conflict between "traditional" and "modern" female roles. The
modern women tend to be unsuccessful in their struggle to move
beyond patriarchal relations and finally return home in shame.
The alternatives presented to women are either childlike
dependence on one's parents or childlike dependence on a "sugar
daddy" provider. There are two basic agruments embedded in the
analysis: firstly, that the active role of women as full
participants in struggles to change society in the interests
of the masses and to liberate women, has been given inadequate
attention in drama; and secondly, that "the struggle against
sexual discrimination cannot operate on its own but must take
place alongside class struggle and this struggle must have clear
perceptions of class interests. It is only then that changes in

women's image will occur because the perception will be of a
different new women and the portrayal will be of new expectations
and values".

189. LIHAMBA, AMANDINA (1981), "The Politics of Women and Theatre
    Production in Tanzania". University of Dar es Salaam, Paper
    presented to IDS seminar series, January 9th, 24 pp.

    Begins with a brief analysis of the relationship between the
    material base of production, the content of ideology and
    materials of culture like theatre. Women's issues with regard
    to culture, as in other spheres of society, must be related to
    class and gender relations, ans class and gender struggles.
    Describes the transformation of theatre and art in general as
    art is separated from religion, magic and ritual. The question
    of the participation of women as producers and consumers of
    theatre is situated within the context of colonial and post-
    colonial changes. One consequence of these changes is the
    destruction of the creative power of the people, and the tribal
    identity which once sustained it. Women's involvement in
    theatre of the past and present is related to the sexual division
    of labour and the subordination of women. The limited participa-
    tion of women in various drama groups, and the sex stereotyping
    of female roles in the drama itself is analysed using summaries
    of several plays to illustrate the argument. There is also a
    general critique not only of the limited support given to
    theatre by the government, but also of the quality of drama
    produced. More emphasis is put on "what to say" than on "how to
    say it" so as to educate, entertain and politicize the audience
    and fully involve them in the drama experience.
       Out of a total of 50 plays surveyed, only eight had central
    female characters, and only three concentrated on women's issues
    as central themes. Notes the need for drama to go beyond the
    analysis of women's problems, and also project what is possible
    for women. Argues that "art might just be ahead of life,
    looking at it and presenting it back critically. Theatre and
    literature can also project possibilities and alternatives...
    (the artist) is often able to break through the forces of
    conditioning. Through the creative imagination theatre can be
    an area where women's perception of themselves and by others
    can be 'critically' exposed together with problems of female
    oppression and exploitation at all levels - economic,
    ideological, political and liberation of men and women from
    patriarchal and other types of domination".

190. LUCAS, STEPHEN (1975), "The Influence of Culture on the Position
    of Women in Tanzania". Dar es Salaam, Ministry of National
    Culture and Youth, Background paper for Directorate of Research
    and Planning, 11 pp.

    Although there were great differences in economy, polity and
    culture in the different pre-colonial societies, women were
    subordinate to men to varying degrees in all of them. The
    ambivalent position of women, as reproducers of life and as
    potentially evil and contaminating agents, is revealed in
    various legends and other ideological institutions. These are
    in turn related to the place of women in the traditional economy.

The development of international trade and later colonial rule reinforced the inequality between men and women. Women became "backward" as they were left out from schooling and from the migrant labour experience – hence, women are sub-peasants and sub-proletariat. The resistance of women during the final decades of the colonial period took the form of spirit possession, "witchcraft" – type behaviour (really the label which "society" gave to single, widowed or otherwise independent, non-subordinated women), and suicide.

191. MATTERU, M.L. (1979), "The Image of Woman in Tanzanian Oral Literature". Paper No. 22, BW, 26 pp.

This is one of the rare works in Tanzanian women studies which critically analyses the nature of sexual relations and poses it as a significant problem. Matteru notes, "The subordination of the female to the male, depends very much on this sexual relation-ship". There are three main themes concerning women in oral literature: the mother; the man's pleasure machine; and the property. Illustrations are provided for each theme. Oral literature is shown to be an expression of the concrete socio-economic relations which subordinate women, and in turn, a means of contributing to their reproduction. The analysis, together with the illustrations, actually suggest to us a fourth theme, the rebellious or resistent women who rejects patriarchal relations and is threatened with punishment, including childlessness and death. It seems crucial to search for oral literature which describes such rebellious women, even if one is forced to transform the direction of the message (see IV: 107). This is necessary to pose as an alternative to the "voice of lamentation and resignation" which, the author notes, dominates oral literature. It also clarifies the qualitative nature and dynamic process of female resistance. The general tendency however in oral literature and modern Tanzanian jazz music is to oppose the transformation of patriarchal relations and the liberation of women from subordination and exploitation. Various specific issues are raised such as barrenness, un-married mothers, sexual relations whereby the male is active and the female passive, and the need for the re-education of radio personnel and jazz and other artists.

192. MBUGHUNI, PATRICIA (1979), "The Image of Women in Kiswahili Prose Fiction". Paper No. 26, BW, 14 pp.

In Kiswahili literature there are two contrasting images of women, the most popular being that of "Eve", the temptress, incontrollable and unsubordinated to any man, the embodiment of evil and social disorder and chaos. The other image of "Mary" is that of submissive, mother-like, domesticated house-wife, often a mere decorative appendage to the male hero. The male represents a higher moral order in either case, hence, "salvation through domestication". In all the novels or stories cited, female independent action, ambition or aggressiveness is punished whereas docility and economic dependence on the male is rewarded. Nearly all the authors cited are male, which reflects male dominance in publication and writing. Such imagery of women "may reflect the problems of this type of male

sensibility in his relations with the female". At the same time,
the problem of male and female audience reaction and the seeming
acceptance of sex stereotypes is posed: "Why should it be
pleasing for either male or female to envision woman as the
source of evil and disorder in society?" One could go further
to question the role of the state in promoting sexist literature
in mass media and schools.

193. MLAMA, PENINA O. (1979), "The Role of Women in Culture
Reproduction: The Case of Tanzanian Art and Literature". Paper
No. 17, BW, 15 pp.

Explores pre-colonial, colonial and post-colonial society with
respect to changing forms and content of art and literature.
Examples are given of songs sung by women to educate as well as
entertain children and young girls during initiation rites, in
order to illustrate the significant role of women in pre-
colonial art and oral literature. The content was related to
the material lives and work of women. During the colonial and
independence periods, women have been separated from their role
as educators and artists, partly due to the development of
commercial art and film industries and schooling. Christianity
led a full attack on indigenous song and dance and substituted
an alien form of art and literature. Commercial art in Tanzania
concentrates on women as sex objects, as found in popular music,
books and films. Women must struggle against these sexist
tendencies, especially if they are working in the mass media
like Radio Tanzania. The analysis would be strengthened by a
more critical view of "traditional" art and literature which
showed the way song and dance often reinforced oppressive
patriarchal relations in the family and community.

194. MOREAU, R.E. (1941), "Suicide by 'Breaking the Cooking Pot'".
TNR, No. 12 (December): 49-50.

Details are provided on the procedures followed and the
"speech" spoken in this form of suicide. As noted in IV:106
"cooking pot suicide" must be perceived to be one form of
female resistance to the oppression of women, in conditions
which tend to render women powerless. Moreau describes
contemporary action and its immediate causes: "the woman still
young, could not bear her husband to take a second wife", "the
woman was neglected by her husband".

195. MWENDA, DEBORAH (1979), "The Woman's Image in the Tanzania Mass
Media: Radio". Paper No. 38, BW, 5 pp.

The "Voice of Tanzania" has four main departments, Engineering,
News and Current Affairs, Programmes and Administration. Women
are found in all four departments, including engineering, but
face severe problems such as discriminatory attitudes of male
and sometimes female colleagues and listeners and husband
resistance to night duty and travel. Women are mainly delegated
to women and children's programmes. Women listeners are reluctant
to participate themselves in women's programmes, and do not
provide feedback, despite the openness of Radio Tanzania to
constructive criticism.

196. TANNER, R.E.S. (1958), "Sukuma Ancestor Worship and Its
     Relationship to Social Structure". TNR, No. 50 (June): 52-62.

The ancestor cult and the threat of curses especially by a
father or mother, contribute to maintaining patriarch relations
in spite of the inevitable conflicts which arise. They also
ensure the biological reproduction of the lineage and clan by
legitimising the children of divorced and widowed women as
lineage members, regardless of biological paternity. Argues
that ancestor worship and its accompanying institutions like
the curse are a stabilizing force under contemporary conditions
of colonial rule. They are "positive" in that they help to
maintain patriarch family and deter social deviation, which he
clearly perceives to be potential threats to the stability of
colonial rule itself. This is another example of the way
anthropology becomes a tool to maintain exploitative relations
in colonial society.

VIII.   EDUCATION

Women have historically been discriminated against in formal
education in Tanzania at all levels, as well as in out-of-school
programmes like agricultural extension services and technical or
vocational training. The issue of sex differences in education has
been investigated according to the following set of problems: access
to education and training; subject specialisation; sex differentiation in hiring of qualified teachers; historical analysis of the
causes for sex discrimination in education; and sex differentiation
in the social relations of school.

Access to Educational Places

There is ample documentation of the structural inequalities in
provision of places at all levels of the formal schooling system:
at primary level (VIII:214, 215, 216, 218, 228); at secondary level
(VIII:205, 220, 225, 230, 231) and at university level (VIII:197,
205, 211, 213, 224, 225). The impact of differential access to
education on wage employment is noted in different sections especially sections V and VI. Less attention has been placed on the
relationship between class and sex. For example, Mbilinyi found
in the 1960's that it was impossible to generalise about unequal
opportunities for primary schooling among girls in the rural areas
(VIII:214-216, 218). Rich peasants, kulaks, traders, primary school
teachers and other government functionaries enrolled all of their
children in school. Poor peasants in Mwanza tended to select one or
two boys to go to school, whereas in Tanga poor peasants did not
invest in schooling for any of their children. Boy preference
persisted among middle peasants in Mwanza, but in Tanga both boys
and girls were sent to school up to standard IV, after which time
girls were married off.
     Universal Primary Education (UPE) begun in 1974/75 has led to
the massive enrolment of girls and boys in primary school, offsetting
earlier sex and class differences (VIII:231). Resistance to enrolment of girls remains among pastoralists, however, for reasons
thoroughly discussed in IV:116. The wastage rate (i.e. the rate at
which students drop out of school) is much higher for girls than for
boys in urban and rural areas. One of the major reasons for this is
pregnancy of school girls leading to expulsion, an issue to be
discussed in Section XI below.
     The number of boarding school places for girls is much lower
than for boys at secondary level. This necessarily leads to structural discrimination against peasant girls who depend on such
facilities. Whereas peasant households may invest in private
schooling for boys, and allow them to rent private rooms in towns
to attend private day schools, they are not likely to allow girls
to live alone in towns. Boarding facilities need to be expanded at
secondary level for girls as well as boys. If this is not done,
the government's policy of deliberate promotion of girls to Form I
will only expand educational opportunities for urban-based girls.
Research has also shown that class background or class position has
an even greater impact on girls' access to secondary schooling than

boys, similar to the findings with respect to primary schooling
(VIII:220). Petty bourgeois families not only invest more in
secondary schooling for girls (and boys), but they also have been
able to manipulate the school system so as to transfer their children
from private schools to higher performing government schools. The
government directive on secondary schools has now made this "back
door" entry point illegal. Differential resources for petty bourgeois
children, like school books, special tutoring at primary level to
"pass" the Standard VII examination (i.e. be selected for Form I),
parental knowledge about the mechanics of schooling and school success,
and exposure to English at home all contribute to higher chances for
(1) selection to Form I on the basis of examination; (2) higher
secondary school performance.

Women have also had fewer places open to them in vocational training programmes run by missions as well as the government and other
agencies (VIII:201, 202). Fewer women have participated in the
correspondence courses run by the Institute of Adult Education (VIII:
213), and in the early mass radio campaigns (VIII:209); partly because of the heavier burdens of work for women peasants and workers
as compared to men.

Subject Specialisation

The issue of access to places in the education system is only one
aspect of the problem. It is also essential to examine what kind of
subjects or training is given to girls and women. Subject specialisation must also be related to opportunities for higher education and
employment. Studies have shown that sex differentiation exists in
subject specialisation at secondary and post-secondary levels, and
argue that it leads to lesser employment and educational opportunities
for women (VIII:197, 203-205, 220, 224). Moreover, the case of
mathematics at High School level (204) shows how less access to math
combinations has led to the lack of women graduate teachers to teach
math.

The establishment of Domestic Science as one of the four major
biases in secondary schooling has been especially controversial. It
is only taught to girls, and has tended to be regarded in practice
as a lesser subject choice, with fewer returns so far as higher
education and employment are concerned. The efforts to increase
"employable" components like catering, tailoring, and so
on, and to upgrade domestic science to a university course, are
important developments. A very simple question to ask, however, is
why only girls? Otherwise, domestic science can only be understood
as a mechanism to reinforce sex differentiation not only in education,
but in work and in the home. This also underlies the criticisms of
agricultural extension and vocational education programmes (VIII:201,
202). Men are taught agriculture, mechanics, carpentry, etc; women
are taught cookery, sewing, and child care. Even on the radio,
educational programmes for women emphasise subject matter which
reflects the sexual division of labour at home. Why should only
women be taught about good nutrition for children, signs of disease
and measures of preventing as well as treatment, and the importance
of cleanliness in the home? Such ideological practices not only
reflect sexual difference in domestic responsibilities, they also
reinforce and actively promote sexual differences in opposition to

basic socialist principles (see section VII for further discussion
of ideology).

Sex Differentiation in Teaching Staff

Much less attention has been given to the problem of training, hiring
and promoting practices of teaching staff. The social dynamics of
the school do effect girls' perceptions of themselves and their
future expectations as will be discussed below. The impact of having
a predominance of male teachers at secondary and post-secondary
levels on female (and male) students can be surmised, though more
concrete investigation is necessary. The whole issue of sex discrimination in hiring and promotions of teaching staff at the University
of Dar es Salaam has been recently raised by women academics (VIII:
195). Only 11 % of academicians are women, the majority of them at
junior levels of the professional hierarchy. Less than 20 % of tutors
at Colleges of National Education are women. The proportion of female
graduate teachers at secondary level is only slightly higher (VIII:
231). Research is necessary to explain why so few women move on into
University and teacher education positions. Comparisons of university
student output and female ratios in other professional and social
service occupations indicate that sexual differentiation and discrimination at the University is particularly high and requires specific
analysis and action. Since the university trains high level personnel
for government and other employers, as well as for other tertiary
educational institutions, the problem becomes even more significant.

Causes of Sex Differentiation and Sex Discrimination in Education

Sex differentiation and sex discrimination in education have been
attributed to a combination of forces: patriarchal relations; the
sexual division of labour in peasant production systems and in wage
labour and structural inequalites in the number of places offered to
girls and women (VIII:199, 214-216, 218, 219, 221, 224). The
differential impact of class differences on girls and boys schooling
has already been noted. In addition, there has been limited investigation of the impact of girls' own expectations for themselves
in comparison to boys on their motivation and school performance.

Young girls and women undervalue themselves and adjust their own
goals downwards in accordance with a lower estimation of their own
abilities. Moreover, academic and work performance tends to be
considered a secondary consideration for most women. For example,
secondary schoolgirls explained that school performance was not important,
after all, after graduation they would find a "bwana", a "sugar daddy",
to provide them with economic support. Indeed, a large number of
school girls engage in prostitution while still in school, to meet
schooling costs like uniforms, travel and lunch as well as to take
part in town recreational facilities like discos (VIII:198,219). The
idea that university graduates are not "marriageable", due to age
plus male preferences for wives with lesser education and occupational
status, is also discussed informally as an explanation for lowered
"struggle" to attend the University. Patriarchal ideologies about
male superiority obviously conflict with having a wife with higher
education, higher occupational status and more pay. Although cases
are informally known of women rejecting educational or employment
opportunities because of husband resistance or outright refusal, or

because of the woman's inability to cope with the expected conflict,
concrete investigation about such ideological issues (and struggles)
is needed. This is not only an issue at university level. Radio
Tanzania has run special announcements encouraging women to attend
adult literacy classes, and asking husbands to "allow" them to do
so. Women factory workers complain that their husbands are not
"happy" about their leaving the home to go to work, even though the
family needs their income (section V). NBC employees have discussed
the ambivalence of their husbands, who want to control all their
movements after office hours (V:143). Such evidence suggests that
there is a major conflict between performance and behaviour demands
at home and at work. The impact of such conflicts on marital
stability and on women's own mental state requires specific analysis.
It is important to note here that Dr. Mere Nakateregga Kiseeka
intends to carry out comparative research on female psychology and
"insanity", based at Ahmadu Bello University, Nigeria but including
Tanzania.

Social Relations of the School or Educational Institution

This is another problem area which has been inadequately researched.
Student teachers of the university have noted the effect of sexual
divisions and conflicts on students in secondary schools, especially
in single sex girls schools (VIII:207). Sexist patterns of socialisation in home and community are said to reinforce sexist relations
in the school (224). The implications of female devaluing of themselves on school performance has already been noted. It is crucial
however, to actually explore sexual relations in the school, and
their impact on the behaviour of teachers, students and non-teaching
staff, and on school performance overall.

----

197. ACADEMIC STAFF ASSEMBLY (1980), "Report of the Ad-Hoc Committee
on Women Representation in Academic Staff Assembly". University
of Dar es Salaam, mimeo, 20 pp.

The result of research by the four members of the Ad-Hoc
Committee (R. Besha, D. Bryceson, M. Matteru and M. Mbilinyi,
Convenor) and other colleagues who assisted, together with a
meeting of women academic staff on 11th October, 1980. Presented
at the Academic Staff Assembly Meeting in November 1980 and
adopted with minor changes in the recommendations for the upgrading of the ad-hoc committee into a standing committee.
Provides a statistical breakdown of female/male staffing ratios
by department, faculty, national and expatriate status and position. Only 11 % of academic staff on the main campus are women,
and the percentage rapidly declines as one moves up the hierarchy
of positions within each Faculty. There is only one woman full
Professor (a Tanzanian) and two Associate Professors (non-Tanzan-
ians), and the majority of women are tutorial assistants and
assistant lecturers. The Faculty of Law has only two female
academics out of twenty-five, and the History Department none,
although these are among the oldest departments and faculties.
Further research is needed to establish sex discrimination
in recruitment, promotion and staff development plans, though

examples were cited during preliminary meetings of women academics. The report attempts to note anomalies within hiring and firing procedures, and decision-making about staff development and research grants which rely on subjective bases, thus allowing sex prejudices to operate. The paper argues that "whereas men are treated first as academics and only secondly if at all as men, women are all too often considered first as women, and secondly if at all, as academicians". There is also a brief analysis of the entire schooling system, subject specialization and wage employment patterns, to clarify some of the structural causes.

198. ANONYMOUS (1976), "The Pregnant School Girls". Weekend Commentary, Daily News, 11 December, 1976, reproduced as mimeo, 4 pp.

Examines the issue of pregnant schoolgirls from the point of view of oppression as women and general class oppression. Feminism is a form of bourgeois ideology which divides'the working class because it emphasises only the one aspect of women's oppression, oppression as women, and ignores the class aspect. Schoolgirls aspire to become bourgeois and imitate bourgeois women consumption patterns (platform shoes, imported dresses and so on). They provide sexual pleasure to sugar daddies in exchange for money and imported commodities. Only "big men" can provide such returns. Schoolgirls like office workers and others share similar interests as workers and peasants against the bourgeoisie who oppress them.

199. ASAYEHGN, D. (1979), "The Role of Women in Tanzania: Their Access to Higher Education and Participation in the Labour Force". IIEP, Research Report No. 33, UNESCO: Paris, 31 pp.

Focuses on women's participation in post-secondary institutions and in the labour force. Examines the socio-economic background of Tanzanian women enrolled in these institutions; the differences in curricula between men and women; and the differences that exist between the sexes in the labour market in terms of waiting period prior to employment, pay scale and current earnings. Findings, although not empirically tested, point to socio-economic factors as contributing to the lack of participation of women in these programmes despite government policies calling for equality of the sexes. Recommends government sponsorship of certain programmes for women to bring in balance, performance and participation of women with government objectives.

200. CHENGELELA, R. (1979), "Adult Education's Impact on Women". Paper No. 16, BW, 8 pp.

Women are portrayed as the second sex, the inferior sex, with the material base of this position rooted in double exploitation as workers and in the home. "What women need to know is: How this bondage came about and who or what is responsible?" Historical analysis of changing human society shows that women's oppression has a social basis and is not natural nor biological. The women's Education Section of the Institute of Adult Education was started in 1974 to further the process of women's liberation from such bondage through education combined with productive activities. Three production training projects have been monitored by the section in Moshi, Geita and Ilala (Dar es Salaam).

201. CHRISTIAN COUNCIL OF TANZANIA (1975), Rural Vocational Education in Tanzania. Dar es Salaam, 1976. 187 pp. plus appendices. Mimeo. Also produced in Swahili, Elimu ya Ufundi.

Prepared for the National Workshop on Rural Vocational Education in Tanzania, Kicheba Village 27th June - 3rd July, 1977. The historical development of vocational education in the colonial and post-colonial periods is provided, followed by an extremely detailed examination of vocational programmes offered today. Sex specificity in curriculum is noted in today's programmes, as well as in earlier periods. Girls in general have less access to vocational education and the kinds of programmes open to girls tend to be related to women's work in domestic labour: cooking, sewing, and child-care are reflected in domestic science courses. On access, the report claims that "sex is an important access regulator to vocational schools ... Out of 12,261 students identified in December 1975 only 3,917 (31.9 %) were girls. The situation has quantitatively improved after the introduction of Vocational Wings in 1975 which added almost 2700 new opportunities for girls through domestic science". However, inspite of the vocational wings, access for girls is often restricted by entrance requirements of training institutions. Out of a total of 38 institutions, 17 were male only, 16 admitted both and 5 were for females only. Even in vocational wings, boys are enrolled for carpentry and masonry while girls for domestic science only. On sexism the report claims that the entire management of vocational education is controlled by men. There are no women on the National Vocational Training Council.
    Appendices include vocational training activities by training authorities and by sex (position at December 1975). It is significant that no girls were enrolled in agriculture, masonry, carpentry, auto mechanics, air-conditioning etc.

202.   CHRISTIAN COUNCIL OF TANZANIA (1977), Rural Vocational Education in Tanzania, Conclusions, Recommendations and Implementation. Also available in Swahili, Elimu ni Ufundi: Mapendekezo na Utekelezaji, Dar es Salaam.

Summarises the findings of the CCT (1976) report, and then develops concrete recommendations and proposals for implementation. The recommendations are situated in the context of the basic industrialisation strategy of Tanzania, and indicate how, for example, the development of producer goods industry could happen at village level based on local material and human resources. The need to integrate training programmes with production is continually stressed. Inadequate attention is given in the recommendations to the mobilization of women for industrial development and for women's liberation. Indeed, it is never directly posed as an issue although the early work clearly showed the need for such attention. Nevertheless, this is valuable as an example of the construction of short-term and long-term technical and structural recommendations and implementation proposals. Many of the recommendations and proposals are relevant to potential women's programmes, or women can be inserted into them.

203. COULSON, J.C. (1974), "Some Reflections on the Girls' Examination Results in Mathematics 1973". University of Dar es Salaam, mimeo attached as Appendix to Duwi et al. (1974) and reproduced in Chem Chem No. 1 (1975).

The differential results of boys and girls on Form 4 and 6 Mathematics Examinations of 1973 are presented and discussed. Causes are due to inadequate staffing of girls' secondary schools. Output of women maths graduates from the University of Dar es Salaam over the past four years and future three years is then analysed, as well as output from Chang'ombe College. The staffing situation will remain poor, because of the few women who enter into maths training at University level.

204. COULSON, JUDY (1976), "Some Further Reflections on the Mathematical Education of Girls". Paper No. 5, BW, 9 pp.

Results of Form 4 Examinations in Mathematics are analysed in detail for 1973, 1974 and 1975, and broken down to look at differences in single sex boys and girls schools and coeducational schools. The performance of girls was much lower than boys for all three years, and in fact less than 25 % of all candidates were girls. Recommendations in the 1974 paper were taken up in this one, partly by discussing them with schoolgirls and teachers. Problems of staffing and unequal access to subject combinations are stressed. Girls seemed to perform better in coeducational schools as shown by Form 4 and Form 6 results. The paper is a good example of the kind of information readers can acquire from secondary analysis of statistics such as examination results. By very simple summation of results for schools clustered in terms of sex categories it is possible to learn a great deal. The Examination Council provides excellent annual reports on Form 4 and 6 Examinations results which can be used for this purpose.

205. DUWI, C.; I.S. MANYAHI and R.R. KAWAWA (1974), "Policy and Implementation of Women Education in Tanzania". University of Dar es Salaam, paper presented to Education Department seminar series (authors were Third Year students in Sociology of Education). Reproduced in Chem Chem No. 1 (1975).

Beginning with the historical background to the women's question in Tanzania, the authors go on to explore the problems of secondary and university education for girls and women. Documentation is provided of unequal access to subject combinations and levels of education.

206. EDUCATION DEPARTMENT (1976), Teaching Practice Study Exercise (1975) Report. No. 2, University of Dar es Salaam, 20 pp. mimeo.

Based upon student teachers' journals and reports on their teaching practice experience, provides rich descriptions of secondary and primary schools and colleges of national education. The problems of being a male student teacher posted to a single girls secondary school are explored briefly.

207. EDUCATION DEPARTMENT (1977), Teaching Practice Study Exercise Report. No. 3 (BTP 1976), 64 pp. mimeo.

This is the most detailed report of the three produced by the Department of Education, both concerning women in education as teachers and students and schooling in general. Probes the tensions between male and female teachers and students, at single sex girls schools, and their impact on the learning process.

208. FAO (1971), Report to the Government of Tanzania on the Home Economics Training Centre, Buhare, Musoma, Tanzania. Rome, FAO, 59 pp. Illus.

The Home Economics Training Centre was set up in 1964 initially with the support of FAO and the government of Sweden. Its purpose is to train women rural development workers and other female staff of the Ministry of Regional Administration and Rural Development and related ministries and agencies, in skills and approaches needed for raising living standards of families and communities in Tanzania and to train women leaders for "Ujamaa" villages and other development projects of the government. The report describes and evaluates the courses run by the centre from its inception to 1971. During this period the centre ran courses in Rural Economics, Day Care Centre Assistants, Institutional Management and Catering and ad-hoc refresher courses and seminars of various lengths for women leaders. It is significant that the evaluation came to the conclusion that the Rural Home Economics course should be taught to all family members rather than just women's groups.

209. HALL, BUDD L. (1974), "Who Participates in University Adult Education", in Mbilinyi ed. (1974): 73-79 and Mbilinyi ed. (1976). Originally published in Studies in Adult Education, No. 5, (February 1973). Institute of Adult Education, Dar es Salaam.

A comparison is made of participation in adult literacy classes, extramural type programmes and the Wakati wa Furaha Radio Campaign. It was found that women outnumber men in the regular adult literacy classes, 2 to 1, whereas the average breakdown for the mass radio campaign was 62 % men and 38 % women. Possible reasons for the differences are given.

210. HOME ECONOMICS TRAINING CENTRE (BUHARE) (1974), "Prospectus: The Home Economics Training Centre - Buhare, Musoma". Ujamaa and Cooperative Development Department, PMO (mimeo).

Buhare trains "Home Economics Assistants" to be "activators" who "encourage improvement in all aspects of home and family life". The Centre is under the Prime Minister's Office and runs courses in Rural Home Economics, Day Care Centre Assistants plus special leadership and other short courses. Subject content and time allocation for theory and practical work is given. The same curriculum was used as of the 1977 PMO/SIDA evaluation report.

211. ISHUMI, ABEL G.M. (1974), "The Educated Elite: A Survey of East African Students at a Higher Institution of Learning", in Mbilinyi ed. (1974): 65-72 and in Mbilinyi ed. (1976).

The sample of students in the study reflected the overall
student composition at the University, with 17 % women. There
was much less even spread of women by age, all falling between
20 and 29 years; whereas nearly a third of the men were found
in the age group of 30 to 45 years. Differential marital
status for the sexes was not analysed, nor social background
and aspiration.

212. LINJEWILE, R.M. (1976), "Sociological Aspects of Education for
Rural Women". Paper presented to the International Workshop on
Education for Rural Women, Lushoto, Tanzania (PMO/UNICEF), 12 pp.

The following issues are relevant to the problem of rural women
and development: women's roles, self-perception, ascribed and
achieved statuses, the importance of social networks in which
rural women exist. However, the workshop participants are
themselves members of an educated and urban-based group discussing the problems of rural women. The power and ability of rural
women to plan for themselves is underestimated. At the same
time, the workshop participants are strategically located to
mobilize resources and struggle ideologically in order to
articulate the needs and conditions of poor village women.
Women are exploited and subordinated as a result of the division of labour which forces women to work harder without receiving a fair share of benefits of their labour. Cut off from
formal education and from the learning which takes place while
participating in employment, women require a new strategy for
education. "Hit and run seminars" conducted in villages by
urban women are inadequate and tend to subordinate village
women further. A village-based cadre is needed to educate
rural women, and the rural women primary school teachers are the
most appropriate, partly because they are educated and numerous.
The problems involved in using such personnel are explored, as
well as the need to transform teaching methods so that adults
are not treated as passive school children, and that of winning
the confidence of older, married village women by the younger and
often unmarried schoolteachers.

213. MASAWE, N.G.E.(1976), "Adult Education Programmes and Their
Contribution to Women Activities in Tanzania" paper presented
to International Workshop on Education for Rural Tanzania,
Lushoto, Tanzania (PMO/UNICEF), 16 pp.

Institute of Adult Education programmes are described, including
the radio mass campaigns and special projects like that of
Chiwanda, where production was combined with training. Reasons
for low participation of women in the correspondence programme
are given, which include higher illiteracy rates and lack of
primary schooling, the lack of cash to pay for the courses,
domestic work and irrelevant coursework. A women's section in
the Institute has been opened, which will conduct nationwide
seminars to identify learning needs of women and seek solutions.
There will also be a regional survey of the women's question.
The possibility of a national radio mass campaign on women,
their needs and aspirations, is mentioned.

214. MBILINYI, MARJORIE (1969), The Education of Girls in Tanzania:
A Study of Attitudes of Tanzanian Girls and Their Fathers Towards
Education, Dar es Salaam, Institute of Education, 82 pp.

Identifies attitudinal and socio-economic factors acting as
barriers to the education of girls. It is based on a sample
survey of girls in the fourth year of primary education, taken
from 2 urban areas and 2 rural areas, Dar es Salaam urban and
Mzizima District, and Mwanza urban and rural. Girls in schools
came from homes representing a higher socio-economic status. A
fairly large proportion of rural non-schoolgoers and their parents
mentioned the need for girls' assistance at home. Urban-rural
differences were found throughout the findings in relation to
socio-economic as well as attitudinal data.

215. MBILINYI, MARJORIE J. (1972), The Decision to Educate in Rural
Tanzania. University of Dar es Salaam, unpublished Ph. D.
dissertation, 768 pp.

Based on a survey of peasant households in nine different districts
of Tanzania, the study found that children had unequal access to
primary school depending upon their sex and their class and strata.
There was a definite preference to send boys to school among
poorer peasants and even middle peasants, because of the reliance
of families on sons for future husbands. Begins with an historical analysis of schooling and women in development, in order to
situate the findings of the survey itself. The chapter on
research methodology is a useful introduction to techniques of
making questionnaires and interviewing.

216. MBILINYI, MARJORIE J. (1973), Attitudes, Expectations and the
Decision to Educate in Rural Tanzania. University of Dar es
Salaam, BRALUP Research Paper No. 3/1, 50 pp.

In essence a summary of The Decision to Educate in Rural Tanzania
the paper focuses on attitudes and expectations of and about
primary school girls. The ideas the young girls and their
fathers have about the virtues of school education and "traditional" education in preparing girls for their future roles in
society are compared, as well as preferences for educated and
uneducated husbands, differential values given to school work
and domestic labour of schoolgirls, the perceived relevance of
different school subjects for women's work, are examined and
discussed. In general, schoolgirls are caught in a web of
contradictory demands reflecting the world of school and
employment, and the world of peasant patriarch relations and
the sexual division of labour at home.

217. MBILINYI, M.J. (ed.) (1974), Access to Education in East Africa.
Rural Africana. No. 25, Michigan State University, African
Studies Centre (Fall), 128 pp.

Articles on schooling and non-formal education in Tanzania relevant
to issues of girls and women in education are cited in this
volume.

218. MBILINYI, MARJORIE, J. (1974), "The Problem of Unequal Access
to Primary Education in Tanzania", in Mbilinyi (1974): 5-28,
and Mbilinyi ed. (1976).

Summarises findings of research reported on in items 215 and
216.

219. MBILINYI, MARJORIE (1975), "Where Do We Go From Here?". Kenya
Education Review, 2 (2): 69-78, University of Nairobi, Faculty
of Education, special issue edited by Abigail Krystall and
Achola Pala.

Analyses the place of women in subsistence economies, changes
brought about by the development of "dependency capitalism",
and issues concerning the education of women. Drawing on
research in a girls secondary school in Dar es Salaam, girls'
expectations for themselves and their perceptions of male-female
relationships are explored. The "sugar daddy" pattern of sexual
relationships between schoolgirls and "big men" is analysed partly
though the eyes of schoolgirls themselves.

220. MBILINYI, MARJORIE (ed.), (1976), Who Goes to School in East
Africa? University of Dar es Salaam, bound mimeo, 14 chapters,
Department of Education.

The articles published in Mbilinyi ed. 1974 are included, as
well as additional materials on the issue of access to education.
Sexism in secondary schooling is analysed in M. Mbilinyi et al.,
"Secondary Education as Cultural Imperialism" (Ch. 10). The
relationship between class and sex and schooling is explored
in terms of access to secondary schooling and the social relations
in the school itself. Findings indicate that petty bourgeois
children have more access to secondary schooling than children
of workers and peasants, and this is especially true for girls.

221. MBILINYI, MARJORIE (1980), "Towards a Methodology in Political
Economy of Adult Education in Tanzania". Toronto, International
Council of Adult Education (ICAE), Working Papers on Political
Economy of Adult Education Series, 31 pp.

Stresses the need for theoretical clarity in the analysis of
adult education, and problematises the question of research
methodology. The debates within historical materialism on
methodology, ideology, modes of production, the agrarian question,
and gender relations are highly relevant to the investigation of
the political economy of adult education. The necessity to
specifically analyse the relationship between class and gender
relations in the context of different stages of capitalist
development is argued and has been adopted within the comparative
framework of the Political Economy of Adult Education Research
Project organised by the ICAE. Examines the historical development of class and gender relations in Tanzania, with emphasis on
the transformation of peasant production and reproduction.
Detailed information of a descriptive nature on the education
system, education reform, and adult education programmes is also
presented.

222. MCHARU, N.E. (1977), Literacy: a Tool for the Development of
Rural Women in Tanzania. (Studies in Adult Education, No. 27)
Dar es Salaam, Institute of Adult Education.

Argues that literacy has contributed quite significantly to the
development of women in Tanzania, socially, healthwise, politically

and even technically. Unfortunately the study does not back any
of these assertions by fact. Nor does it show how adult education
has or will change the overall status of women. Other studies
have in fact pointed out that the lack of women's participation
in politics, agricultural extension, and adult education classes
as well as their inability to implement health improvements is
rooted in their status in the family and the dominant capitalist
relations. This is not to discredit the role of adult education
in the integration of women in national development but rather to
put it in a more realistic perspective.

223. MMARI, G. (1976), "Implementation of the Musoma Resolutions:
The University of Dar es Salaam Admissions". Papers in Education
and Development, No. 3: 15-51. A summary version with up-dated
information is found in Prospects, IX (1): 1979:69-77, but lacks
the original tables in full.

Traces the historical development of the new admissions policy
to the University of Dar es Salaam which arose with the Musoma
Resolutions in 1974. All new entrants must have had one year
National Service and two years work experience and be selected
by the Party branch at the work place and cleared by employers,
with reference to Form 6 leavers. The Mature Age Entry Scheme
expanded as well to include many more entrants with work experience and some form of professional or vocational training. The
paper analyses the backgrounds of the first year intake in 1975/
76 under the new admissions policy and their examination perform-
ances. An important finding of the paper was the drastic drop
in women entrants as a result of the new procedures. Throughout
the author provides sex breakdowns in the statistics presented
on applicants, performance, degree course and so on, which can
be used by others for further analysis. Since the publication
of this paper and its earlier seminar presentation, the policy
has been altered to allow women to enter the university immediately after National Service Training which follows form 6
education. This has been done to offset the imbalance found in
enrolment.

224. MUNUO, EDITH MALLYA (1979), "Education for Equality". Paper
No. 14, BW, 19 pp.

The author, the Deputy Secretary General of UWT, argues that the
structure and content of education depends on the socio-economic
context. As modes of production in Tanzania have been transformed, education has changed to meet the interests of the
dominant exploitative classes. Historical analysis of colonial
and post-colonial education shows how education has been
structured to provide a differentiated education system,
differentiated by the urban-rural situation, sex, class, and
during the colonial period, race. With respect to women,
content is focused on women's work in the home, especially
in non-formal education programmes but also in the diversified
secondary school programme, and even more significant, women
have unequal access to post-primary education at all levels.
Statistics are presented to document unequal access overall,
and the sexist pattern of subject combinations in Form V/VI and
Technical Colleges in 1979, where women have no places or signif-

icantly fewer places in all of the basic science combinations.
Education contributes to the reproduction of a class of exploited illiterate women who provide most of the manual labour
in the rural villages. Sexist patterns of socialisation in the
home and community reinforce the sexism in the formal educational
system, where young girls are taught to "sit politely with your
husband/don't bother him when he talks/don't answer back to
him ... satisfy his needs". (Utendi wa Mwana Kupona 1972)
Progressive reforms to equalise educational opportunities for
women and men, and for the rural poor, are inadequate, especially
if the question is posed, what kind of education? The questions
raised in the paper are significant, backed as they are by
historical analysis of the problem and statistical data to
document the overall argument.

225. OLE KAMBAINE, P. (1979), "Women and Education in Tanzania".
Paper No. 30, BW, 9 pp.

The formal and non-formal education system is discriminatory
towards women in terms of access and content of instruction.
This reflects the place of women in production and reproduction
in society, and is shown in secondary and university enrolment
figures for 1961-1975/6 provided. Recommends that women must
organise themselves in groups and use UWT to channel their
problems to the government; they must struggle to get influential
positions in which they will have more power to struggle for
women's liberation; schoolgirls should receive sex education;
girls and women should demand opportunities in formerly male-
dominated school and university level subjects.

226. PMO/SIDA (1977), Report on the UCD-Workers' Evaluation of Their
Training and Education at Buhare Home Economics Training Centre.
Dodoma, PMO/Stockholm, SIDA.

The historical development of the Centre is briefly analysed,
beginning in 1966 when courses were mainly 10 months in duration, and through 1974-1975 when the two years Advanced Home
Economics Certificate Course had been instituted. Whereas
previously intake was mainly ex-standard VII/VIII graduates,
beginning in 1974 it became Form IV leavers with domestic
science bias. Fifty-two ex-Buhare trainees were interviewed
to evaluate their training and its relevance to present work as
UCD workers. The general consensus was that the training was
useful but too short. Specific recommendations were given for
each course, reflecting their present work. Although UCD workers
reveal high moral commitment to their work in rural areas, they
also share very high dissatisfaction with their promotion status.
There was also unease if not dislike for the present emphasis in
their work on management of development-oriented production
projects rather than "home economics" per se. This includes
auditing and book-keeping for which they were inadequately
prepared. The kinds of women's projects found in each sample
region are noted, as well as impressions of changes which have
occurred in the districts where posted. Changes reflected higher
standards of living: better food habits, better dress, and better
child care. Specific recommendations are made by the survey team
in the light of UCD workers' own suggestions.

227. REICHEL, GERTRAUD (1977), Some Ideas and Concerns of Tanzanian
Pre-adolescent and Adolescent Children. University of Dar es
Salaam, unpublished M.A. dissertation.

The purpose of the study was to gain some knowledge about school
adolescents' ideas and areas of concerns in their relations to
parents, school, future occupation, and peers. Differences in
answers occurred between urban and rural adolescents as well as
between boys and girls.

228. SHANN, G.N. (1956), "The Early Development of Education Among
the Chagga". TNR, 45 (December) 21-32.

Emphasis is placed on the developments of Catholic German Mission
schooling in the Kilimanjaro areas during the German Colonial
period. From the beginning girls received a third or more of
the places in the schools at all levels. There was sex specificity in curriculum, reflecting the missionary conception of
appropriate sex stereotypes: boys learning agriculture, girls
learning domestic science. For all students a great deal of time
was spent on rural vocation skills and manual work. Concern was
expressed about the effects of the schooling on the girls, who
began to reject their "traditional" obligations as women, such
as their responsibility to produce cultivated foods for the
household.

229. SHEKELAGHE, M.M. (1973), "Community Development, Home Economics
and Women's Organisations". UTAFITI, The Young Child in Tanzania,
Dar es Salaam, UNICEF, pp. 84-165.

Discusses training programmes for home economics through adult
education, run both by voluntary agencies and national programmes.
Under the former it includes women's groups, homecraft centres,
maendeleo clubs, YWCA and UWT; while under the latter it describes
the scope and programmes of the Regional Home Economics Training
Centres at Buhare and Rugemba as well as those of the Rural
Development Division.

230. TANZANIA (1976), Annual Manpower Report to the President 1975.
Dar es Salaam.

Includes specific attention to sexual imbalance in secondary
education and university. Figures provided on secondary and
high school enrolment with boy/girl breakdowns. Every year
such a manpower report is published and they tend to provide
valuable information on education and employment. Inadequate
attention to male-female differences is fairly common, however,
and this was an exceptional report.

231. TANZANIA, MINISTRY OF NATIONAL EDUCATION, "Hotuba ya Waziri wa
Elimu ya Taifa Ndugu Tabitha Siwale, Mbunge, kuhusu Makadirio
ya Fedha kwa mwaka 1980/81" 36 pp. 29 pp. of statistics.

Each year the budget speech of the Ministry of National Education
presents valuable information and statistics concerning the
education system. Male/female breakdowns are provided for all
sectors in the schooling system except for the University in the
1980/81 speech. These are combined with regional and private/
government breakdowns, allowing the reader to compare different

trends in access to schooling for the different regions and in the two sectors of schooling. Although the government has announced a deliberate policy of selection to Form I which would correct the previous sexual imbalance, this has mainly been implemented in urban areas where day schools are situated. Overall, the number of places for rural based girls in secondary school remains much smaller than for boys. This can only be offset by expanding the number of coeducational and girls boarding schools. The government policy to expand day in preference to boarding schools needs to be re-examined, since far fewer boarding facilities exist at present for girls.

232. TANZANIA: PMO and UNICEF (1976), International Workshop on Education for Rural Women, Lushoto, Tanzania 13-27 November 1976. Report, Dar es Salaam, 110 pp.

The workshop had 26 participants from 11 different countries of Africa, and was organised by the Prime Minister's Office. The report presents summaries of all papers, workshop recommendations and the final action plan. The areas covered were broad, and generated provocative and meaningful recommendations which tend to be technically oriented and could be promoted for immediate adoption and implementation. Some of the papers are cited in this section. To our understanding the report has not yet been widely circulated, and is in mimeograph form. The CCT reports exemplify the way such mimeographed reports become more permanent and durable items after binding. It is hoped that the Workshop report can be salvaged and circulated as widely as possible, and translated into Swahili for wider impact.

233. UNITED NATIONS CHILDREN'S FUND (1975), "Training Programme for Women, Development and Home Improvement". Project Working Document UNICEF, Dar es Salaam, Tanzania, 10 pp.

Describes a joint UNICEF/Tanzania government one-year project to train village women in shop management, handicraft and textile production, leadership, home economics and food preservation and storage techniques.

IX. LEGAL QUESTIONS

Many social injustices are rooted in the historical economic processes
that have shaped the societies in which these injustices take place.
However, the injustices are reinforced and given permanence through
legal systems. For instance, the exclusive right of men to vote was
established by law and could only be changed by law. Legal systems
can thus be a major obstacle to meaningful change and those that
struggle against any form of oppression and injustice must therefore, find out to what extent the injustices are enmeshed in the
legal systems that operate. However, the de jure position of a
situation may be negatively affected by strongly ingrained prejudicial practices so that the law may be powerless to bring about
the necessary change. This is particularly true if the victim has
neither the knowledge of the law nor the ability to appeal to the
law. The legal system also becomes ineffective if there is any
ambiguity or conflict. In Tanzania, ambiguity and conflict is
facilitated by the existence of more than one code of law and by
what appears to be an inordinate desire to maintain the customary
law even when it is seen to be unfair and unjust (IX:236).

Law and the Socio-Economic Status of Women

Several studies have discussed the close relationship between the
legal system and the socio-economic status of women in the country
(IX:235-237, 241, 246, 248 and section II). James and Fimbo examine
how patriarchal relations have affected customary land tenure. Eight
of the tribes in Tanzania are patrilineal and in these groups descent
is almost exclusively through males. In matrilineal societies the
principal heirs are uterine brothers (same mother, same father) and
sister's sons. Even where changes have occurred, women usually get
usufruct rights rather than outright ownership with full rights to
dispose of the property by grant, will or sale. The subordinate
position of women in production relations is discussed in several
studies with varying degrees of critical analysis (IX:235, 237, 241).
Rwezaura draws special attention to the relationship of law and the
reproductive role of women (IX:246, 248). In cases of separation
or divorce, the law, particularly customary law, ensures that the
men take the children. He shows how this is related to the traditional value of children as a source of labour and the role of women
as mere producers of these children. Women have also legally been
kept out of cooperative agricultural marketing societies and thus
deprived of the right to participate in the sale of cash crops
(VI:174).

Law and the Changing Socio-Economic Political Situation

A number of studies have shown that the law has not kept pace with
the political and social changes taking place (IX:237, 241). Since
1967 the country has adopted the policy of socialism based on the
fundamental rights of the individual woman and man, yet this is not
reflected for example in villages and villagisation land tenure
practices. Ownership of land in ujamaa and development villages in
practice is still vested in the heads of household, usually male,

despite the Villagization Act of 1975. There are also other
contradictions that have not been resolved: the division of labour
at the household level; the division of proceeds obtained from joint
labour on individual plots; the divisions of the family income
obtained from wages; the rights of widows and divorcees etc. The
1971 Marriage Act has some progressive measures but the Act will
remain ineffective as long as these provisions are in many cases
paralleled by provisions in the customary law and the contrary
interpretation is subjective (IX:247).

On the other hand some laws enacted to alleviate the conditions
of women backfire on them because legal changes cannot change societal
values and prejudices. For example, legislation providing working
women with 84 days paid maternity leave has resulted in some employers
preferring male instead of female employees (IX:234, 241 and section
V).

The Need for Legal Aid and Information

Among the reasons why the provisions of the Marriage Act may not be
used in preference to those of the more discriminatory customary
law, is the fact that the legal provisions of this Act are not widely
known or used by the women concerned. A great deal needs to be done
in the form of free legal aid groups and dissemination of legal
information. The work done by the Legal Aid Committee (IX:238-240)
is a model in this respect. Comprehensive works like those summa-
rising key legislation affecting women are useful (See Rwezaura 1981
and IX:244, 245), but even in the more developed countries it has
been found that simplified and published versions of legislation as
pamphlets are necessary instruments of change. On the more academic
level, the legal system needs to be critically analysed in order to
expose sections that contribute to the subordination of women and a
denial of their basic human rights as individual members of society.

REFERENCE

B.A. Rwezaura (1981), Sheria ya Ndoa Tanzania, Dar es Salaam, Taasisi
ya Uchunguzi wa Kiswahili.

———————————

234. BRYCESON, D.F. (1980), "A Review of Maternity Protection
Legislation in Tanzania". Infant Feeding Practices in Dar es
Salaam, edited by O. Mgaza and H. Bantje. TFNC Report No. 484
and BRALUP Research Paper No. 66. Dar es Salaam, TFNC and
BRALUP, 168-181.

Reviews maternity legislation from its first limited provision
in 1956 to the current situation where a woman is entitled to
84 days maternity leave with full pay every 3 years; outlines
problems related to the implementation of the legislation using
the Friendship Textile Mill as a case study and discusses the
implications of these problems. Employers incur financial loss
as a result of the maternity leave provisions. The study
recommends that maternity leave should be a burden shared

equally by all employers through a uniform system of taxation,
the proceeds of which could then be used to compensate employers
for losses incurred through maternity leave.

235. DOBSON, E.B. (1940), "Land Tenure of the Wasambaa". TNR, No. 10
(December): 1-27.

A thorough analysis of land tenure systems in one sub-chiefdom
of Vugiri, relying on interviews with sub-chiefs, elders and
missionaries as well as measurement and marking out of fields
concerned. Elements of feudal relations are noted, such as
tribute and labour service exacted by the chiefs and their
agents. Information on what can be called patriarch relations
and sex specificity of tasks and activities are detailed,
together with accompanying ideological justifications for male
dominance.

236. JAMES, R.W. and FIMBO, G.M. (1963), Customary Land Law of
Tanzania; a Source Book. Nairobi, East African Literature
Bureau, 1973, 678 pp.

"An attempt is made in this work to deal with some of the
important rules and principles of the land tenure system in the
traditional sector and to take the reader by comments and
arrangement of the cases and legislation through historical,
social and political changes that are taking place and are
affecting the land laws". Authors' preface.

237. JOHNSTON, P.H. (1946), "Some Notes on Land Tenure on Kilimanjaro
and the Vihamba of the Wachagga". TNR, No. 21 (June): 1-20.
Includes Appendix: "Case Law and the Kihamba Land".

Land tenure has changed as a result of growing commoditisation
of crop production, the demands for coffee cultivation which
take precedence over food production, and so on. The impact
of changing land tenure on women is shown, such as loss of right
to Kihamba for each wife. Conflicts between patriarchs and sons
as well as patriarchs/husbands and wives are rooted in altering
conceptions of land and labour use. Details about sex
specificity in tasks and activities are given. The Appendix
begins with a section entitled "Rights of Women" which provides
case histories.

238. KAMATI YA MSAADA WA KISHERIA (1979), "Aina za Mikataba ya Kazi
na Haki Mbalimbali za Wafanyakazi Wapatao Mshahara Usiozidi Shs
700/= kwa Mwezi". Ufafanuzi wa Sheria zinazohusu Wafanyakazi
wa Tanzania (Bara) Toleo No. 2, 5 pp. Mimeo.

Distinguishes between kibarua, daily, weekly and monthly-paid
employee status. It then describes the rights of each, including
minimum pay (now out of date), days off, holidays, leave,
compensation, severance allowances and overtime pay.

239. KAMATI YA MSAADA WA HISHERIA/LEGAL AID COMMITTEE (1979),
"Vibarua". Ufafanuzi wa Sheria zinazohusu Wafanyakazi wa
Tanzania Toleo No. 1, Chuo Kikuu cha Dar es Salaam, Kitivo cha
Sheria (Faculty of Law), 2 pp. Mimeo.

Outlines the legal definition of a daily worker or kibarua, and
a monthly employee, as well as their respective rights and

salaries. The daily paid worker must be paid at least the
minimum daily pay set by law at the end of each day (Employment
Ordinance Cap. 366). If injured on the job, she/he is to be
paid compensation by the employer. The daily worker has no
other rights under the present law. Once a daily worker has
worked at least 280 days during a period of twelve months, she/
he is recategorised legally as a monthly employee, with all the
respective rights (Sheria ya Kazi Na. 1 ya 1975). These rights
are listed in the paper and include one day of rest after every
six work days with no cut in pay; all holidays with full pay;
seven days leave every four months of work and so on. It is
noted that many workers are illegally hired on a daily paid
basis even after working for a year or more.

This is the first of a series of papers available free from
the Legal Aid Committee, see item 238, 240. They are written
in Kiswahili in a straightforward, easy to understand style and
are a valuable means of educating workers about their rights
under the law. It is hoped that there will be special numbers
concerning the question of women's rights as workers under the
law: for example, maternity leave provisions, and protection
against sexual discrimination in employment, promotion and on-
the-job training. A similar series on issues related to the
marriage act would also be a major contribution. The papers
are out of date with respect to details on actual wage rates.
Another problem is the format, mimeographed, unbound, and in
regular type-face which may be difficult for semi-literates to
read. Support should be provided to the Legal Aid Committee
for this important work, so that they could put out pamphlets
on newsprint paper, for example using large size print. These
could be sold at a subsidized price of T. Shs. 1/=, and thus
circulate through newstands around the country.

240. KAMATI YA MSAADA WA KISHERIA (1980), "Kiinua Mgongo" Ufafanuzi
wa Sheria zinazohusu Wafanyakazi wa Tanzania (Bara) Toleo No. 3,
Chuo Kikuu, Kitivo cha Sheria, 4 pp. Mimeo.

Explains which workers have the right to receive severance
allowance when fired (e.g. have worked a minimum of 3 months or
more; receive shs. 700/= or less per month (1980); are not on
pensionable terms; are not vibarua; did not voluntarily quit
work etc). It also covers payments for such workers at time
of death or disabling injury, when the severance allowance is
paid directly to dependents and/or trustees of minors. The
formula used to calculate severance allowance is also given with
clear examples of how to use it.

241. KIKOPA, JANE R.K. (1979), "Human Rights: The Position of Women
and Children in Tanzania" University of Dar es Salaam, Faculty
of Law Seminar Paper (March 22), 15 pp. Also presented as
Paper No. 33, BW, 11 pp.

The subordinate position of women in production is reflected in
Tanzanian laws and these in turn reinforce or reproduce women's
subordinate position in all spheres. Areas surveyed include
land tenure, inheritance, the Employment Ordinance, the maternity
benefits, travel allowances and the family law in its various
aspects. The United Nations Declaration on Elimination of

Discrimination against Women (1967) is appended, together with a section of Customary Land Law dealing with inheritance.

242. LUHANGA, EMILY (1979), "Law and the Status of Women in Tanzania" Paper No. 36, BW, 7 pp.

A brief description of relevant laws categorized as political and civil rights, civil law, family welfare and education and employment. Notable among these are that marriage must be voluntary on both sides, and that no spouse has the right to inflict corporal punishment on the other. Abortion is a criminal offence, although there are conflicting sections of the law. It is noted that "the patriarchal customs and religious influences have made it difficult for the Government to have the laws fully implemented".

243. MUNUO, E.N. (1977), Sheria za Haki za Wanawake. Dar es Salaam, Tanzania Publishing House, 86 pp.

Summarises the salient features of the Tanzania Marriage Act of 1971 and other related legislation pertaining to women's rights in marriage; inheritance; right to children born in and out of wedlock, care and support for children; divorce; distribution of assets in marriage; and maternity leave. Discusses the disadvantages to women arising out of the custom of bride-price and recommends that the government should set up legislation to abolish it.

244. MWAKASUNGULA, N.E.R. (1975), Sheria za Ndoa na Talaka. Tabora, T.M.P. Book Department.

Summarises the 1971 Marriage Act and other legislation regulating marriage and divorce.

245. MWAKASUNGULA, N.E.R. (1979), Kesi za Ndoa na Talaka. Tabora, T.M.P. Book Department.

Provides cases to illustrate legislation regulating marriage and divorce. These also reveal the oppressive nature of court proceedings as well as of the laws themselves.

246. RWEZAURA, BARTHAZAR A. (1977), "Recent Cases and Conflicts: A Short Study of the New Tanzania Divorce Law". Dar es Salaam University Law Journal, 6, pp. 71-97.

The paper examines the procedural and substantive law governing divorce. The aim is to find out whether (i) the provisions of the law are observed by the courts, (ii) whether there exist factors that influence the observance or breach of the existing law by the courts e.g. procedural defects in the law, institutional inadequacy to cope with the new demands, ignorance of the law, unsuitability of the law to the prevailing social and economic conditions. Through an examination of specific cases, the study shows that there appears to be a conflict between primary and high courts. The primary courts appear to be more understanding of the human problem, whereas the high courts seem more concerned with the procedural aspects.

247. RWEZAURA, BARTHAZAR A. (1977), "Law and Population Policy in Tanzania". Paper presented to the Seminar on Population in

Decision Making for Development, organized by the Centre for
African Family Studies, from 24th Oct. to 5th Nov. 1977. 25 pp.

Shows how, although there is no official population policy in
Tanzania, a number of statements by the President; the
establishment of the Family Planning Association and maternal
and child health care centres; and laws like those regulating
maternity leave can be taken to constitute a population policy.

248. RWEZAURA, BARTHAZAR A. (1978), "Family Law and Family Welfare
in Tanzania". Paper presented to the IPPF African Regional
Workshop on Law, Status of Women and Family Welfare, Nairobi,
June 26-29, 1978. 29 pp.

Shows how customary laws relating to the family were evolved
as direct responses to social and economic forces. In the
traditional society children were considered as a source of
labour and women as sources of children. The introduction of
the cash economy, private ownership of land, urbanisation and
other aspects of modernisation have had a profound effect on
changing the value of children.

249. TANZANIA (1971), "The Law of Marriage Act, 1971". Dar es
Salaam, Acts Supplement to the Gazette, No. 5 (Swahili Issue:
"Sheria ya Ndoa" 59 pp. Government Bookshop, Jamhuri Street,
Box 1801, Dar es Salaam).

The sections covered in the law include the following:
restrictions on marriage (e.g. minimum age, no marriage save of
free will); preliminaries to marriage; the different forms of
contracting marriage; property, rights, liabilities and status
(e.g. equality between wives, duty to maintain spouse, no right
to spouse to inflict corporal punishment, separate property of
husband and wife and so on); miscellaneous rights (e.g. right
to damages for adultery); matrimonial proceedings (e.g. separation and divorce, division of assets and maintenance as between
husband and wife, custody and maintenance of children); offences
(e.g. coercion, minimum age). Detailed knowledge about all
aspects of the law is essential for all women in order to
protect themselves and their children. Many aspects of the
law are inherently progressive but remain paperwork until they
become incorporated as mass knowledge and put into practice.
Women themselves must put them into practice, and can then
decide which aspects are not progressive but instead violate
socialist principles of equality between men and women.

X. POLITICAL PARTICIPATION

The participation of women in politics and leadership positions in
Tanzania is very low, whether at national or local level (X:250-252,
262). The 1979 village survey carried out on behalf of the Prime
Minister's office has shown, for instance, that only 6.5 percent of
the village managers were female while there was not a single female
chairman or secretary (X:260). At the national level, out of over
200 members of parliament elected in 1980, less than 15 were women
(see election results discussed in the Daily News, October 1980).
Nor have the new policies of ujamaa and villagisation made much
difference. Discussing ujamaa village development in Mwanza Region,
Mapolu discovered that although the ratio of women to men was 2:3
in 55 percent of the villages surveyed, women constituted less than
10 percent of the membership of all the committees (IV:103). Similar
situations are described in many of the studies included under the
section on "women peasants". The low level of participation is
rooted in the women's role in production and reproduction. The
sexual division of labour assures that women are tied to household
activities while men have more mobility and leisure. This element
of time and leisure is clearly illustrated by Lewin when he states
that "while the men debate enthusiastically, women fall asleep
during ujamaa meetings. They have worked so hard in the course of
the day to make ujamaa living a reality that they are too exhausted
to stay awake" (IV:102). An analysis of cell leaders in Kigombe
Village sums it up succinctly when it concludes by saying that unlike men, women usually do not take up leadership roles until middle
age. Until then their domestic and farming activities impose a
severe limit on the participation in extra-familial duties and
responsibilities (X:252).

The cultural values that assign sex-specific roles to men and
women in society have led to the popular belief that politics is
for men. It has been shown elsewhere that socialisation processes
and the ideology of male dominance were necessary to maintain the
subordinate position of women in the productive and reproductive
sector. It followed therefore that women were perpetual jural and
political minors, their grievances usually taken up by male relatives.

Some studies have mentioned the existence of women's groups which
acted as a forum for women's grievances but not enough research has
been done on this aspect to see how effective these groups were in
redressing the grievances. It is possible that women in some societies were more forthright than in others, reflected in their
representation in parliament and elsewhere, where women are
"surprisingly" occupying positions like the regional police commander
or a district party secretary. That historical and cultural factors
are important is illustrated by O'Barr with respect to the greater
participation of women in politics in Usangi (X:258). However, one
wonders which was the more important factor: the fact that women had
historically been important in politics even though to a very limited
extent, or the fact that with male out-migration, a greater number
of women were de facto heads of household. Nevertheless, this question
does not deny the need for research into the background of women
leaders, in pre-colonial, colonial and post-colonial societies.

Mobilisation of women through the national women's organisation, the UWT, is the subject of many papers (X:250, 251, 253, 261-266). The UWT has been given political backing through recognition as a national mass organisation. It has undoubtedly had some achievements, for instance, its successful campaign to obtain paid maternity leave for women workers and to allow female students to enter the university directly after National Service. It has also tried to improve the situation of women by organising various activities centred mainly around child care, health and nutrition, income earning activities and education. On the whole, the income earning activities have not been successful. Several reasons are posed for the failure of these activities ranging from lack of funds and lack of skills, to inherent weaknesses in the organisation and leadership. Whatever the individual or cumulative effect of these reasons, the fact remains that UWT has failed to mobilise the women, particularly in the rural areas. Membership figures show that UWT has managed to reach a very small percentage of the women of Tanzania and very often these figures do not represent active members. Fuller mobilisation is constrained by conflicts in the multiple role of women as worker, provider of household needs and producer of children. It is also constrained by conflicts between varying age groups and classes of women - showing yet again that the struggle of women has to be sited within the wider context of class struggles and the processes of capitalist development that have affected and continue to affect the political practices of different groups and classes of women.

UWT has begun to recognise these weaknesses and some attempts are being made to eliminate them. The proposals for a new structure, if accepted, will give the organisation women with better managerial and administrative abilities (X:243). The recent attempts to incorporate university women in joint research projects is also breaking down barriers between the highly educated and the less educated (IV:90). However, the full participation of women in politics will not depend on the success of a few economic ventures run by women but on fundamental changes in the attitudes of women and men towards politics, and even more, on fundamental changes in the production and other social relations that currently give women a less participatory role in society.

---

250. KODA, BERTHA (1975), Emancipation of Women in Tanzania and the Role of the UWT. University of Dar es Salaam, unpublished M.A. dissertation, 183 pp.

Tanzania is characterised by an agrarian economy in which women have been assigned very distinct roles. The division of labour is such that women remain shackled to individual households while men have chances of mobility and links with the world outside their immediate environment. Women are considered as a possession, a source of labour and of wealth earned by her children - a status perpetuated by traditional practices like brideprice, and customary laws. Since independence, the country's political party and administrative organization have effected a number of measures designed to give women equality in education, employment and participation in politics. Evaluates

the role of the women's organization, Umoja wa Wanawake wa
Tanzania (UWT) in bringing about unity among women, and their
integration into the economic, cultural and political activities
of the country.

251. KODA, BERTHA (1979), "The Role of UWT in Rural Development".
Paper No. 19, BW, 8 pp.

A summary of Koda's MA. dissertation (item 250), the major
problems of UWT were identified as: (1) lack of adequate
education and training at all levels, accompanied by conservative attitudes especially among older members, and reflected in
the leadership courses which emphasise the domestic and domesticated role of women in the home; (2) inadequate funding for cooperative projects, day-care centres and other services; (3)
inadequate transport facilities; (4) the double workload of
women in the workplace or on the farm and in the home, which
hinders full participation; (5) lack of capacity and resources
to successfully administer responsibilities such as day care
centres; (6) national conditions dominated by capitalist
relations of production and the low level of development of
productive forces which affect all of the above.

252. LANDBERG, PAMELA WEAVER (date unknown), Cell Leadership in a
Coastal Tanzania Community. 38 pp.

Most political and authority positions in Swahili coastal
communities, particularly those involving contact with government officials, institutions and organizations outside the
community are allocated to men. It was, therefore, not
surprising that only two of the cell leaders in Kigombe village
on the northern coast of Tanzania were women. Cell leadership
in the community is defined and constrained by traditional norms
and values. The two cell leaders were selected because their
personal and sociological characteristics were very closely
related to these norms. They were bona fide citizens born in
the village, were already considered as leaders within their
traditional women's activities such as dance groups, were the
right age and had no children. Both were in their fifties.
Until then domestic and farming activities impose a severe
limit on women's participation in extra-familial duties and
responsibilities.

253. MADABIDA, R.R. (1974), The Umoja wa Wanawake wa Tanganyika -
Its Role in Tanzania. University of Dar es Salaam, unpublished
undergraduate Political Science dissertation, 59 pp.

Describes the history; functions and objectives; organisational
structure; and strengths and weaknesses of the UWT. The
effectiveness of the organization in fulfilling its goals is
evaluated and attempts are made to explain the failures. The
chief drawback to success is identified as the failure by UWT
to unite all women in Tanganyika.

254. MAKWETA, JACKSON (1974), The Role of the UWT in the Mobilization
of Women for Economic Development in Tanzania. Thesis, (M.A.)
University of Dar es Salaam, 82 pp.

Summarises briefly the role of women in Tanzania before the emergence of colonialism and during the colonial period. Shows how women were prevented from participating in the retail trade or taking up white collar jobs. Analyses the role that UWT has been playing in mobilizing women for economic development from 1962 to the present day. The emphasis is on UWT attempts to involve women in retail trade of the locally produced textiles such as khangas/vitenges. This is followed by an examination of the women's shops in Morogoro Region. The problems in this region are compared with those faced by women in other regions.

255. MANASE, S. (1980), "Hali Iliyopo ya Shughuli za Uchumi". UWT, MAKAO MAKUU, Dodoma (15th February), 4 pp. mimeo.

Provides a thorough brief analysis of problems which have arisen in some of the more common economic activities run by UWT. Hotel enterprises are rarely run by women, and tend to be begun too quickly without adequate feasibility studies, and lack of proper accounts. Capital is inadequate and rates too high, combined with difficulties of getting the necessary materials. Coffee places tend to use inadequate capital, do not have proper book-keeping and have problems of materials. There is a high demand for hostels from regions and districts, but they require a lot of money and expert assistance for acquiring loans. Vegetable gardens tend to produce on inadequate acreage and lack full cooperation of members. Agriculture extension workers are not used. Shops have depended too much on sales of khanga and kitenge, and only operate when these are available. They tend to be licensed without insurance, have insecure premises and lack guards, lack bookkeeping and regular accounting procedures, and the Shop Committees do not meet regularly. Small industries suffer from unequal access that women have to modern equipment, and often inadequate planning and assistance from SIDO and other relevant bodies.

256. MHANGO, B.P. (Secretary-General, UWT) (1976), "The Role of Women's Organizations". Paper presented to the International Workshop of Education for Rural Women, Lushoto, Tanzania (PMO/UNICEF), 6 pp.

The problem of the role of women's organizations must be situated in the context of a particular society. The characteristics of the colonial economy and culture have continued during the post-colonial period and need changing. Women were instrumental in the struggles for national liberation during the colonial period, and must not be left out during the period of struggles for self-determination and nation-building. Women's organizations like UWT "must not wait for their role to be determined and assigned by their men folk; they must assert it through their own organizations, and make government a recipient of institutional advice and responsive to popular need". Objectives of UWT are: to educate women about their economic, political, social and cultural roles; to deal with all matters concerning women with the Party and the government; "to campaign for and preserve women's rights and dignity" nationally and internationally. The administrative structure includes both elected and appointed leaders, the Secretary General being a Presidential appointee.

257. O'BARR, JEAN F. (1970), "The Cell-Leaders of Usangi-Kighare
and Mbaga Mshewa". In: Ten-House Party Cells and Their Leaders.
Northwestern University, Evanston, Illinois, unpublished Ph.D.
dissertation, see pp. 96-108.

A study of two wards in the Pare District, Tanzania, showed that
women accounted for approximately one-fourth of the ten-house
cell leaders in one of the wards, Usangi. This was remarkable
in a district where politics was considered to be the preserve
of men. Since their participation in the anti-tax riots of 1940
in which they marched in support of their husbands protesting
against a new tax, Usangi women have been accepted as a political
force. The second factor favouring female cell leaders is the
disequilibrium in the male-female ratio of cell composition. Men
in Usangi generally go outside their home areas to earn wages,
giving women the opportunity to hold political leadership
positions.

258. O'BARR, JEAN (1976), "Pare Women: A Case of Political
Involvement". Rural Africana, No. 9: 121-134.

Discusses factors likely to affect women's participation in
politics, and describes the political involvement of Usangi
women in the Pare District, Tanzania, during the colonial period.
This involvement, the author claims, has been reinforced and
continued into current times through out-migration of males
leaving women as heads of households. The study argues that
the reason for Usangi women's political participation was
originally to maintain the traditional way of life. However,
their very participation in politics brings them into contact
with new networks and perspectives and makes them more responsive
to social changes. Women cell leaders are more systematic in
performing their duties and more keen to initiate community
development projects than male cell leaders.

259. SANGA, EDDA WILLIAMS (1976), "Women in the Revolution: Women
Groups is the Answer". New Outlook, No. 1: 20-24.

Asserts that women's contribution to development is best achieved
through women's groups. No suggestions are offered as to how to
organize such groups, except to say that prospective groups
should seek advice from the Umoja wa Wanawake wa Tanzania, (UWT)
and the Young Women's Christian Association (YWCA).

260. TANZANIA, PMO. Ujamaa and Cooperative Development Dept. (1980),
Report on Village Survey. Dodoma, PMO, 2 vols.

The village Survey was carried out primarily to provide the
Prime Minister's Office (PMO) with essential data regarding
village activities and development. Data was collected on the
following aspects: general information about the village; village
organization and functionaries, economic activities in the
villages; storage and office facilities; management assistance;
bookkeeping and transportation.
        The data is based on a random sample of 514 villages in 19
regions. In addition to providing useful overall data about
village organisation in Tanzania, the publication illustrates
the role of women in village decision-making. A sex breakdown

for all the village leaders and officials shows that although not altogether absent, women form a small percentage of such personnel.

261. UWT (1971), Shughuli za UWT Katika Mwongozo Mpya wa TANU. Ripoti ya Semina Iliyoandaliwa na UWT, Kuendeshwa Katika Chuo Kikuu. Dar es Salaam, 16-17 April, 1971. 91 pp.

Proceedings of a seminar held to discuss the TANU directive of 1971 known as the TANU Guidelines, and ways and means of implementing it. Also includes a lengthy discussion on the implications of the Marriage Act of 1971.

262. UWT, Taarifa ya UWT - 1975/76. Dodoma, 20 pp.

Gives a breakdown of how women fared in the national elections of 1975. Other sections cover membership (176, 210) total number of branches, meetings held during the year; operation of child care centres, seminars held, economic projects and co-operation between UWT and other women's organisations. It is significant to note that the total grant for child care centres was roughly 1,000/= per region while the number of centres in each region varied greatly. Lack of adequate finance is a major constraint for the successful operation of these centres. It is not clear why the grant was so small nor why UWT did not press for larger grants.

263. UWT (1977), "Maazimio ya UWT Yaliyotekelezwa na Yasiyotekelezwa". Dodoma, 36 pp.

The major policies decided upon in the meetings of the Mikutano Mikuu from 1962 to 1976, and of the Halmashauri Kuu from 1969 to 1976 are presented with a brief note on implementation of each one. This becomes a historical record of the kinds of issues faced by women in Tanzania during that time as understood and taken up by the national women's organisation, and the positions actually taken. Some insight is also provided into constraints on the implementation of specific policies emanating from government organs or from national economic conditions. Issues covered range from the organisational structure of the UWT to problems of schoolgirl pregnancies.

264. UWT, Taarifa ya Mwaka, 1978 na 1979. Dodoma, 22 pp.

Covers the first two years following the union of the women of Tanzania mainland and Tanzania Islands into one mass organization affiliated to CCM. Gives staff breakdowns, figures on membership (275, 537), number of branches (total 4,083 by 1979), and UWT activities. The main activities appear to be operating child health care centres (3,065 by 1978/79), organising economic projects and holding seminars. It is interesting to note that 39,824 women earned 6,268,727/80 shillings. Of this they spent 2,685,535/25; banked 3,785,040/15 and distributed shs. 202,275/50. In other words the net profit was approximately 100/= per head. If the aim was to obtain cash earnings then the results are not very encouraging and would explain why so many projects start well but then peter out. The problems facing UWT are also described.

265. UWT (1980), <u>Makadirio ya Mapato na Matumizi ya Mwaka Unaoanzia</u>
<u>1 Julai, 1980 mpaka 30 Juni, 1981</u>

Provides breakdowns of revenue for 1978/79, and estimated revenue
for 1979/80 and 1980/81. Membership fees is the largest estimated
source of funds, but was much lower in 1978/79 than the estimates
for the next two years, exclusive of development funds for
building a hostel and lodging and government support. The
Government provides the greatest input of funds into the development and recurrent budget of UWT. It also includes reports from
the Regions, which are particularly detailed for Morogoro and
Mbeya. The total number of new members in 1980/81 is expected
to be 448,010.

266. UWT (1980), <u>Mapendekezo Kuhusu Muundo ya Makao Makuu ya Jumuiya</u>
<u>ya UWT na Miundo ya Utumishi kwa Wafanyakazi wa Jumuiya</u> (UWT).
Dar es Salaam, UWT, 60 pp.

The proposals for a reorganisation of UWT and its personnel came
as a direct response to a request from the national political
party, <u>Chama cha Mapinduzi</u> (CCM) and as thus reflects the national
concern in the inability of UWT to mobilise women in Tanzania.
 The proposals identify the basic need as being that of
obtaining personnel with better education skills and commitment.
The proposed organisation also recognises the need for research
and has made provision for a separate section for research. The
qualifications for the personnel and the provision of salaries
for these personnel will contribute greatly towards giving the
organisation more capable personnel.
 However, given the generally small number of women that will
qualify according to the new specifications and the traditional
scepticism against "Women's Organisations" by men and women due
to historical economic and cultural processes, the new organisation may not be able to effect changes immediately.

Recent References on Politics

Marjorie Mbilinyi with Mary Kabelele (1982), <u>Women in the Rural</u>
 <u>Development of Mbeya Region</u>. Mbeya RIDEP Project, PMO/<u>FAO</u>.

Liz Wily (1981), <u>Women and Development, A Case Study of Ten</u>
 <u>Tanzanian Villages</u>. A Report for Arusha Planning and Village
 Development Project, Arusha (USAID).

XI. BIOLOGICAL REPRODUCTION AND SEXUALITY

In the last ten years there has been a significant increase in
funding of research and seminar activities on the broad problem
area of biological reproduction and sexuality in Tanzania and in
Africa as a whole. Anthropological case studies in the colonial
and early post-colonial periods concentrated on functionalist
analysis of the economic, political and ideological structures or
system in "tribal society". Bridewealth, marriage and traditional
sex education practices were all posed as aspects of the society.
What is a recent development in social sciences is the posing of
sexuality and fertility as specific problems of analysis in and of·
themselves. The significance of the establishment of demography
as a separate social science discipline at the University of Dar
es Salaam should be seen in this light. At the same time, state
intervention in practices of sexuality and fertility is growing.
It is therefore important to clarify the kinds of issues being
raised, and to pose two related problems which require explanation:
(1) changing practices of sexuality and fertility for different
classes in Tanzania; (2) the practices of international agencies,
the state and social scientists when their attention is focused on
sexuality and fertility. The materials included in this and other
sections provide an adequate basis for beginning this inquiry. It
is appropriate to stress here that issues of sexuality and
fertility are posed both as class and gender issues.

Statistical Analyses of the Relationship Between Fertility and Child Mortality and Socio-Economic Factors

Statistical analyses of demographic patterns have been mainly based
on either macro-level census data or on micro-level surveys relying
heavily on structured interviews. The 1967 and 1978 Population
Censuses and the 1973 National Demographic Survey provide a wealth
of information on demographic relationships (XI:291, 299, 304, 312).
Sembajwe's secondary analysis of census data (304) indicates that
there is a curvilinear relationship between fertility and women's
educational and occupational levels. Women with Standard IV education have higher fertility rates than those with less or no schooling, and rates then drop for women with more schooling. With
respect to occupational levels, petty bourgeois salariat women
including teachers, medical and religious workers, agronomists,
veterinarians, government officials and management directors have
the highest fertility rate, and agricultural producers, be they
peasants or hired labourers, have the lowest. Infant and child
mortality rates are statistically related in the opposite direction,
being highest for agricultural producers and lowest for professional
women. Hence, petty bourgeois women bear more children who are also
most likely to survive. Sembajwe points out that the relationship
found between fertility rates and occupational levels differs from
the fertility trends presented by comparative statistical analyses
at a worldwide level. These trends suggest a negative relationship
between fertility and child mortality and women's educational and
occupational level. That is, women with more education and higher

"status" occupations tend to bear fewer children, and their children have a higher survival rate. For example, Monsted and Walji found that fertility and child mortality rates in Tanzania (1967 Census) and Kenya dropped in relationship to urbanisation and educational levels (XI:289). It is possible that regression models assuming a linear relationship between the factors included in the mathematical equation were adopted in this work, thereby missing the kind of mixed set of statistical relations found by Sembajwe.

Such findings based on macro-level statistical analysis need to be thoroughly problematised, however. One problem lies with the conceptual categories underlying the measures of education and occupation. For example, is it correct to lump together, for example, primary school teachers and nurses and professional lawyers, doctors and Ministers as members of one occupational category labelled "professionals"? Another, more substantive problem rests with the methodology adopted. Statistical analyses of correlations describe the way different characteristics of a sampled group are statistically associated with each other. The analysis depends on the conceptual categories adopted and the measures ultimately used to quantify those categories. The findings represent associations of characteristics and not cause - effect relationships. Explanations for the different fertility trends found among different categories of people become speculative so long as they are not derived from historical analysis of changing patterns of fertility. Account must be taken of such issues as the following: differential access to health services including contraceptives; the fluidity and insecurity of family class position such that many so-called "professionals" like teachers and nurses continue to rely on agricultural production as a future means of subsistence, as well as a complementary basis of subsistence at the current period; inadequate development of state social welfare services and the relatively low incomes to be derived from pensions for those with access to them, so that security of subsistence in old age continues to depend on support from adult children; the rapidity of social change, whose effect on fertility practices cannot be measured by examining total birth rates of women between the ages 45-49 years.

Sembajwe has recently carried out a major survey in Mara, Kilimanjaro and Morogoro Regions on related issues (XI:305). He found that child mortality rates statistically fell in relation to higher educational and income levels of husband and wife, the amount of food resources in families and its distribution to children (breakfast before school), and having access to clean sources of water. No clearly separate factors were related statistically to fertility levels.

In Kocher's survey in Lushoto and Moshi Rural District (XI:281) in the late 1970's no relationship was found between birth and infant child mortality rates and levels of education and other factors which he used as a "modernity" index. The few villages included were ranked as being least or most traditional or modern, with no statistical significance in birth or child mortality rates at village level. However, there were very different "ideologies" about marriage and fertility, and changing marital practices. In the "modern" village in Moshi District, there was a rapid drop in polygamy over two generations, a rise in the age of women at their first marriage, an expressed desire for smaller numbers of children,

and the perception that children's survival rate had risen. Jonge
(XI:279) found in Rungwe in the early 1970's a very high fertility
rate, related to high child mortality rates among peasant households,
an early age of marriage, the "universality" of marriage, the absence
of modern contraceptive techniques, and the organisation of agriculture production. Child labour was an essential input into
cultivation and livestock - keeping, and the labour of adult children
was relied upon in old age as well.

In a study of migrant labourers on sisal estates during the late
1950s, Roberts and Tanner (XI:299) found very low fertility rates
and high infant mortality rates. The low fertility rates were partly
explained by a low female ratio and the tendency not to marry, as
well as high divorce rates. However, it was also found that there
was a high infertility rate among married couples, who were unable
to conceive children. Mburu (XI:285) notes that infertility is,
in fact a major problem in Africa. With reference to Sembajwe's
findings noted above, we could therefore ask what the relationship
is between infertility and different class position? The evidence
clearly suggests that the harsh conditions in which peasant and
working class families live and work negatively affect the capacity
to conceive and bear healthy children, and the capacity of their
children to survive. Bantje's investigation of seasonal variations
in birth weight of infants is extremely pertinent here (XI:268). He
found that the labour input of pregnant women in peasant production
was the major cause of low birth weight. This was so, even during
periods of ample food supply. Low birth weight infants also have
higher mortality rates, as shown in items in section XIII below.

There is scope therefore for more research on the effects of
differential labour demands on peasant women and food consumption
on their general health condition, their capacity to conceive and
carry a pregnancy full-term, to deliver safely under the usual home
conditions of delivery, to adequately breast-feed their infants; and
on the birth weights of their infants and their infants general health
condition during the first one to two years of life. Such research
would need to be comparative, with samples of different class
categories of peasant as well as working class and petty bourgeois
women, and include the health services which are available and their
accessibility. For example, Everett (XI:275) found that higher
maternal mortality rates were found in rural hospitals compared to
Ocean Road Hospital in Dar es Salaam. Most of the deaths in the
rural hospitals were due to post-partum bleeding, usually following
home delivery.

Patterns of Sexuality and Fertility in "Precapitalist" Social Relations

The diversity in social relations of sexuality and fertility is
revealed in anthropological and survey research acounts of "precapitalist" relations (XI:268, 272, 273, 277, 284, 286-288, 292,
300, 307, 310, 311). These relations of sexuality and fertility
appear to vary according to different kinds of property relations,
and relations of exploitation, as revealed for example in descriptions of lineage systems and so on. The form and degree of
commoditisation, absorption into long distance trade, and class
formation are also significant factors to consider. For example,
in coastal areas like on Mafia Island, which experienced centuries

of involvement in long-distance trade and commoditisation of production systems, a cognate principle of inheritance and lineage membership developed (XI:272, 273). This meant that inheritance and lineage membership followed the lines of both mother and father. Although conditions made premarital sexual relations for girls very difficult, due to seclusion after puberty, extramarital relations were expected for both women and men. Girls were taught to be sexually active, and sexual intercourse was understood to be a pleasurable activity for women. At the same time, sexual relations were understood to be a commodity relationship, whereby the woman exchanged her sexual services for a payment from men. In the case of marriage, bridewealth represented a payment for access to the wife's sexual services. There was no boy preference, infertility was not considered a major calamity for women, and a large proportion of children were "fostered" by adults other than their biological parents. Divorce rates were also very high.

In comparison, in Bukoba patrilineal society, mechanisms were developed to attempt to ensure the husband's exclusive access to and control over his wife's sexuality and fertility (XI:286, 300). Adulterous practices of wives were punishable by death in several patrilineal groups (e.g. XII:333). In other groups (and sometimes the same), premarital sexual relations were encouraged among girls and boys, but combined with rigid prohibitions against pregnancy (XI:307, 310). Trial marriages were often practiced to ensure the fertility of a new wife; and infertility usually led to divorce (XI:287, 307, 310). Boy preference with regards to offspring was prevalent, and could contribute to either divorce or the selection of an additional wife to produce male heirs.

Analyses of pastoralist sexual practices indicate a complex pattern whereby young pre-puberty girls had love affairs with young warriors, and after marriage to male elders had extramarital relations with warriors of their own age-set (IV:116). Divorce was very unusual. Even in the case of infertility, additional wives provided the desired male heirs. At the same time, clitorectomy was practiced in order to control female sexuality by lowering female sexual desire, according to ideological explanations of the practice (see XIII:377).

In matrilineal groups the girls were controlled by severe seclusion practices which were harsh and "punitive" according to Brain (XI:269). His accounts of the mwali rites are similar to those of other matrilineal groups in the Eastern Zone of Tanzania (III:70), with stress on pleasing the husband. At the same time, women retained important rights to productive property and children, and relatively high divorce rates were found. Clitorectomy was practiced among matrilineal groups in Southeastern and South central zones, but combined with emphasis on the pleasurable nature of sex (XI:277).

In order to explain the different patterns of sexuality and fertility practices described above, it is necessary to relate them to concrete historical analyses of the production systems in which they were situated, and the underlying relations of production. In subsistence economies based on cultivation or livestock - rearing, the biological reproduction of the labour force was as vital to the overall reproduction of the group as production of adequate food (XI:284, 307). The significance of reproduction of human labour, and of control over exchange of women as "reproducers" has been analysed at length by Meillassoux with reference to West African

subsistence economies. The demand for as many offspring as possible
is therefore rooted in the reliance on human labour in particular
forms of production systems. Also at issue however is the reproduction of ownership or control over productive property and living
labour, or producers of living labour (that is, women). Hence the
significance attached to different mechanisms of inheritance both
of property and wives as well as lineage "membership". Understanding
of the development of different mechanisms of control over female
sexuality and fertility needs to be ground in concrete analyses of
specific precapitalist social formations. The Mafia Island case is
quite different, in that production was formerly based on slave
labour and peasant subsistence is more recently based on cash
purchases from proceeds of sale of coconuts and other commodities
as well as subsistence agriculture. Historical analysis is   ·
necessary, however, to clarify, for example, the different sexuality
and fertility practices for the different classes in the slave
production system.

Needless to say, most of the items included in this section have
a tendency to attribute sexuality and fertility practices to
"traditional values" of different tribes, thereby situating them
as cultural characteristics (e.g. XI:287, 288). Alternatively, these
practices are described and not explained; they are taken as "givens".
If one accepts a psychological cultural explanation for sexuality
and fertility, then changing such behaviour becomes a matter of
changing "attitudes", it becomes an educational problem. The
emphasis given to "population" or "family life education" in research
and in government programmes reveals the predominance of a psycho-
cultural analysis of the problem among social scientists and state
functionaries.

Changing Sexuality and Fertility Practices

Several items note major changes taking place in sexuality and
fertility practices or beliefs/ideologies (XI:276, 277, 281, 284,
294, 299, 310). These include fewer polygamous marriages, higher
divorce rates, later ages at first marriage among women, the growing
number of unwed mothers ·and never-married women, as well as
divorced women who remain unmarried "female heads of household",
female adolescent promiscuity and prostitution. Sumra and Omari
(310) record the concern expressed by male elders about the growing
independence of children and youth, who are no longer willing to be
subservient. Parents continue to subvert the state's demand that
all children attend a full seven years of education, especially with
respect to girls (see also section VIII). The reason given by
parents is that schoolgirls are less controllable. They are likely
to refuse to marry the spouse chosen by the father, and from whom
bridewealth has been received, and tend to go to towns and marry or
stay with men of their own choice. The significance of this
rationale is the recognition that schoolgirls are rejecting
patriarchal control over their sexuality and fertility.

The high incidence of induced abortions among young (15-29 years)
married women was attributed by Hathi to growing hostility or
ambivalence towards bearing children (XI:276). Husband - wife
relations and relations with in-laws were other possible explanations.
The objectively worsening conditions of existence for working class

women in towns, be they married or unmarried, could be another and
more potent explanation. The cost of living has risen dramatically.
A working woman depends on milk substitutes and other infant foods
for infant feeding which are either not available or else very
costly. There is a lack of supportive services at home as well
at the workplace to relieve working mothers from some of the burdens
and anxieties of child bearing, nursing sick children, and providing
food and other necessities. The family does not rely on child labour
in the same way that a peasant family does. Children represent a
cost as well as a labour burden. Moreover, marital instability or
conflict in towns combined with economic problems contribute to less
security and may well effect a woman's mental and physical health.
These are lines of possible investigation, oriented not so much
towards the explanation of induced abortions; but rather towards
understanding the changing conditions of existence of working class
women, and their own actions.

Intervention in Sexuality and Fertility by the State and International Agencies

One sign of growing intervention by international agencies in
practices of sexuality and fertility is the number of conferences
and workshops recently held on "population" issues (XI:267, 278, 296,
304, 307, 308). I. Omari (XI:295) rationalises the Tanzanian state's
intervention in biological reproduction by giving examples of the
practices of socialist (China, Czechoslovakia and the USSR) and
African states. In general, a Malthusian analysis of population and
development predominates this work: population growth rates are
growing much too rapidly, and do not match the pace of economic
development. If left uncontrolled, population growth will put an
intolerable strain on the state's capacity to provide basic services.
Unemployment will rise, food scarcity will grow, and political unrest
will be an inevitable outcome (e.g. XI:295 and the World Bank).

Sumra (XI:309) attacks this position and points out that it is
because the poor are poor that they bear as many children as possible.
He notes that the underlying concern of such population programmes
is the revolutionary potential of the massive unemployed and hungry
population which is so rapidly growing in the third world. He also
argues that a socialist approach to population planning would include as a major priority the emancipation of women through control
over their bodies. Sterkenburg and Jonge also reject the argument
that reduction in population growth in itself leads to higher incomes and generally improved economic development (XI:306). They
found that staple crop prices and other economic changes had a
greater impact on per capita income than declines in population
growth rate in Rungwe District.

State intervention in sexuality and fertility has taken several
different forms in Tanzania. The active struggle of the colonial
state and missions to destroy matrilineal systems and transform them
into patrilineal systems is discussed by Hokororo (XI:277) and Huber
(III:77). In each case, the missions expressed disapproval of
female sexual promiscuity, lack of morality (meaning bourgeois
sexual morality), and resulting high divorce rates. Bryceson and
Mbilinyi (II:28, 29) point out the response of the colonial state
to increased adultery cases in labour reserve zones. Special measures

were adopted to attempt to control female sexuality in the context
of the absence of migrant labourers from home and the general breakdown of old patriarchal mechanisms of control. A new set of morals
concerning sex itself was propagated in school curriculum and in
Christian instruction. The former methods of traditional religious
rituals with their heavy sexual component; of explicit sex instruction in puberty rites; premarital sexual relations often associated
with bweni or separate boarding arrangements for unmarried adolescent
boys and girls, and ngoma/dances; and polygamy were all attacked as
"heathen" and "uncivilised". In many Christian missions, an African
could not become "baptized" into the church until she/he renounced
all such practices and showed through her/his behaviour that she/he
had accepted the bourgeois morality underlying Christian concepts
of sexuality and fertility. Failure to follow the acceptable
practices led to the threat of excommunication from the Church,
with social and economic consequences for those so affected (see
section III). Great concern is expressed in colonial files over
the effect of "urbanisation" (i.e. proletariation) on marital
stability. More research is necessary to establish the concrete
measures taken by the colonial state and missions to construct a
new, bourgeois morality (see Corrigan and Sayer's 1981 analysis of
the significance of bourgeois struggles to construct a new,
bourgeois morality; Lasch's 1977 analysis of state intervention
in reproduction and the reconstruction of the family).

The post-colonial state intervenes far more actively. For
example, contraceptive services are available free to members of
UMATI, the national family planning organisation. UMATI operates
through the state Maternal and Child Health Services, and provides
"family life" education as well as contraceptive devices, regular
medical check-ups and assistance in cases of infertility (XI:282,
290, 293, 313, 317). The emphasis in their literature is placed
on child spacing, in order to safeguard the health of the mother
and the children. This is related to the negative impact of frequent
child bearing, which not only weakens the woman's health, and leads
to greater risks for the unborn infant; but also stops the lactation
process so that the youngest infant can no longer breast-feed. Child
spacing is also linked to reduction in total numbers of offspring in
order to improve a family's economic capacity to provide for each
child's needs (see UMATI materials, XI:313, 317). A similar rationale
for child spacing is adopted by the materials produced under the PMO
Population/Family Life Education Project oriented to village-level
mass education (XI:267, 296). The UMATI materials, like similar
products of the CCT and the Catholic Church, also stress bourgeois
morality with respect to sexuality, similar to the line adopted
during the colonial period.

Research has been conducted to find out the attitudes of different
groups to modern "family life" education and contraceptive practices
(XI:282, 287, 288, 292, 310). Most of the studies have said that
both young people and adults, including peasants, express their
desire for sex education to be taught in the schools. The major
issue is that of age, and whether it should be taught in coed or
in single sex groups. The authors note that young people are already engaging in sexual intercourse, often in ignorance of conception and contraception, and that parents are particularly concerned
about the rise in expulsion of pregnant schoolgirls at primary and

secondary levels. It could be however, that there are different
concepts of the purpose, content of and form which family life
education should take. One approach is to stress knowledge about
conception and the unfortunate consequences of unwanted pregnancy,
in order to discourage premarital sexual relations among girls.
Another is to stress information about conception and contraception as well as provision of contraceptives in order to increase
a woman's power to make decisions. Rarely is family life education
perceived to include explicit sex instruction, as found in mwali
rites, or to emphasise the pleasurable aspects of sexual relations
(XI:271).

The Tanzanian state has intervened in practices of sexuality and
fertility in more indirect ways as well, outlined by Sumra (XI:309)
and others. Maternity leave benefits provide married and unmarried
women with three months paid leave, with security of job and
position. These benefits are restricted to three - year periods.
Tax allowances for children are limited to four children or less.
The legal age limit for marriage for girls is fifteen years, which
can be reduced to fourteen years in certain cases; and eighteen
years for boys. In Zanzibar, married girls are expected to continue
their primary and secondary schooling, and they cannot be withdrawn
from school to get married. On the Mainland, a girl cannot legally
be withdrawn from school to get married, but no pronounced position
has been taken concerning marriage while in school. A pregnant
schoolgirl on the mainland is automatically expelled from school,
with no effective punitive action taken against the father of her
child, as found in Zanzibar in the case of unmarried girls.
Schooling regulations on the mainland appear to aim at delaying
marriage until after completion of schooling, be it 7 years of
primary or an additional 4 years of secondary (by which time a girl
would be at least 18 years of age).

Social Reproduction

Several items included in this section and elsewhere argue that the
control over biological reproduction is a fundamental aspect of
women's subordination and of the reproduction of social relations
of production (XI:270, 284, 287, 309, 318; II:29, 35). The latter
refers to social reproduction. In their analysis of women's role
in economic development in third world countries including Africa,
Beneria and Sen argue that "in order to control social reproduction
- through inheritance systems for example - most societies have
developed different forms of control over female sexuality and over
women's reproductive activities, and that this control is at the
root of women's subordination" (Beneria and Sen 1980: n. 18).

The problem of (control over) sexuality and fertility needs to
be related to the different ways in which women and men produce
their subsistence, and reproduce the necessary conditions of
production. Human labour is a universally necessary condition of
production, and the reproduction of any society depends on the
reproduction of human labour. As noted earlier, in precapitalist
societies production was primarily based on the input of human
(living) labour. Maintenance and expansion of society depended on
the accumulation of human labour. Mechanisms of control over
sexuality and fertility indicate major pressure to increase fertility

by accumulating more women as wives. The forms of control varied
however, given different historical material conditions of existence.
Capitalist relations have not only led to a revolutionary transformation of technology and the overall organisation of the labour process,
so that "dead labour" or machines takes the place of living labour
in the production process. Capitalist relations have also transformed
the technology of health and fertility. Greater human capacity to
counteract disease and promote physical health is matched by the
capacity to control conception with contraceptive devices. The mass
distribution of contraceptives and birth control practices is a
recent phenomenon of the last two decades in the developed capitalist
countries. Moreover, the technical capacity now exists to replace
women as "producers" of offspring by machinery (test-tube babies).
The issue therefore becomes one of who controls sexuality and
fertility. In whose interests? If population issues and programmes
are separated from those having to do with the emancipation of women
(and men), then forms of state intervention are likely to become
manipulative and oppressive. Much more research is necessary on
the whole question of sexuality and fertility, to be posed as a
materialist problem of analysis.

That control over fertility is an issue for peasant women has
been emphasised in recent research in Morogoro villages by Oomen-
Myin (IV:119, 120). The majority of peasant women argued that the
major constraint on production was the burden of child - bearing
and child - rearing, having too many children. They scoffed at the
idea that peasant women do not want to use modern contraceptives,
and said those city - dwellers saying such things don't know about
the conditions in the rural areas, they should come to the villages
and see for themselves. They said that the problem was not that
peasant women did not want contraceptives, but rather that the
contraceptives were not available to them.

REFERENCES

Lourdes Beneria and Gita Sen (1980), "Accumulation, Reproduction
    and Women's Role in Economic Development: Boserup Revisited".
    Paper presented to Burg Wartenstein Symposium No. 85. "The
    Sex Division of Labour, Development, and Women's Status",
    August 2-10.

Philip Corrigan and Dered Sayer (1981), "The Real Peculiarities
    of the English: Once Again on Capitalism, State Formation and
    Cultural Relations". Paper presented to History Department
    Seminar Series, July 30th, University of Dar es Salaam.

Christopher Lasch (1977), Haven in a Heartless World, The Family
    Besieged. New York, Basic Books, Inc.

Claude Meillassoux (1978), "The Social Organisation of the
    Peasantry: The Economic Basis of Kinship" and "Kinship
    Relations of Production" in David Setton (ed.); Relations of
    Production: Marxist Approaches to Economic Anthropology.
    London, Frank Cass.

267. ABBAS, ELMA R.D. (1980), "Population and Family Life Education
in Integrated Rural Development". ECA National Seminar on
Population and Development, Arusha, 17-24 February, 17 pp.

Presents the overall rationale for the population/family life
education project situated within three regions, Morogoro,
Kilimanjaro and Mara under the Prime Minister's Office. The
need for an integrated approach is stressed which focuses on
rural development. The objectives of family life education
are as follows:

1. to explain the health and welfare value of child spacing
   to family members;

2. to explain the biological and social aspects of sex and
   marriage with a view to improving marital relations and
   family health;

3. to discuss the laws and customs relating to marriage,
   inheritance and adoption within the community;

4. to discuss the types and prevention of sexually transmitted
   diseases and their relationship to fertility;

5. to exercise responsible parenthood by example.

Stress is laid throughout on the need to maintain the family as
the pivot of development. Different strategies of integrating
population/family life education into basic education programmes
are evaluated.
    This represents the more enlightened, sophisticated approach to
the whole question of population education, but does not raise
such issues as the contradictory nature of transformed
patriarchal relations in peasant households today which operate
to subordinate women and children, nor the question of underlying exploitative relations which explain both high fertility
rates and high mortality rates among the Tanzanian population.
See XI:297, 298, below for products of this project.

268. BANTJE, HAN (1980), "Seasonal Variations in Birthweight
Distribution in Ikwiriri Village". BRALUP Research Paper, No. 43
(new Series), Dar es Salaam, University of Dar es Salaam. 23 pp.

Examines seasonal variations in birth weight distribution over a
seven-year period in Ikwiriri and correlates these with rainfall,
female labour output in agriculture and food availability. The
findings revealed that average birth weight responds to the
combined intensity of labour output and food availability. It
was also discovered that changes in average birth weight were
very sudden so that birth weight was affected by conditions even
as late as just before delivery. This was very significant since
women tend to work almost to the onset of labour pains. The data
also revealed that even when food was plentiful but agricultural
labour was also demanding, low birth weight were more common.
Alternatively, when food was low due to bad harvests but with
resulting low level of agricultural acitivity, birth weights
tended to be high. The paper therefore concludes that labour
output is the more dominant variable affecting birth weight, and
that availability of food would be the more dominant factor only

if food scarcity was a prolonged phenomenon.

The implications of this study are obvious. Low birth weights
are one of the chief causes of infant mortality. If low birth
weights are so significantly affected by the mothers' labour
output, there is a great need to look into the sexual division
of labour at the household level.

269. BRAIN, JAMES L. (1978), "Symbolic Rebirth: The Mwali Rite Among
the Luguru of Eastern Tanzania". Africa, 48 (2): 176.188,
biblio.

Beginning with a useful brief description of the historical
development of the Luguru, including slave relations and
matrilineal relations, the article goes on to give a detailed
account of seclusion and coming out rituals of young girls. The
analysis clarifies the contradiction between matrilineal relations at the level of the "tribe", "clan" and "lineage" and
patriarch relations at the level of the homestead. It is
worthwhile to quote at length the effects of the initiation
rites: "(1) To clarify status and ease the transition through
the symbolically dangerous liminal period of adolescence,
(2) To clarify male and female roles, (3) To give instruction
in traditional lore and sexual conduct, (4) To prevent any
possibility that women might gain a dominant position, (5) To
uphold the authority of older women over younger, and to
emphasise the subservience of all women to all men, using the
mystical authority of the male ancestors to buttress this".

An otherwise enlightening analysis is marred by the
author's reliance on psychologism to explain the origins of
such rites in "male envy of female procreativity". He goes to
great lengths to prove his theory with illustrations from the
rites, but the same illustrations could be explained as efforts
to emphasise over and over again the subservient and dependent
position of women towards men.

270. BRYCESON, DEBORAH FAHY and ULLA VUORELA (1980), "Outside the
Domestic Labour Debate: Towards up Materialist Theory of Modes
of Human Reproduction". University of Dar es Salaam: Paper
presented to the BRALUP Seminar, 40 pp.

A very provocative and controversial analysis which argues for
the development of a concept of modes of human reproduction in
order to explain women's oppression within different epochs
and different modes of production. Begins with a critique of
Maxine Molyneux's "Beyond the Domestic Labour Debate" (1979,
New Left Review), analyses some of the major problematiques
of the women's question and then builds up the argument for
modes of human reproduction. The concept is then used to analyse
and explain the sexual division of labour and alienation of
women. The articulation of the mode of production and the mode
of human reproduction is analysed in the context of articulated
precapitalist and capitalist modes of production in the third
world, using diagrams to illustrate the argument.

This paper raises fundamental questions about women's
subordination although the "leap" towards adoption of the concept
mode of human reproduction, is highly problematic. The paper
errs towards over-generalisation and the adoption of a trans-

historical analysis of women's oppression. It ignores recent
developments towards a materialist analysis of precapitalist
and capitalist relations in Tanzania and elsewhere which
emphasise analyses of concrete, specific social formations.
Nevertheless, it is an extremely important contribution towards
the development of theory adequate to explore the women's
question in the Tanzanian context.

271. BWATWA, Y.D.M. (1981), "Sex Education in Tanzania Primary
Schools", in S. Sumra (ed.), Final Report, Workshop on Population, Education and Curriculum Changes, Arusha, 15-20 December,
1980. University of Dar es Salaam, Department of Education,
bound mimeo: 208-239.

Summarises basic arguments for sex education in Tanzanian
primary schools, including the growing rate of expulsion of
girls from schools because of pregnancy.

272. CAPLAN, A.P. (1976), "Boys' Circumcision and Girls' Puberty
Rites Among the Swahili of Mafia Island, Tanzania". Africa,
46 (1), pp. 21-33.

The similarities of the two sets of rites are stressed by the
author. However, the descriptions indicate different content,
especially concerning the issue of social relations of subordination within the marriage. For example, a girl is taught
in unyago how to conduct herself during menstruation, so as
not to "endanger" her husband and others with her "dangerous"
blood. She is also taught never to refuse her husband sexually,
"nor to gossip about his sexual behaviour". Caplan compares
the more ritual nature of the male unyago and suggests that the
boys' rite is more "transformative" since his status has changed
from being an uncircumcised to a circumcised boy. The girls'
rites are merely "confirmatory" of her "status as a young
marriageable woman, a status which physiologically she has
already achieved". One could go further, and argue that the
male rite expresses a transformation from child to adult male,
whereas women do not undergo such a transformation because of
their "minor" juridical position, always a child to be represented
by adult males. Two major themes dominate both the male and
female unyago: sexuality and cognate descent (see item 295 on
the significance of cognate descent). Girls and boys are both
taught to be sexually active and encouraged to have extra-marital
relations. Stress is on the pleasurable aspects of sex, and not
the reproductive, "fertility" aspect. However, they are also
taught that sexual relations is one of exchange, whereby the
woman exchanges her sexual services for commodities including
bridewealth   presented by the male partner.
   The analysis of the politics of practicing unyago by different
groups in the village power structure is also important. The
significance of "cultural" practices in constructing power or
class relations is made clear in a concrete way.

273. CAPLAN, PATRICIA (1978), "The Swahili of Chole Island, Tanzania",
in Anne Sutherland (ed.), Face Values, Some Anthropological Themes.
London, British Broadcasting Corporation, pp. 140-175.

An anthropologic account based on a case study of Kanga Village
on Mafia (Chole) Island. The Mafia lineage pattern is <u>cognate</u>,
meaning that inheritance lines run along both the husband's
(father) and wife's (mother) set of relations. The complex set
of social relations based in part on the six major descent
groups as well as different processes of class differentiation
and gender relations are analysed. The article is particularly
rich in information about relations of sexuality and fertility.
The prevalent practice of fostering children; sex differentiation
in traditional educational practices, including circumcision
practices for boys and puberty rituals and seclusion of girls;
marriage and bridewealth practices; divorce (which is high);
childbirth and child-rearing practices - details are given on
all of these areas. There is also discussion of spirit
possession curative practices, usually dominated by male elders.
The property relations based on cognate lineage principles
combined with Islamic law mean that women have independent
access to productive property, and there is no boy preference
with regards to fertility. Rigid sex differentiation in
particular spheres of production and reproduction and the
subordination of women in terms, for example, of household
social relations, suggest that more research is needed to
clarify the material basis of female subordination. This text
is based on a BBC series, and includes photographic illustrations
taken from it. The photos often speak louder than the words;
particularly in portraying the sexual division of labour.

274. CULWICK, A.T. and A.M. CULWICK (1936), "Fostermothers in
Ulanga". TNR, No. 1 (April): 19-24.

The means by which Ulanga women are able to induce artificial
lactation in middle-aged women are explored. The need historically arose in the case of a deceased mother of a new-born infant,
or her illness or otherwise inability to nurse. The procedure
includes the use of particular herbs as ointment on the breasts
and a combination of herbs, spices and other ingredients in a
special soup to be consumed in large quantities by the foster
mother.

275. EVERETT, V.J (1979), "Maternal Mortality in Tanzania". Dar es
Salaam Medical Journal, Vol. 6, No. 1, p. 7-8.

Forms requesting particulars of maternal deaths occurring in
1972/73 and their causes were distributed to over 100 government
and voluntary agency hospitals in Tanzania. The results of 45
of these hospitals are presented, together with those from Ocean
Road Hospital, for the same two-year period. The findings
revealed that rural hospitals had a high mortality rate of 4.8
per 1000 deliveries, compared to 1.8 at Ocean Road Hospital.
The causes of death are discussed and some geographical correlation has been noted. Most of the deaths in the rural
hospitals were due to post-partum bleeding and in many cases
the women were brought in a serious condition after having
delivered at home. Most of the cases could have been prevented
by early and efficient hospital care, adequate blood transfusions
and good intrapartum management. Anemia was considered to be
the direct cause of death of 35 women and also affected deaths

from hemorrhage. The study points out these deaths are
preventable through better transport facilities, better
attendance of antenatal clinics, and improved hospitals (These
recommendations in turn, cannot be discussed outside the socio-
economic context of the Tanzanian society today).

276. HATHI, J.G. (1979), "Medical Factors Associated with Abortions
at Muhimbili Medical Centre (June 1978)". Paper No. 41, BW,
7 pp.

Induced and spontaneous abortions rank as first among the top ten
causes of admission in gynecology wards at Muhimbili and formed
55 % of admissions in 1977. The majority of these were presumed
to have been induced illegally, and are categorised in practice
as "incomplete" abortions. Three-quarters of these were found
between the ages of fifteen and twenty-nine years. Where marital
status was recorded, all unmarried women were found in this
"incomplete" category, comprising nearly one-fourth of the total
number here. Given social and economic sanctions against unwed
motherhood, one would have expected a larger percentage. The
fact that about 70 % of incomplete abortions and all threatened
abortions occurred among married women reveals the ambivalence and
hostility many women feel towards bearing children, which is
affected by hostility towards their husbands or their family
situation. A possible relation may exist between careless and
unprofessionally induced abortion and later spontaneous abortion,
thus affecting the woman's capacity to bear healthy children
later. Women must "struggle for universal contraception and
for legalising abortions in public hospitals".

277. HOKORORO, A.M. (1960), "The Influence of the Church on Tribal
Customs at Lukuledi". TNR, No. 54 (March): 1-13.

The Lukuledi Mission practiced among Wamwera, Wayao and Wamakua,
all matrilineal peoples experiencing pressure towards becoming
patrilineal. The article focuses on female initiation and
circumcision, the ceremony at the time of first conception or
pregnancy, and marriage customs in general. Clitorectomy was
practiced, and sometimes deformation of the labia minora, which
led to lessened sexual pleasure for women and presumedly greater
sexual control over women as a result. The ceremony during the
first pregnancy provides the young woman with education about
child birth, with emphasis on the pain to be anticipated.
Understanding that women have an active desire for sex is
revealed in the ceremonial dance and songs which imitate sexual
intercourse and delivery. Marriage was ordinarily preceded by
an experimental period of sleeping together, followed by the
potential groom's period of labour service and "trials" to prove
himself to the wife's family and particularly her maternal
uncle. Outlines the church's selective approval and disapproval
of different procedures and customs, which tended to reflect
patriarchist values and puritanical bourgeois notions of sex.
There was constant struggle by the church to uphold the power
of the husband versus the traditional power and control of the
maternal uncle or wife's brother.

278. ILO and UNFPA, National Symposium on Population and Development, Tanga, Tanzania, 14-20 October, 1974. Report, Dar es Salaam, 133 pp.

Discusses the country's population trends in relationship to economic development and family welfare. One of the papers deals with the organization and work of the Tanzania Family Planning Association (UMATI).

279. JONGE, KLAAS (1974), "Fertility: Dependable Variable, a Case Study of a Rural Area in Tanzania". Kronick van Afrika, 1974/1. Special Issue: 61-71, Leiden, Afrika Studiecentrum.

Data from a demographic survey in Rungwe involving 496 households was used to show the inter-relationship of socio-economic development and attitudes towards fertility control. The findings revealed that Rungwe had a high fertility due to the following factors: young age at first marriage; universal character of marriage; short interval before remarrying; absence of the use of modern contraceptive techniques; and the desire for many children. The findings also revealed that the desire for a large number of children was linked to the high rate of child mortality and to the current agricultural practices in the region.

280. KABAGAMBE, JOHN C. (1979), "Demographic Trends and Family Planning in Africa". Africa Link, July: 4-8.

Examines demographic trends and population and family planning policies in 18 African countries in the IPPF Africa Region. Tanzania is one of the countries covered. The findings reveal that in almost all the African countries surveyed, family planning is permitted and practised. In Tanzania, the government encourages family planning.

281. KOCHER, JAMES E. (1976), "Social, Economic and Demographic Characteristics of some Rural Areas in Lushoto and Moshi Districts". University of Dar es Salaam, BRALUP Research Paper No. 44, 82 pp.

Comparative analyses of changing demographic patterns and family structures in four rural areas, Bumbuli and Soni of Lushoto and Kibosho and Vunjo of Moshi. Vunjo is the most "modern" according to such indicators as age of women's first marriage, incidence of polygamy, educational attainment, type of prenatal care, where babies are delivered, changes in breast-feeding practices, perceptions about changes in infant and child mortality rates, desire for smaller families and participation in new technology. According to such indicators, Bumbuli is the least modern and has the lowest "material well-being". Information is provided about significant and objectively real changes taking place in relations of sexuality and fertility. Valuable as the data produced in this survey is, the techniques of data interpretation and shallowness of explanation are a problem. For example, the so-called indicators of modernity are a random cluster of statistics which have been found clustered together in one sample. What is called modern is clearly what shows signs of "development", with the concept of modernity or development non-problematised. Underlying the indicators has been a historical process of commoditisation which has transformed social relations in Moshi. The differential nature of precapitalist social relations and the different processes of transformation which may/ may not have occurred in these four specific localities require analysis in order to explain the phenomena measured in the survey.

282. MAKOBWE, KELLEN MPONGULIANA (1975), Towards Family Life Education in Tanzanian Schools: Possibilities and Constraints. University of Dar es Salaam, unpublished M.A. dissertation, 295 pp. biblio.

The aim of the research was to explore the possibilities and constraints of introducing Family Life (FL) Education into the school curriculum. Samples of youth and adults were interviewed or responded to questionnaires in Ngara and Kisarawe Districts and in Dar es Salaam about a wide range of related topics. A combination of short-answer and probing questions allowed for in-depth information on such questions as amount of information already acquired, source of information, opinions towards having family life education taught in school, what level of schooling preferred, what its content should be. By combining literature citations with anecdotal information derived from interviews and responses on the questionnaires, the author presents a very readable and informative account of issues related to the biological reproduction function of women.

   Among the important findings of the study were (1) a very positive reaction to having FL Education in Schools, but concern about having it taught at primary school level, (2) home is not adequate as the sole place for FL education, (3) despite concern about teaching young people or primary school children FL education, a large proportion are already engaged in sexual intercourse, often in ignorance of how to prevent unwanted pregnancies, (4) the problem not only of unwanted pregnancies but of adequate knowledge about sexuality itself was noted to be a significant problem area for all age groups and sexes, in urban and rural areas. Contrary to the stereotyped assumption of peasant conservatism, the vast majority of peasants wanted family life education taught at primary school level upwards. Based on her analysis of different aspects of the problem, the author calls for the development of family life education in schools at all levels. Useful ideas are provided on how it should be taught and what content it should have, derived from the views of the people surveyed.

283. MAMUYA, S.J. (n.d.), Uzazi wa Majira. Dar es Salaam, UMATI, 35 pp.

A simple illustrated handbook explaining the advantages of child spacing and the disadvantages of too frequent pregnancies. A short explanation of why some mothers still have frequent pregnancies is given. Also included are brief notes on the types of modern contraceptives available, their use and how they prevent pregnancies.

284. MBILINYI, MARJORIE (1980), "The Problem of Sexuality and
     Fertility among Female Youth". Paper presented to IDS Staff
     Seminar series, 21st November, University of Dar es Salaam and
     to Workshop on Population Education and Curriculum Changes,
     Arusha, UNESCO, 15-20 December 1980; published in proceedings
     of the Arusha Workshop edited by Suleman Sumra, and in Cuthbert
     K. Omari (ed.), Adolescents and Youth Problems in Tanzania,
     proceedings of workshop of the National Council of Social
     Welfare Services, Moshi, 21st - 27th September 1980; 30 pp.

Relations of sexuality and fertility are posed in relation to
the relations of production within which peasant and working
class women are situated. The significance of the problem of
reproduction is posed, including biological reproduction,
reproduction of the labour force on a daily basis, and social
reproduction. The conflicting demands of sexuality and
fertility made by patriarchal and capitalist relations are
investigated through historical analyses of patriarchal
relations and their subjugation to capitalist relations.
Demographic trends are related to the growing public concern
about "misbehaviour" and promiscuity among female youth. The
high marital and fertility rate of girls aged 15 to 19 years
indicates that such concern must in turn be questioned (half
of the girls in this age groups have been married at least
once). The problem expressed by this public issue is related to
the breakdown of patriarchal (and state) control over girls
and women, as well as male youth, though that does not lead
to the same "alarm".
     Explores the question of socialist morality in sexual
relations: "Is there a socialist sexuality where two human
beings share in a mutually pleasurable and beneficial relationship, a non-oppressive relationship?" Argues that "it is
impossible to practice socialist relations of sexuality under
present conditions of patriarchal and capitalist domination
over sexuality ... It is necessary however for men and women
committed to socialist struggle for women's liberation to
engage together in this analysis of the question of sexuality
and fertility, lest the issue be taken out of our hands
altogether".

285. MBURU, F.M. (1980), "Infertility: The Indelible Cause in Africa".
     Africa Link: 14-15.

Describes the background to the IPPF project on infertility
involving 6 countries in sub-Saharan Africa, Tanzania being one
of the six. Argues that infertility is one of the major
fertility problems in many African countries. In the project
countries primary infertility is as high as 10 % - 15 % while
secondary infertility is 15 % to 25 %. Causes of infertility
and the exact definition of infertility in the African context
are also discussed.

286. MOLLER, M.S.C. (Dr.) (1958), "Bahaya Customs and Beliefs in
     Connection with Pregnancy and Childbirth". TNR, No. 50 (June):
     112-117.

Various customs surrounding the period of time after marriage and before the birth of the first child, and during pregnancy and childbirth itself, performed to protect the interests of the husband's lineage in ensuring its biological reproduction. For example, the bride of seventeen or eighteen years was secluded until the birth of her first child to control sexual access to her person. The first individual to be informed of her pregnancy was her mother-in-law, not her husband or her own mother. There were multitudinous food and other taboos ostensibly to ensure a safe delivery, though some reinforced the fact that women did not have access to meat which remained food for the male patriarchs. The skills and knowledge of local midwives about pregnancy and delivery are shown.

287. MOLNOS, ANGELA (1968), Attitudes Towards Family Planning in East Africa. Munich, Institut für Wirtschaftsforschung. Afrika-Studien, no. 26. 414 pp.

Presents the traditional and present position and role of women among the Ganda, Kikuyu, Luo and Sukuma, and current attitudes to children and family planning among 2,648 pupils of 43 primary and secondary schools in rural and urban areas around Lake Victoria and in Nairobi. The possible influence of religious beliefs, both traditional and new are also discussed. Major factors which seem to correlate with attitudes towards family planning are education, ethnic origin, actual living conditions and exposure to information about modern birth control techniques. Also includes suggestions for a psychological approach to family planning promotions.

288. MOLNOS, ANGELA (1972-73), Cultural Source Materials for Population Planning in East Africa. Nairobi, East African Publishing House, 4 volumes.

Vol. 1. Review of Cultural Research. 1952-1972, 335 pp. Rewiews social science research relevant to fertility carried out between 1952-1972 in Kenya, Tanzania and Uganda and describes the author's own survey during 1970-72 among social anthropologists who worked in East Africa. The survey covered 28 ethnic groups including for Tanzania, the Haya, Sukuma, Nyamwezi, Nyakyusa, Kaguru and Chagga. Research action and priorities are also identified.

Vol. II Innovations and Communications. 396 pp. Discusses factors that affect "innovations and communications".

Vol. III Beliefs and Practices. Deals with beliefs and practices covering sex, marriage, conception, pregnancy, child-rearing, and value of children, for the 28 ethnic groups covered by the survey.

Vol. IV Bibliography. Bibliography of writings on the 28 ethnic groups. The emphasis is on topics more closely related to the socio-cultural background to fertility, population trends and population planning such as health and nutrition, education and training, urban problems, traditional beliefs and practices concerning sex, marriage, kinship, family and children, customary law, and modern legislation, psychology, mass media and communication.

289. MONSTED, METTE and PARVEEN WALJI (1978), A Demographic Analysis of East Africa: A Sociological Interpretation. Uppsala, Scandinavian Institute of African Studies, 211 pp.

A wide range of demographic aspects of the population of East Africa are covered. These include: Source and nature of demographic data, age/sex distribution, rural/urban distribution, factors affecting mortality, nunptuality, fertility, migration, age/sex structure of the labour force, dependency ratio and socio-economic rural/urban differentials. For each aspect, the authors use examples from Kenya and Tanzania.
   The Tanzania data is based mainly on volume six of the Population Census, 1967 edited by R. Henin and B. Egero.

290. MUZE, SIPHIWE (1979), "Family Life Education: A Growing Need in Tanzania". Paper No. 21, BW 4 pp.

An integrated programme of family life education (FLE) is needed to be inserted in existing school curricula and in seminar programmes run by relevant organisations. Youth and parents should be involved in setting up FLE from the planning stage to implementation. The objectives include development and prep-aration for the rights and responsibilities of adults; develop-ment of communication, evaluation and decision-making skills; overcoming anxiety and fallacies concerning sexual development; providing knowledge and understanding concerning sexual parental and civic responsibility.

291. NGALLABA, SYLVESTER A.M. (1980), "Review of Population Situation in Tanzania". ECA National Seminar on Population and Development, Arusha, 17-24 February, 19 pp.

Provides vital statistics drawn from the 1978 Population Census, including fertility rates, distribution of population by age and sex, regional sex ratios, population growth and regional growth rates. The census procedures adopted in 1978 are also described.

292. NGUMA, JUSTIN KAZYAMEKA (1976), Attitudes of Parents Towards Family Planning. University of Dar es Salaam, unpublished M.A. dissertation, 136 pp.

Attempts to find the reasons behind the slow progress in the acceptance of modern methods of family planning among Tanzanian parents. The area of study is Bagamoyo District. Among the reasons discussed are traditional attitudes towards fertility and children, religious prejudices towards birth control and the current programmes for dissemination of knowledge about birth control devices. Traditional methods of child spacing and birth control are also described. These methods were traditionally taught to young girls before their marriages. Monogamy and urbanisation are slowly eroding these practices. At the same time resistance to modern methods leads to women having children at very short intervals and thus causing serious health problems to both mother and child.

293. NTUYABALIWE, E.N. (1975), "Child Spacing in Tanzania". In: The Ten Top Childhood Diseases and Child Health Priorities, Volume I. Dar es Salaam, Department of Child Health, University of Dar es Salaam, p. 45-54.

Describes the organization, function and work of UMATI (The Family Planning Association of Tanzania). Its main failing is lack of information about its services as well as a lack of evaluation of the support of its services on child spacing in Tanzania. Suggests that Family Planning should be introduced in school curricula as one possible way of strengthening the information services of UMATI.

294. OMARI, C.K. (1980), Some Aspects of Family Life Education in African Society: The Tanzania Case. University of Dar es Salaam, Department of Sociology, bound mimeo, 90 pp.

Based on a survey of 1,188 men and women in five regions, the research report covers such issues as changing family structures, family size and fertility control, contraception for youth and married women and family life education. Adds little to the knowledge already provided in the reports of the national demographic surveys. However, some of the information such as knowledge about and use of family planning services is useful. The sample is a more educated population than that of the nation, and not representative. At the same time, information about changing patterns of sexuality and fertility among primary school and secondary school graduates is valuable.

The author's own views on various controversial issues are stated in a straight-forward way, and are significant given his position as head of the National Council of Social Welfare Services and Professor of Sociology. For example, on the question of provision of information about contraceptives and contraceptive services to young boys and girls, he asks: "Is it right to refuse the youths the services of family planning and instead expel them from school because of resultant pregnancies? And is it justifiable to let a child be born to a girl when she is not yet able to care for it?"

295. OMARI, I.M. (1981), "Revamping Teacher Education Through Population Education: New Dimensions for Increasing Responsiveness to Current Human Needs". In S. Sumra (ed.) Final Report, Workshop on Population, Education and Curriculum Changes, Arusha, 15-20 December, 1980. University of Dar es Salaam, Department of Education, bound mimeo, pp. 240-287.

Provides examples of state intervention to control fertility in China, Czechoslovakia, USSR, and selected African countries to back up his argument that population is a development issue and that development is a population issue. "Influx of school leavers into towns is creating slums and unemployment" is the style of argument adopted, which ends up attributing problems of poverty and proletariation to high birth rates, rather than the other way around. As argued elsewhere, the problems of development in Tanzania are a product of underlying exploitative relations at national and international levels. In this case, the poor have as many children as possible because they are poor, and rely on their children's labour for subsistence production and/or their earnings as wage labourers, etc.

296. PRIME MINISTER'S OFFICE (1981), "Population/Family Life
     Education Manual" draft, Population/Family Life Education,
     Communication and Applied Research in Integrated Rural
     Development UNFPA/URT 701, Arusha, 69 pp.

The manual is to be used in training village-level cadres who
will integrate population/family life education into the
curriculum of adult education, cooperative education and
agriculture extension in their village-level work in three
regions of Tanzania, Kilimanjaro, Musoma and Morogoro. The
manual will be used in pre-service institutional training
and will also become a village-level resource. Presents socio-
economic factors related to family size and other population
factors, and the dynamics of change in peasant production and
reproduction with growing commoditisation. The sexual division
of labour and the significance of child labour in production
are analysed, together with the impact of villagisation. The
nature of different demographic measures and their use at local
and national levels are described as well. Examines human
growth and development, with a straight-forward description of
basic physiological changes during puberty for women and men,
the nature of conception, practical guidelines on home delivery
in the village, and child development. Discusses basic
conditions for family health such as safe and clean water,
nutrition, and the major health problems which contribute to
high infant mortality and which are subject to preventable
measures.
     Presents a conservative view of family structure complete
with the male head of the household. However, the growth of
female-headed households is noted, as well as the way many
former family responsibilities are now being taken over by the
village government and the state as a whole, like education,
and health. The advantages of child spacing are presented,
with stress on the health of mother and infant and the changing
significance of children in peasant household production and
reproduction. Family Management outlines basic significance
of human labour as being a fundamental aspect of production.
Included are family budgeting and joint-decision making about
incomes and expenditures.
     The manual is an important contribution towards the develop-
ment of literature oriented to villagers and village-level cadres
which raise issues of sexual relations in the context of
changing social relations as a whole. It also provides much
needed information about physiological changes and biological
reproduction and family health. However, there are no
references to capitalist exploitation outside of the colonial
context. The stress is on stated objectives with respect to
the villagisation programme rather than practices. It is
accompanied by several giant photo books or poster books as
well as poster, cassette and slide show programmes and a film
series. The poster books and posters will be invaluable visual
aids at village level (297, 298 are examples).

297. PRIME MINISTER'S OFFICE (n.d.), Gharama ya Kila Mtoto
     Anayeongezeka. Tanzania na FAO kwa Msaada wa UNFPA, 20 pp.

One of the series of seven photo books referred to in item 318, this is the only one using coloured illustrations. The theme is the rising costs of child-bearing and child-rearing, related to standards of living which seem decidedly middle-class (re: clothing, furniture, etc.) in the Tanzanian context. The argument is to plan families wisely so children can be cared for adequately, since children (and pregnancy) are so costly.

298. PRIME MINISTER'S OFFICE (n.d.), Siku Baada ya Siku. Tanzania and FAO with Assistance from UNFPA, 13 pp.

Laid out like still-life photos from a cinema with fifty-four pictures, this tells the story of two factory workers, Ali Omari and his wife Margaret. Ali tells the story about work conditions, family budgeting and joint decision-making and family planning. Every day he foregoes a canteen lunch so that Margaret can have a proper lunch of ugali and meat each day at the subsidized price. The two share household duties at home, with Ali taking over child care while Margaret cooks dinner, and both participating in feeding and putting to bed the two children at home. Ali notes how tired Margaret is, and worries about her getting pregnant again. Their three children, aged six, four and two, are already a lot to take care of, and their mother has low blood pressure. In the end they decide to go to UMATI for advice and services of family planning.

299. ROBERTS, D.F. and TANNER, R.E.S. (1959), "A Demographic Study in Low Fertility in N.E. Tanganyika". Population Studies, V. 15, pp. 61-80.

Three villages in Pangani District with varying distances from large sisal estates were selected to study the extent of infertility in the area and identify factors responsible for it. The demographic characteristics showed that infertility was high specially in the village that was dependent on the estates. Average number of children was as low as 1.82 with the highest average being 2.05. Reasons for the infertility are: (1) excess of immigrants specially male, resulting in a high male/female ratio, (2) tendency to refrain from marriage, (3) marriage instability, (4) high infant mortality, and (5) the high proportion of infertile marriages.

Instability of marriages was very high. In one village about fifty per cent were terminated within the first five years; of the rest about half were terminated before the 10th year. The chief reason for marriage instability was the attitude of men towards women. In addition, men were accused of not providing for the women's material needs as required by tradition and Islam, even though the women were contributing towards the maintenance of the household through their production of rice and cassava.

300. RWIZA, K.J. (1958), "Natal Customs in Bukoba". TNR, No. 50 (June): 104-105.

Ritual sanctions are depended upon to ensure the husband's paternity of a newly born child, a theme found in Moller (item 286) as well. The husband's exclusive sexual access to his wife is the major issue.

301. SEMBAJWE, ISRAEL S.L. (1973), Impact of Urbanization on Fertility and Child Mortality: The Case Studies of Tanzania and Uganda. University of Dar es Salaam, unpublished M.A. Dissertation, 267 pp.

Deals with the impact of urbanization on fertility and child mortality. Based on the 1967 Population Census in Tanzania and 1969 Population Census for Uganda. It describes levels of fertility and child mortality in rural and urban areas and rural-urban differences. Discusses social and economic factors causing rural-urban differentials in fertility and child mortality. For instance, it shows that "Longer education of women in the urban areas than in the rural areas leads to lower urban than rural child mortality". Similarly, it concludes that the lower fertility in towns is due to the fact that urban dwellers are non-farmers and have more education.
    The findings would have been even more useful if other factors were included like distance to medical services and water sources, differential quality of medical services, nutrition level of mother and child, differential household incomes and so on. Education interacts very highly with other factors like occupation and income levels, which may in fact be the more important determinants of child mortality.

302. SEMBAJWE, ISRAEL S.L. (1974), "An Analysis of Rural - Urban Differentials in Fertility and Child Mortality in Tanzania". BRALUP Research Paper, no. 28.

Attempts to assess the affect of urbanization on fertility and child mortality by establishing the levels of these two demographic characteristics in rural and urban areas of Tanzania. The findings show that fertility and mortality are both lower in the urban areas. The author argues that the low mortality in urban areas is the direct cause of low fertility in these areas. He also suggests that with improvements in the social and economic development of rural areas, the urban-rural differentials can be reduced. This is already evident in areas surrounding large urban centres which benefit from the better health and associated services of these centres.

303. SEMBAJWE, ISRAEL L. (1979), "The 1978 Population Census of Tanzania: A Preliminary Assessment of its Implications". University of Dar es Salaam, BRALUP Service Paper No. 79/7, 12 pp. + tables.

Argues that there is a population problem in Africa of fairly recent origin, which is related to rising unemployment, rising consumer demand for local products, and higher demand for basic needs in a context of limited or scarce national resources, despite relatively low population density. Prior to the 1940's, high fertility and high mortality rates combined to give relatively low population growth rates, whereas post-1940's declines in mortality rates and high fertility rates have led to very high population growth rates. His central argument is the need for demographic planning to control population growth so that it matches with the resources available to provide basic services.

304. SEMBAJWE, I.S.L. (1980), "The Relationship between Changing Roles and Status of Women and Childbearing and Child Survival in Tanzania". ECA National Seminar on Population and Development, Arusha, 17-24 February, 13 pp.

Discusses the significance of women's studies in Africa, the need for development of indicators to measure changing roles of women, and analyses education and employment figures to measure sexual inequality. Statistical analysis of the relationship between fertility (number of live births per women aged 45-49) and education, employment and urban-rural location shows a curvilinear trend, with rises in fertility as women get lower primary education followed by a drop as they get higher, post-St. IV education. Professional women have the highest fertility rate of all, and agricultural labourers (employed and self-employed) in general the lowest, contrary to expectations. At the same time, infant mortality is lowest for the professionals and highest for the latter. The author's conclusion, that there is an inverse relationship between high education and high occupational status and large family size and child mortality is therefore only partially correct. More research is needed on the relationship between class and fertility, including differential access to the means of subsistence beginning with adequate and nutrituous food and health services which ensure both high fertility capacity and high child survival rates. A useful list of suggested research areas is presented at the end of the paper.

305. SEMBAJWE, I.S.L. (1981), "Population & Family Life Welfare: Beliefs, Attitudes and Felt Needs in Rural Tanzania". University of Dar es Salaam, BRALUP, 151 pp.

A detailed survey analysis of the relationship between socio-economic indicators and child mortality and fertility in eleven villages situated in Kilimanjaro, Mara and Morogoro. A wealth of data is presented on such factors as education, occupation, sources of income, nutrition, health and sanitation, knowledge and practices of family planning and demographic indicators such as mortality and fertility rates. Correlations were found between child mortality rates and education of mother and father's income, the number of meals per day and providing breakfast for children before going to school. As these measures went up, child mortality statistically went down. Child mortality was also higher in households with a bad source of water. The author notes that these statistical relationships require further social analysis, in that the factors measured ultimately relate to different family socio-economic conditions. Child mortality and fertility rates are ultimately related to different income (or class) positions of families. The report includes copies of the Interview Schedules used. The data provided is very useful in further analysis of social relations in production and reproduction in peasant households.

306. STERKENBURG, J. & CLAAS JONGE (1974), "Population Growth and Economic Development in Africa". Kronick van Afrika, 1974/1, (special issue) Leiden, Afrika Studiecentrum.

This special Issue of <u>Kronick van Afrika</u> focuses on Population Growth and Economic Development in tropical Africa. Nine papers are presented discussing case studies or theories about population and economic growth. The papers question the assumption that underlie the argument that population control is a prerequisite for economic development. They posit other reasons for under-development and illustrate these with case studies. For instance, Sterkenburg and Luning show that prices and other changes in the economic structure have a greater impact on per capita income than a lower population growth rate. This volume is important to understand family planning in its correct perspective, as opposed to a Malthusian perspective.

307. SUMRA, S. (1979), "Values and Concepts in Traditional Population Education in Africa" in UNESCO, <u>Final Report, Seminar on Population Education and the Reform of Educational Systems in Africa South of the Sahara.</u> Nairobi, 10-15 December, 1979.

Relates relations of sexuality and fertility to relations of production and the division of labour by age and sex in the analysis of cultivating societies organised by kinship. The control of elders was based not on ownership of landed property, but on their control over the labour of individuals under them and the product of their labour. Drawing on Meillassoux's work, he stresses the objective necessity of continual replacement of the population for the continued existence of the group, expressed ideologically by the stress on continuity of clan or tribe. Biological reproduction of the labour force was as essential as adequate production of food. Elders therefore sought to control procreative women as "the producer of the producer" and to control the distribution and storage of food. The relatively small size of most groups meant it was crucial to develop a mechanism of exchange of women, which developed into the marriage contract and the medium of bridewealth. Bridewealth represented a "replacement" of the "procreative power" of women. Bridewealth legalised the marriage and conferred upon the husband the right of sexual access and control over progeny, the last being the most important (but also access to labour services of the women in production of use values and exchange values; OM/MM). Traditional forms of population education included pre-adolescence games of sex, joking relationships between grandparents and grandchildren which included sexual instruction, initiation ceremonies, and premarital sexual relations. Although Sumra does not stress this point, the combination of premarital sexual relations with a prohibition against pregnancy meant that girls and boys necessarily were instructed in methods of contraception and sexual techniques during intercourse which would avoid conception. He recommends at the end that children should receive sexual and family life education in school, a responsibility that used to be handled by elders in the past.

308. SUMRA, S. (1981), <u>Final Report, Workshop on Population, Education and Curriculum Changes, Arusha, 15-20 December, 1980.</u> University of Dar es Salaam, Department of Education, bound mimeo, 302 pp.

Contains ten papers, four of which are included in this section
(by Sumra, Mbilinyi, Bwatwa and Omari). The Workshop was
sponsored by UNESCO and UNFPA. The summary observations and
recommendations of the workshop include: that population issues
have already been taken up by the party and government, and
related topics are taught in separate school subjects; that
there is global concern and support for population programmes;
and therefore the government should strengthen its population
policy; there be a centralized institution for coordinating and
monitoring population activities; that an integrated problem
oriented population education curriculum be introduced in the
formal education system; that mass population education be
developed by party and government; that a committee be formed
to be convened by the head of the Department of Education.

309. SUMRA, SULEMAN (1981), "Population Education and the Tanzanian
System", in S. Sumra (ed.) Final Report, Workshop on Population,
Education and Curriculum Changes, Arusha 15-20 December, 1980.
University of Dar es Salaam, Department of Education, bound
mimeo.

Argues that a distinction must be made between population
education as a part of a programme to control population growth
against the interests of the masses, and one which relates
population issues to socialist transformation. Most current
population education programmes reflect the former position.
What is ultimately at issue is poverty, the causes of poverty,
and the potential revolutionary character of a massive unemployed, underemployed and hungry world population. The argument
that an individual family can break out of poverty by reducing
the number of children is firmly rejected. Rather it is often
in the interests of the poorest peasants to have as many children
as possible, due to the significance of child labour in production
and the support of children in old age. High infant mortality
rates also force the poor to have as many children as possible
so that some may survive. Population policy in Tanzania is
analysed, in relation to the impact of villagisation, women's
role in production, the expansion of MCH clinics with UMATI
services attached, the 1971 Marriage Act, maternity leave
benefits spaced every three years and limited tax allowances
for children.

Emphasises the relationship between population education
and women's emancipation, which is absolutely necessary for
socialist revolution. The biological aspect of reproduction
is seen as the basis for the sexual division of labour, and
the objectification and commoditisation of women. He concludes
that "any population education which does not look at women's
question would be of little value. Boys and girls should be
provided with education that will instill self-confidence in
themselves and provide opportunities to realise their full
potential. This will come about only if women are given the
most necessary freedom, i.e. freedom over their own bodies. The
kind of population education we provide in Tanzania should be
in line with our ideological commitment, it should aim at
liberating man (i.e. human beings)".

310. SUMRA, SULEMAN A. and ISSA M. OMARI (1980), "Social-Cultural
Case Study for Population Education in Tanzania". Paris,
Population Education Section, UNESCO, 108 pp. draft, to be
published by UNESCO.

Presents a wealth of material, including basic demographic
statistics and findings of the surveys done in Kilimanjaro,
"Sukumaland", Ubarabaig and in Zanzibar. Background information
on national socio-economic characteristics, development and
educational policies is presented. The relationship between
"kinship and productive systems" is analysed in the context of
the socio-economic characteristics in each area. Traditional
socialisation processes as they relate to sexuality and
fertility, and the impact of the schooling system are examined
in detail. Recommendations on educational planning and training
for population education are provided. The inclusion of quota-
tions from interviews highlights major points of controversy
and strengthens the overall impact of the research findings.
Teachers, parents and students were all included in the survey.
On the whole, all groups in the four areas were positive about
the desirability of introducing population education into schools
and elsewhere. However, many parents in Sukumaland and Ubarabaig
are still reluctant to school their daughters, for different
reasons. Many of the issues raised by the interviewees centered
around changing relations of sexuality and fertility and the
breakdown of patriarchal relations. Concern was especially
expressed over the growing independence of young people and
children, no longer subservient to their parents and other
elders as in the past.
    Such views of elders were confirmed by the differences in
behaviour and attitudes as reported by the youth compared with
the elders. For example, young and "educated" people preferred
monogamous marriages, smaller families and spouses who were
educated and employed, even if there were not members of their
own tribe.

311. TANNER, R.E.S. (1956), "Suduma Fertility". East African
Medical Journal, v. 33, no. 3, pp. 96-99.

One hundred and forty-eight marriages in 3 parishes in Mwanza
District were examined in 1953 and revealed interesting variations in fertility, infertility and infant mortality between
polygamous and monogamous marriages. The length of marriage
and the locality of the women also appeared to be significant.
Monogamous marriages appeared to place greater emphasis on
women not having illegitimate children before marriage whereas
this did not seem to matter in polygamous marriages. The former
type of union seemed to be more stable and this was reflected
in a smoother curve in child bearing. However, monogamous
husbands were less tolerant of childlessness and the divorce
rate for this cause was therefore higher in monogamous
marriages. Monogamous marriages also had higher rates of
child mortality in the first 10 years of marriage ostensibly
because of less assistance in work.

312. TANZANIA. MINISTRY OF FINANCE AND PLANNING (Bureau of Statistics
and Bureau of Resource Assessment) and (Land Use Planning,

University of Dar es Salaam), (1973), <u>National Demographic</u>
<u>Survey of Tanzania</u>. Vol. I <u>Regional and National Data</u>, Dar
es Salaam.

As noted in the Foreword to the various (6) volumes of the
1973 national demographic survey, the survey was based on a
2 % sample of the total population and was intended to estimate
levels of fertility and mortality for each region of the Mainland
(iii). Volume I presents tables with breakdowns of women by age
and education, age and occupation, husband's age and income/
employment, and so on; facts concerning fertility and mortality
of women and of children and new born infants, and much else.
Regional figures are given for each set of breakdowns, as well
as national totals. Hence, someone interested in studying women
in one area would find basic demographic information to draw
upon in this volume. The tables are somewhat difficult to read,
however, and readers will want to refer to volume IV, <u>The Methods</u>
<u>Report</u>.
    Tanzania 1973 Vol. II. <u>Data for Socio-Economic Groups</u>. The
basic data of the demographic survey are clustered in this volume
according to "modes of life", tribes, educational groups,
religious groups and related to different aspects of fertility
and mortality, such as marital conditions and infant mortality
rates. There are problems with the clustering according to
modes of life, such as the lumping together of all Kigoma and
West Lake Region Districts despite the different levels of
development and commoditisation in the two regions. Through
careful and critical study of the data provided, however, the
reader will find potentially useful information.
    Tanzania 1973 Vol. III. <u>Summary Data for Survey Clusters</u>.
The Foreword notes that the data provided here is based on
summaries of basic demographic estimates from the household
schedule and information on socio-economic conditions drawn
from meetings with regional and district officials. The
information summarised for each rural cluster and for twenty-
two towns includes the major tribes, major religions, percentage
of husbands polygamous, percentage of women childless, age and
distribution and average number of live births for women in
each age group (parity), demographic estimates including
expectation of life at birth, the infant mortality rate, the
crude birthrate, and the total fertility rate; occupation of husbands and percentage wage earners and education of women and
their husbands. These are drawn from the household surveys
and appear more reliable than the information drawn from the
meetings with regional and district officials. For example,
the proportion of women following sexual abstinence during
lactation is estimated by the male officials, as well as the
proportion owning a radio, watch, etc. It is difficult to take
such estimates seriously.

313. UMATI (Family Planning Association of Tanzania) (1976),
    "Family Planning Association of Tanzania". Report presented
    to the International Workshop on Education for Rural Women,
    Lushoto, Tanzania (PMO/UNICEF), 5 pp.

The organization and administrative structure is described, as

well as the relationship of UMATI to the government. In 1975
there were 50,000 members, belonging to 35 branches in the
country. Activities include information and education,
training of medical and paramedical and auxiliary staff,
medical and clinical work, including an infertility clinic.
Abortion is illegal in Tanzania. The need for sex education
or family life education in schools is noted.

314. UMARI (n.d.), Jee Unafahamu Umati ni Nini? Dar es Salaam,
4 pp.

An informative folder; explaining the functions of UMATI, the
advantages of child spacing and a cautious reminder that UMATI
can advise and offer services to those wishing to space their
children.

315. UMATI (n.d.), Sifa za Jamii Bora. Dar es Salaam, 4 pp., folder.

The pamphlet idealises the behaviour of the mother, father and
children in a healthy middle class family. The conclusion is
that such behaviour is only possible if the family practices
child spacing. Ignores the socio-economic factors which cause
poverty and high birth rates.

316. UMATI (n.d.), Uzazi wa Majira ni Kama Ukulima Bora. Dar es
Salaam, 4 pp.

A 4-page folder pamphlet showing how frequent pregnancies is
like bad maize growing practices. Good spacing in children is
just as essential as good spacing in maize culture. The analogy
between the fertility of women and the fertility of the soil
reproduces the reification of women as objects, as means to
produce children and other labour products.

317. UMATI (n.d.), Wasemayo Viongozi Kuhusu Uzazi wa Majira. Dar
es Salaam, 4 pp., folder.

A collection of official statements on child spacing and on
UMATI. The statements include those made by President Julius
Nyerere, the Prime Minister, other Ministers. Concludes that
the statements show the importance of child spacing in family
health and the health of the nation.

318. VUORELA, ULLA (1979), "Women's Role in Production and Reproduction, Some Reflections on Relationships between Men and
Women in Tanzania and Finland". Paper No. 28, BW, 19 pp.

The major thesis is that women under Tanzanian patriarchal
relations are means of production and means of reproduction,
and have full status neither as producers or reproducers. A
brief analysis of changing sex relations in the family and at
work in Finland is included to provide some perspective on the
nature of sex relations in Tanzania. Class differentiation
among women is considered with special emphasis on the relationship between labour (power) and sexual power, and the exchange
of each for commodities or for access to the means of
subsistence. The romanticisation of the traditional place of
women as "mother" ("oppression through elevation") as a mechanism
of social control of women is among the many insightful issues

raised. Reproduction is considered with respect to both ideological reproduction of capitalist and patriarchal social relations, and biological reproduction.

XII. FAMILY AND DOMESTIC LABOUR

Analysis of social relations within the family and the labour input
into maintenance of the family have already been referred to in
other sections. Only a few items focus specifically on the family
or on marital relations, and these have been included here. In
addition, we have included materials about child care in the home
as well as in state-run institutions. The issue of child care is
fundamental to the question of domestic labour, but also to that
of sexuality and fertility.

Stress in Family Relations

One expression of the social transformation in Tanzania during the
19th and 20th centuries is the number of studies which focus on,
and document, the rise in marital instability and/or family tensions
(XII:324, 330, 333, 334, 342). In Rungwe villages, for example, the
individualisation of the family from its extended to its nuclear
form is related to commoditisation in peasant production and reproduction. Parent-child-youth and husband-wife conflicts are not
new, but the old mechanisms of social control have lost their potency.
The result has been open violence of sons against fathers and an
increasing number of divorce and adultery accusations.
   As early as 1932, divorce was identified as an important
problem (XII:330). In the colonial period, the colonial administrators as well as the Christian religious functionaries tried to
explain the growing incidence of divorce by referring to the spread
of Islam (330) or the practices of matrilineality (324), as well as
the migrant labour system (II:28). Women's growing (or changed)
consciousness has also been noted as having an impact among peasants
as well as workers and petty bourgeois (XII:333, 334, 342). The
phenomenon of divorce is linked to that of unmarried mothers,
schoolgirl pregnancies and prostitution. What is lacking in most
of these studies is an analysis of the changing basis of subsistence
or reproduction of peasant, and working class and petty bourgeois
households and women in each class, as a possible source of explanation for these phenomena. Bader noted the significance of prostitution as an alternative basis of subsistence and accumulation of cash
income for peasant women, who moved out of peasant production to
engage in prostitution, and returned to invest their savings in
land and coffee trees in Bukoba (IV:86). Bujra found that women
turned to prostitution as a means of subsistence and investment in
real estate in Nairobi and in Coastal villages in Kenya. Bryceson
and Mbilinyi (II:28, 29) pointed out that women factory workers and
other proletariat women were rejecting patriarchal marriage as an
unnecessary labour burden and consumption cost. Much more research
is necessary however to relate changing marriage and family practices
to the changing conditions of existence of the different classes in
Tanzanian society, and women within each.

Child Care

Overcrowded housing conditions, and the growing difficulty to
adequately feed, clothe and maintain children and other relatives

in urban working class and "sub-working class" families has contributed to alienation between parents and children (XII:320). This
alienation is expressed by parents who say they are "tired of their
children". One result of adverse living conditions is that children
and youth steal and engage in prostitution as a means of maintaining
themselves. Once ensnared in the state machinery, these young
people are labelled as "juvenile delinquents". The author points
out that petty bourgeois children engaged in similar practices are
less likely to become court cases or to be sentenced to remand
schools, because of the financial leverage their parents have.

Most of the other items concerning child care in the family
focus on peasant households (XII:325-327, 335, 338, 343-345). Women
are primarily responsible for rearing children, whether their own
biological children or those of the husband or others. Many
children are raised by stepmothers, grandmothers, older sisters,
etc. Children are given a "secondary" place in terms of allocation
of resources at family and national level (XII:327, 336, 345). Sex
differentiation is found in allocation of resources like food and
schooling, with girls being discriminated against. At the same
time, girls contribute more labour than boys in domestic labour
(XII:327, 335, 338, 345 and sections above).

The problem with the concept of "child care" is that it connotes
child dependency. In poor peasant and working class families,
children contribute their labour to production activities as well
as to the maintenance of the family in domestic labour. Hence, the
concept of child care must not be adopted as a non-problematic
concept from literature of industrialised capital countries.

Socialisation of Child Care

State intervention in child care is most immediately visible with
respect to the development of day care centres. The government
established a policy of having at least one day care centre in
every ujamaa village in 1976, and aimed to have 4,000 centres by
1980 (XII:346). Even when non-government institutions like missions
provide such services, they are state-regulated. Day care leaders
and nursery school teachers are all to be trained within state-
regulated training institutions. The need for children's literature
and toys to be produced by local industry is emphasised, as well as
the development of recreation facilities.

The Maternal and Child Health Clinics provide health education
which has implications for the labour burdens of child care. For
example, the home preparation of weaning food (like pounding fruits,
vegetables and later, meat) require additional labour inputs on a
daily basis for women already over-worked. As Billau (XII:321)
notes, it is necessary to query MCH advice to mothers to feed their
children fruits, eggs and milk, when they are forced to sell these
in order to buy other necessary consumption items like soap and
salt. Directing the attention of health education and health
services related to children's health only to mothers is misplaced,
since they do not control the major cash income in the household,
nor are they in control of the distribution of food supplies.
Attention must be directed to patriarchal relations and the steady
impoverishment of peasant and working class families. Child care,
like other aspects of domestic labour (cooking, water provision, and

energy provision), must be conceptualised as a social responsibility
and <u>not</u> a <u>maternal</u> responsibility (XII:331, 336). The direction
taken by state intervention then becomes the crucial question: a
direction in line with socialist principles of the liberation of
all human beings, women, men, girls and boys; or in line with
capitalist principles of creating a more malleable, exploitable,
productive labour force·

REFERENCE

Janet M. Bujra, "Production, Property, Prostitution. Sexual
    Politics in Atu". <u>Cahiers d'Etudes Africaines</u>, 65, XVII
    (1): 13-39.

---

319. ARENS, W. and DIANA ANTOS ARENS (1978), "Kinship and Marriage
    in Polyethnic Community". <u>Africa</u>, 48 (2): 149-160.

Analysis of the historical development of a rural settlement,
Mto wa Mbu, at different periods provides illustration of the
breakdown of ethnic and religious distinctions as a basis for
marriage. Other issues of marriage, possible changes in
marital social relations and so on, are not explored by the
authors. The different flows of immigrants correspond to
specific conditions which "pushed" them from their home areas:
poverty, landlessness, famine and so on. However, the authors
err in providing psychological explanations which end up to be
apologetics for colonial rule. For example, the second wave of
immigrants came from drought-stricken areas, as noted by the
authors themselves, but their explanation is that they "took
advantage of the increased individual mobility afforded by
colonial presence". The third wave "responded to the new
opportunities made available by the coming of independence"
when in fact these were traders leaving areas of land scarcity
to engage in retail trade and commercial farming.

320. BAKENGESA, S.K.S. (1980), "Delinquency and Social Development".
    Paper presented to the National Council of Social Welfare
    Services Workshop on Adolescent and Youth Problems in Tanzania,
    Moshi, 21st-27th September, 17 pp. to be published in proceedings
    edited by C.K. Omari.

The major problems noted as juvenile delinquency are thieving
and prostitution. The circumstances which lead to such behaviour
are analysed, such as the nature of family life in town, overcrowded housing of the poor where there is no privacy for sexual
relations among parents and others, high unemployment rates
among youth, and high rate of family breakdown and the alienation between parents and children. Peer groups are highly
influential, and the development of urban gangs consisting of
girls and boys is noted here. Poverty forces young people to
steal or to prostitute themselves, and poverty itself is the
result of an exploitative economic system. The analysis is

based on interviews of youth in 11 urban centres of Tanzania.
Fifty percent of the youth in remand homes come from the Coastal
belt and Kilimanjaro and Morogoro Regions, and most of the rest
from along the central railway line. The author's explanation
is that youth find transport systems easy to get to town. A
more likely explanation is that traditional patriarchal relations have been more completely destroyed in these areas and
the process of commoditisation in production and other social
relations has been more developed, combined with growing
alienation of youth from land, livestock or other means of
production. The paper is important in outlining changing
family structures in urban areas, and the specific problems
of youth. A major weakness is the total disregard of sexual
differences in reporting on family, parental or youth problems.

321. BILLAU, G.M. (1977), "Child Care in Manyoni". Dar es Salaam,
Department of Sociology, University of Dar es Salaam. 351 pp.

The study shows how child care is closely related to the socio-
economic status of the families. This is reflected in several
ways. Attendance of M.C.H. clinics is associated with the
economically better off and attendance and delivery at the
Rural Health Centre reflect the economic base. Nutritional
education obtained at the clinics cannot always be implemented,
partly because it is not relevant to the area and partly because
economic conditions are such that highly nutritious foods such as
eggs and milk are sold in order to provide essentials like soap
and salt. Cultural taboos and the desire for more children or
more male children also act against family planning affecting
the health of both mother and children. The situation is
exacerbated by the unsympathetic attitude of the nurses at the
M.C.H. clinics who appear to be unaware of the realities of life
and ignore traditional foods etc., in their nutritional education
classes.

322. BRAIN, J.L. (1969), "Matrilineal Descent and Marital Stability:
a Tanzanian Case". Journal of Asian and African Studies, Vol. 4
No. 2 pp. 122-131.

Examines the divorce rate among three groups of the Luguru in
order to test J. Clyde Mitchell's theory that marriages in
matrilineal societies are less stable than in patrilineal
societies. Mitchell argues that in the matrilineal situation
where initial uxorilocality is followed by verilocal, the wife
is removed from her descent group. When her sons marry they
in turn return to the clan land after the birth of the first
child, i.e. to the descent group of the mother. When they do
this, there is a tendency of the mother to follow her sons,
thus resulting in a high divorce rate. Since this occurs only
when children reach adulthold, the greater the duration of
marriage, the greater the likelihood of divorce. The study
concludes that this pattern continues and is unaffected by the
conversion to Roman Catholicism or proximity of dwelling.

323. BUJRA, ABDALLA, S. (n.d.), (1973 research), "The Young Child
in Ujamaa Villages: Dodoma District". University of Dar es
Salaam, Sociology Department mimeo, 43 pp.

The first part of this paper deals with the nutrition and health conditions of young children and infants prior to ujamaa village developments in Dodoma Region in 1971. In the second part on changes which have taken place as a result of ujamaa villagisation, there is detailed analysis of customs surrounding the pregnant women, childbirth, infant feeding and child care. The role of women in village politics can be investigated in the case studies attached to the report. The development of day care centres is explored in each village, and specific concrete recommendations are made for day care centres in Dodoma District.

324. CHOWO, H. (1976), Mtoto na Malezi. Dar es Salaam, Wizara ya Elimu ya Taifa - Ministry of National Education, 79 pp.

Describes the characteristic attributes of different kinds of learning disorders or handicaps of children, and the kinds of measures which teachers can adopt to promote learning. Although intended primarily for teachers, the book is also useful for parents. Case studies of children are also included, which are based on the research of primary school teachers participating in the M.T.U.U. Infant Methods Programme.

325. EBRAHIM, G.J. (1978), Breast Feeding, the Biological Option. London, MacMillan Press, 86 pp.

A detailed analysis of the "physiology of lactation", the "physiology of suckling", the role of the health worker in providing assistance to the mother breast-feeding her child, the composition of breast milk compared to other milk sources, the historical development of "artificial feeding" of infants worldwide and in the third world. It has been written to fill the gap in teaching materials for the training of health workers, which has tended to ignore breast-feeding as a subject area. It is also a response to the decline in breast-feeding practices and the promotion of infant foods.
   Breast-feeding is one of the labour inputs of women in domestic labour. The complexities of the issues raised in the book are important to consider. The line taken is that breast-feeding is "natural" whereas feeding with infant foods is "artificial". The dichotomy established is a misleading one, unless we accept that all food consumption other than breast-feeding is artificial at any age. Moreover, to attribute malnutrition and infant mortality to the use of food supplies and the distribution of food, health services, housing and sanitation conditions for the peasants and workers of the third world mystifies the real causes of infant mortality. Finally, the calculation of potential costs in foreign exchange to the Tanzanian state if women switch from breast-feeding to use of powdered milk reveals the way in which women have been reified as "objects producing milk" in the whole debate. It is vitally important to clarify the social forces which lead or force women to use infant foods, and which result in extremely low incomes, in milk being imported in the first place, and sold at unsubsidized prices.

326. ERESUND, PIA and NANCY TESHA (1978/79), The Situation of
Children (0-15 years) in Tanzania. Dar es Salaam, SIDA Report,
95 pp.

Based on a survey of the relevant literature and detailed
studies in selected villages of Dodoma Region, the report
analyses many different aspects of child care, pregnancy and
delivery, health and nutrition, and education. Of particular
interest to the women's question are the following: a survey
of day-care centres, including activities, problems and probing
of needs for toys and crèches; a critical look at the functioning of maternal and child health (MCH) clinics, where staff-
mother relations are found to be oppressive and non-beneficial;
the rich case material based on interviews and observations of
adult women, young girls and children. Much is revealed about
how sexist ideas about women are internalised by women and
young girls, as well as resisted. A mix of techniques were
used, including interviews, observations and administration of
a "draw a man" test to children.

327. FREYHOLD, M. et al. (1973), "Field Study: Moshi District".
TNSRC, The Young Child in Tanzania, Dar es Salaam, UNICEF,
pp. 166-238.

Devoted mainly to the care and up-bringing of children among
the Wachagga of Moshi District, Kilimanjaro Region, but there
is a great deal of material on the socio-economic environment
of the children including the economic and social position of
women. Children are considered to be the property of the man but
the responsibility for their up-bringing lies heavily on the
mother. Women do not have any individual rights to land and
very rarely do they inherit land, yet they do an inordinate
amount of work producing food for domestic consumption and
sale. They also look after the cattle which they cannot own
or sell and put in a substantial amount of work in producing
the cash crop, coffee, the proceeds of the sale of which is
entirely the husband's affair. The article asserts that "60 %
of the women had to support their children and themselves out
of their own income from maize, beans, and bananas without
receiving any help from their husbands," - and this after they
had produced enough food for the household.
    Most of the girls are taken out of school before they
complete primary school, while the majority of boys were
allowed to finish and go beyond. Forced marriages are quite
common and "if the husband mistreats her or neglects her,
there is little a woman can do". Divorce was not sought
because "if the woman leaves her husband, she has to leave
the children with him - whatever the cause of the divorce...."
"Privileges" previously in favour of women such as a three-
month period of rest after childbirth or a special diet of
meat, milk and butter for nursing mothers, are also dying out.
Food habits such as giving the largest portion of the meat to
the men also tend to impoverish the diet of women and girl
children. Many men eat at bars and "therefore have little
interest in what is eaten in their homes".

328. INTERNATIONAL YEAR OF THE CHILD (IYC) SECRETARIAT (1979),
"First Quarterly Report on I.Y.C. Activities in Tanzania:
January to March 1979". Dar es Salaam, 14 pp.

The report presents the organisational structure of IYC in
Tanzania and the role of the National IYC Committee: to
monitor and coordinate national activities implemented for
the benefit of children; to recommend action towards a long
term programme benefiting children. The President's inaugural
address of IYC is summarized (see Nyerere, 1978), as well as
a circular of the Prime Minister which called for an integrated
approach towards developing programmes benefiting children
through the regional administrative structures. Research and
communication activities are listed, as well as publications
arising from IYC. A Swahili version of Where There is no Doctor,
a Village Medical Handbook was published during 1979, together
with Njoo Tukuzindike about immunization and other preventative
services of the Ministry of Health. Lishe had a special issue.
Books of practical use for day care centres are cited. The
problem of publishing children's books is discussed and
emphasised, given the dearth of attractive and relevant
children's literature. Other projects such as toy production,
local weaning foods and so on are mentioned. The report is an
excellent summary of on-going activities effecting both women
and children, and it is hoped there is also a Swahili version
and that it is widely distributed.

329. KAISI, M. (1976), Ukunga na Utunzaji wa Watoto Vijijini
(Midwifery and the care of rural children). Dar es Salaam,
Tanzania Publishing House, 216 pp.

A very practical guide on the various aspects of pregnancy,
child-bearing, the care of newborns, and the conduct of baby
clinics. On pregnancy the book describes the food and care
of pregnant mothers, possible problems associated with
pregnancy and how to deal with them and how to measure the
size of the growing foetus. On childbirth the book describes
how to cope with normal birth and possible problems, nine of
which are identified. Under care of the newborns the author
recommends the traditional 40 days special care. It outlines
the various stages of development of the infant and recommends
measures to prevent and cope with infant diseases. It also
describes how to run baby clinics and keep records of the
baby's progress including vaccination records. Appendices
give practical instructions such as how to prepare milk for
kwashiorkor, marasmus, how to do catheteriation etc. The book
appears to be aimed at medical assistants and midwives but it
could be equally useful to personnel in villages likely to
deal with emergencies such as teachers, family members,
traditional midwives - or for training such person(s),
especially for villages far from medical services. Its
special usefulness lies in its clear instructions written in
easily understandable language and the fact that it is profusely
illustrated.

330. KAYAMBA, H.M. (1932), "The Modern Life of the East African
Native". Africa, 5 (1), January.

Important in documentation of changing family and sexual relations
midway during the colonial period, written by one of the most
prominent African petty bourgeois functionaries of the colonial
state in Tanzania (Tanganyika). He notes that divorce has
risen 100 %, as well as adultery, and related this to the
influence of Islamic Law. Recommends that women should receive
more education, and gives reasons for dissatisfaction in marriage.

331. KIRIMBAI, M.W., "Child Welfare". Paper No. 12, BW, 3 pp.

A set of notes based on the work of the UWT Assistant Secretary
in charge of Legal Rights of Women and Children, the paper noted
that child welfare is situated within the family and within
society, including child clinics, day care centres and family
allowances. However in practice responsibility is delegated
mainly to the family, thus privatised. Child welfare must become
increasingly a social responsibility in order to free women for
more productive work; to contribute to socialist transformation
through early collectivisation of child care and child learning;
to ensure equal provision of adequate early learning and social
experiences, and material needs such as nutritious food, medical
attention and preventative health care. A national policy of
child welfare is necessary which is backed up by a programme
which coordinates various institutions concerned.

332. KOEUNE, ESTHER (1952) (1975), The African Housewife and Her
Home. Dar es Salaam, East African Literature Bureau, 193 pp.

This text is valuable as an example of the way in which the
colonial bourgeois attempted to construct a bourgeois ideology
about the family among petty bourgeois East Africans and
others. At times it is clearly directed to "the African
housewife" at other times appears directed to community
development-type workers. Reading through the table of contents
one gets a list of the kinds of tasks which women do to maintain
and provide for the family in poor peasant households (planning
the home, discusses the problems of grass roofs, and the merits
of papyrus, bati or tiles; the layout of the compound; the
vegetable plot; the family wash; care of children in the home;
sickness in the home; feeding the family) as well as others
which could only have relevance for the petty bourgeois class
in the process of formation (walls and pictures; curtains;
furniture; how to lay the table; preparation for a large party
- serving tea, cakes and biscuits). More importantly however
is that bourgeois concepts of "the family" parent-child relations
and the sexual division of labour permeate the entirety of the
book. Very useful practical suggestions are provided and
accompanied with sketch illustrations. These include a home-
made water filter, a manure pit, a hanging shelf, furniture
like beds and chairs which can be made at home with simple
tools and local materials, and so on. At the same time, the
kinds of consumption items introduced in the book require a
cash income, and hence would lead to pressure to produce more
cash crops or to seek alternative sources of income. The
condescending and generally racist tone of the book is apalling.
That it is still being reprinted twenty years after independence
is intriguing in itself.

333. KONTER, J.H. (1974), <u>Facts and Factors in the Rural Economy of the Nyakyusa, Tanzania</u>. Leiden, 346 pp.

Examines changing social relations of the extended and nuclear family within the context of a detailed examination of land tenure, the organisation of the production process, including the division of labour, distribution of income and consumption patterns. The different economic bases of the two groups of villages provided a context in which to explain breakdowns in old patriarchal relations at clan level, the impact of land scarcity and commoditisation of labour, and the changing sexual division of labour. Patrilineal property relations continue to function, but the control of the <u>nuclear</u> family head over male youth labour has severely diminished. One result of the disintegration of old forms of extended family cooperation in production is the intensification of wives' labour and for those richer peasants, the hiring of labour.

The author asserts that "while women in the subsistence economy often produced more than they personally consumed, they nowadays tend to consume more than they earn by way of agriculture". It is important to clarify the methodological errors which have led to this erroneous conclusion. The problem lies with the conception of production, property relations and the <u>origins</u> of those products consumed within a peasant household. In terms of labour time, he himself notes that women work more hours a day in the fields, than men. Women are solely responsible for producing food for the household, but this labour product is seemingly excluded from his calculation. Although the husbands "own" the coffee or tea or sugar cane produced <u>jointly</u> by themselves <u>and</u> their wives, this labour product <u>is</u> the product of the wives' labour input as well as the husband's. However, a wife's "earnings" are necessarily less, relying as they do on what is left over from household food consumption needs.

Throughout the text there is no attention given to the impact of worsening terms of trade on the peasant households. What <u>is</u> true is that peasants in general are increasingly consuming more in money terms than what they can produce with the means of production at their disposal. The author has also in general adopted ideological statements made by his male respondents as a true reflection of reality, and in so doing, appears to have accepted their specific ideologies as well. For example, whereas it is apparently true that men provide major consumption items to their wives in reality those items purchased by the husband are the products of his wife(ve)'s labour as well as his own.

334. MAKUNDI, K. and E. WARIOBA (1979), "Psychological Relationship between Men and Women". Paper No. 27, <u>BW</u>, 55 pp.

Traditionally the family and social structure was such that men were considered superior, women inferior, men active and rational, women emotional and nurturant. Marital disputes arise today due to pressures to change such old sex role patterns, e.g. over equal decision-making and participation in household finances and in doing housework. Marital relations are negatively affected by differentiation in education, cultural backgrounds, nationality, race and class origins. A stable marriage relationship depends on allowance for self-identity of both spouses; mature attitudes towards sex and economic ventures; and acceptance of each other's strengths and weaknesses. Application of western sociological analysis in an uncritical way to Tanzanian situation.

335. MASCARENHAS, A.C., Participation of Children in Socio-Economic Activities - The Case of Rukwa Region, BRALUP Research Report No. 20.1 (New Series) 20 pp.

The report discusses the participation of children in socio-economic activities in Rukwa Region of Tanzania. The information is based on interviews of 171 families in the administrative divisions of Sumbawanga, Kate and Kirando. Isolates the factors such as location of social services, natural resources, and formal employment including the status of the mother, which may govern the activities of the children. Significant differentiation was found in tasks between girls and boys. Similar studies are proposed for Kilosa, Bagamoyo and Bukoba districts.

336. NYERERE, JULIUS K. (1978), "The President's New Year Address to the Nation, Broadcast over Radio Tanzania on December 31, 1978". Dar es Salaam, International Year of the Child Secretariat, 5 pp.

Although this is a statement about children, it becomes a policy statement about women and sexist practices as well. The uninvolvement of fathers in child care is related at another level to the tendency for different ministries to ignore the implications of their programmes for children. For example, decisions about industrial strategy must take into account the specific needs of working mothers. The importance of UMATI and MCH clinics in providing information and methods of child spacing and proper maternal and child nutrition and health is stressed. Services and information provided by the Tanzania Food and Nutrition Centre are noted. School lunches and Day Care Centres provide for the well-being of the country's children, and also lessen the work load of women at home, thus freeing them to work on farms or elsewhere. Two hundred new MCH clinics are to be opened in 1979 and the expansion of day care centres encouraged. Throughout the speech the emphasis is that children are a social and a national responsibility - that is, not a maternal responsibility alone.

337. OMARI, I.M. (1973), "Childcare and Child Welfare". TNSRC, The Young Child in Tanzania. Dar es Salaam, UNICEF, pp. 108-165.

An overview of the services provided by the government for pre-school children and the history of social services in Tanzania and the need for child care services. Four factors are identified as contributing to the need; weakening of traditional family structure; changing political ideology; education for siblings; and urbanisation, employment of women and educational considerations as well as day care centres and nursery schools, children's homes, and facilities for handicapped children. Useful for the details of the programmes described and the statistics provided.

338. RAUM, O.F. (1940), Chagga Childhood. London, Oxford University Press (Reprinted 1967). 422 pp.

A comprehensive study of the education of the Chagga child from
infancy to childhood and adolescence. It is one of the best
examples of how traditional education was used to inculcate
sex-specific roles in society among children, youth and adults,
This educational process was achieved in several ways:
(1) informally through daily activities within the family,
(2) through group play and age class activities, (3) and
formally through circumcision, initiation and pre-marital rites.
Informally, differentiation of male and female roles was
constantly impressed upon children and youth through activities
and comments. For instance girls and boys would help with housework up to the age of 5-6 years but the mother would deliberately
ignore boys when teaching the children basic domestic skills. If
boys were found playing near the home, the fathers would tell
them to stop their childish ways and seek the company of boys.
Mothers would constantly comment on their daughters' behaviour
with respect to their status as future wives. Girls were
expected to be charming, respectful, peaceful minded, diligent
and to excel in cooking so as to attract suitors, whereas
aggressiveness, competitiveness and hunting skills were
emphasised as male attributes.

339. RUPIA, THERESIA (1979), "Care of the Newborn During First Week
of Life by Mothers Around Mpanda Town". Paper No. 42, BW, 7 pp.

Based on a survey of mothers attending four village dispensaries
and an MCH clinic near Mpanda, it was found that 59 % of
deliveries were at home and attended by female relatives in 78 % of
the cases. Home deliveries relied on unsterilized razor blades
to cut the umbilical cord (which dramatically increases the
possibility of tetanus infection for the infant). In 88 % of
all deliveries, including those in health facilities, newborns
were fed either unboiled water or an uncooked maize flour mixture
prior to breast-feeding (thereby increasing the possibility of
diarrhea).

340. TANZANIA. HOME ECONOMICS TRAINING CENTRE, BUHARE (1969), Report
of a Study and Seminar on Patterns of Living in Musoma Rural
District, Mara Region. Ministry of Regional Administration and
Rural Development.

Community and family life was studied in five villages, most of
them ujamaa villages. Gives information on the general characteristics of the population (religion, age distribution, education,
occupation) as well as on housing and sanitation, family food and
food habits, health, social patterns, attitudes and values and
government services. Includes some interesting material on
family planning, ambitions to study, and day care centres.

341. TANZANIA. HOME ECONOMICS TRAINING COLLEGE, BUHARE (1975), The
Study of the Patterns of Living in Morogoro District. Dar es
Salaam, Office of the Prime Minister and Second Vice President.
34 pp. tables.

Community and family life was studied in 10 villages most of
them ujamaa villages based on a total sample of 100 households.
Gives similar information as in 340.

342. TANZANIA NATIONAL COUNCIL OF SOCIAL WELFARE SERVICES (1971),
The Role of Social Welfare Services in East and Central Africa.
Fourth Social Welfare Seminar held in East and Central Africa.
Dar es Salaam. 277 pp. tables.

The country report on Tanzania discusses the history, policy
and organization of the social services in the country including
both the government services and those run by private and
voluntary organizations. Both types include women's programmes.
Provides a general description of the socio-economic conditions
of the country with a section on "major social problems" in
Tanzania which include marriage breakdowns, unmarried parenthood and prostitution.

343. TANZANIA NATIONAL SCIENTIFIC RESEARCH COUNCIL (1977), The Young
Child in Tanzania. Report on a Study of the Young Child in
Tanzania from Conception to Seven Years. Dar es Salaam, UNICEF.

Includes a number of national and field studies on the physical,
social and economic environment of the young child up to seven
years of age. Since at this stage the mother and child are
physically very much together, the study contains a great deal
of material relevant to conditions of women in Tanzania. Five
field studies are also included and cover mother/child conditions
in Moshi District, the less developed coastal area of Bagamoyo;
the less developed interior area; Singida; Ujamaa Villages in
Dodoma District and the peri-urban settlements around Dar es
Salaam City. Most of the field studies contain information on
the position of women, sexual division of labour, health and
care of expectant mothers and mothers with newly born babies
and other aspects of the mother/child relationship.

344. TANZANIA NATIONAL SCIENTIFIC RESEARCH COUNCIL (1977), The Young
Child in Tanzania Age 7 to 15. Dar es Salaam, 456 pp.

Includes material on Children from seven to fifteen years of
age. Aspects covered are handicapped children, mass health and
nutrition, media and youth, primary school education, problems
of youth and school leavers, youth and youth activities. Five
field studies give considerable insight into traditional
education, differentiating between girls and boys based on a clear
cut sexist division of labour (see especially the study on the
Nyakyusa in Rungwe). The field study on Bagamoyo is especially
revealing on the educational impact of socialisation on girls.

345. TESHA, NANCY E.J. (1979), "Women's Role in Rearing Children
and National Development". Paper No. 39, BW, 4 pp.

UWT should be interested in all aspects of children welfare,
and encourage the development of sports and other clubs. It
must struggle against the secondary place given to children in
society and the home, and in particular the lowest position
given to girls. A set of "shoulds", the paper lacks analysis
of the place of children historically in the family and community in different areas of the country, which would have
clarified the reasons for such recommendations.

346. UNITED NATIONS CHILDREN FUND (1976), "First Addendum to the
Plan of Operation for a Day Care Centre Programme in the United
Republic of Tanzania". UNICEF/Dar es Salaam, 14 pp.

This three-year joint government of Tanzania/UNICEF project
continued an effort begun in 1973; it resulted from the
government's expressed desire to have day care centres
established in every ujamaa village. Specific goals of the
project were (1) to continue day care centres development in
ujamaa villages and to extend the effort to urban areas; (2) to
provide a multi-service programme including medical services,
food supplements and parent education; (3) to develop a cooperative programme for the Tanzania Women's Organization and
various government ministries; (4) to train day care leaders
and assistants; (5) to stimulate self-help day care-construc-
tion programmes; and (6) to establish toy production units.
The project document estimated that there would be 3,500 - 4,000
day care centres by 1980. Nearly 2,000 day care personnel were
scheduled for training over the life of the project.

347. UNICEF (1976), "Basic Services for Children in Developing
Countries". Paper presented to International Workshop on
Education for Rural Women, Lushoto, Tanzania (PMO/UNICEF), 6 pp.

Children and mothers in "under-served" communities in low-income
countries are the priority groups requiring urgent attention.
The basic services identified by UNICEF are maternal and child
health family planning, safe water supply and waste disposal,
production and consumption of more and better quality food,
nutrition education, measures to meet basic education needs, and
introduction of simple technologies to lighten the daily tasks
of women and girls. UNICEF has shifted its approach from
provision of individual sectoral services to different
communities to an integration of several different services to
one community. Priority is given to communities who have
already begun to develop their own resources (human and
material) for development (N.B: "a progressive community"
approach like the "progressive farmer" approach? Will this
approach act to further the differentiation process between
rich and poor communities?). The strategy includes full
participation of communities in identifying needs, planning
and implementation, the use of locally-selected people as
"primary level" workers, and a combination of auxiliaries and
professionals to operate services themselves.

XIII. HEALTH AND NUTRITION

The country's goals in providing basic health services are posing
severe challenges to the country's development planning and policies.
The figures provided in 1980 show that too many people are served by
too few facilities (XIII:379, 380). The problem is particularly
serious in the rural areas where about 60 % of the 8,200 villages
are without any health facilities whatsoever. Services aimed at
protecting the health of children and mothers show similar poor
rates of accessibility. Some studies see the problem as rooted in
the current strategy for the deployment of health resources in the
country. The emphasis on hospitals, rural health centres and
dispensaries is a carry-over from the colonial era and an adoption
of a Western European model of medical and health care. Although
these facilities are indispensable, the current and forseeable
economic conditions make it unrealistic that such facilities could
be adequately provided for the entire nation by the year 2000. A
revolutionary strategy based on the training of rural health workers
and traditional birth attendants appears to be more realistic in
achieving primary health care before the end of this century (XIII:
361, 374, 380).
     In Tanzania one reflection of the country's health conditions
is the high rate of child mortality which ranges from 150 to 300
per 1000. It has been found that the biggest child killer is
malnutrition either directly or indirectly (XIII:351, 354, 356, 362,
363, 365, 366), accounting for 21 % of the fatalities and 74 % of
the hospitalised cases. Indirectly, malnutrition increases
susceptibility to death through other major killers like measles
and malaria. The tendency in the past was to explain malnutrition
by ignorance of food values, balanced diets, good methods of food
preservation and preparation as well as cleanliness. This tendency
is still apparent today (XIII:348, 351, 356). However, while not
denying the value of nutrition education, it must be pointed out
that such an attitude ignores the basic cause of malnutrition, which
is poverty and the inability of a considerable section of the
population to provide themselves with adequate food, let alone
vitamin and protein rich foods. Malnutrition can not be isolated
from the context of increasing impoverishment and separation of the
producers from direct control over the benefits of their labour and
its demoralising effect on production, including food production.
     It is therefore encouraging to see that recent studies in
nutrition and malnutrition are adopting a more critical analysis of
the root causes of malnutrition and a more integrated approach
towards the eradication of malnutrition (XIII:353, 355, 362, 363,
366). Concrete examples are given of how the monetisation of
agricultural production has had an adverse effect on food production
and nutrition. Monetisation has resulted in changing production
relations, making women more solely responsible for food production
yet paradoxically allowing them less say in the allocation of land
and labour towards food production (XIII:348, 353). Reining has
shown how increasing coffee production and a land shortage in Bukoba
have pushed food production into marginal areas (IV:123). Women are
also expected to participate in cash crops production but have

limited access to the cash income thus generated so that the labour
lost in food production cannot be compensated by increased ability
to buy food. In some cases cash is absolutely necessary for household activities and the only alternative may be to sell food or use
it to make beer for sale. In either case the effect on the family
food store is self-evident. Obviously, more concrete examples are
needed before generalisations can be made. At the same time, the
cause and effect of monetisation and malnutrition may not be so
clear cut. A recent study on family life education in three regions
has shown that the standard of nutrition was best in a region with
the highest socio-economic indicators associated with a high degree
of monetisation. The fact remains, however, that food production
is declining in Tanzania and unless this trend can be reversed,
malnutrition and associated diseases and fatalities will persist
in spite of the most comprehensive nutrition education and sophisti-
cated curative services.

Health and Nutrition Education

Some progress has been made in the field of health and nutrition
education through the activities of TFNC and MCH centres (XIII:366).
Evidence from Nigeria also supports the importance of nutrition
education in reducing child mortality (XIII:349). Nevertheless
some basic problems and contradictions are apparent. In the first
place out of the over 8,000 villages only 1,750 had MCH centres in
1979 (XIII:366). The rural areas are also worse off in terms of
transportation so that distances combined with transportation
difficulties effectively prevent women from attending these centres.
A further constraint is their workload in productive and domestic
labour.

Studies dealing with the utilization of MCH centres also point
out other contradictions regarding accessibility associated with
occupational, educational, and income differentials (XIII:359, 373,
375, 382). The contradictions are most apparent where socio-
economic differentials are most pronounced, such as in urban areas
(XIII:382). Attendance of MCH clinics in the rural areas has
shown less contradictions because they were done in areas where
there was more homogeneity in incomes, education and occupations.
A more useful approach would be inter-regional comparisons.

Health and nutrition education is aimed entirely at mothers.
There is an underlying assumption that the supply of food to the
family should be the sole responsibility of women and that the
ignorance of food nutrition practices is the ignorance of women
alone. Thus a woman is blamed if her children suffer from
malnutrition but a man is excused if he uses the cash obtained from
sale of crops to buy non-food items including non-essentials or if
he neglects his share of work in food production. There is a
fundamental contradiction in any policy where women attend
nutrition education and men are allowed to appropriate the cash
surplus that would enable the women to implement what they learn.
The responsibility for the health of the family is the joint
responsibility of men and women and this must apply to information
and education about health and nutrition just as much as it applies
to production. This contradiction is also apparent in national
programmes for improved food storage and agricultural production.

Such programmes are usually aimed at men although women are predominantly or solely responsible for these activities (XIII: 350, 360, and section IV). An integrated approach to production and nutrition cannot be achieved if illogical and indefensible contradictions are not eliminated.

Women in Health and Nutrition Programmes

Improved nutrition in Tanzania is usually interpreted to mean improved nutrition of children. Maletnlema has pointed this out with respect to maternal and child health services (XIII:362). Yet even here the criticism is from the point of view of how the neglect of the care of pregnant women adversely affects the health of the foetus and newborn infant. Even family planning services advocate child spacing as a way to ensure healthy children. It is noteworthy that popular posters showing the benefits of child spacing use the analogy of good agricultural practices in maize spacing in order to obtain a healthy crop. The debate on infant feeding where women are blamed for not breast-feeding their babies for a "reasonable" length of time also underlies the societal conception of women's primary role as producers of children, healthy children. The preoccupation with women as objects of biological reproduction has a dehumanizing effect. It also successfully tends to ignore women's labour in the productive sector.

On the whole not much work has been done on the health and nutritional standards of adults although high mortality and morbidity are recognised as one of the major causes of low productivity. Health and nutrition must be studied as a problem affecting the entire community, and not only under-fives in order to achieve an integrated approach towards health and nutrition. More analysis is also required of health issues arising out of traditional practices such as circumcision (XIII:352, 377), and social problems such as prostitution, drunkenness, physical abuse of women and children, infant killing and suicide. The preoccupation with health as defined in medical terms has to be abandoned to adopt a more critical analysis of the basic causes of malnutrition and ill-health in order to improve the health, welfare and overall development of the nation.

---

348. ATTEMS, M.C. et al. (1969), "Investigations in North East Tanzania". IN: H. KRAUT and H.D. CREMER, Investigations into Health and Nutrition in East Africa. Munich, Weltforum, pp. 15-217.

A community survey of 250 families and 1190 individuals was conducted in 8 survey areas in North-East Tanzania with a mix of highland and lowland areas. Although concerned mainly with the technical aspects of malnutrition, the survey included many questions on the demographic and socio-economic characteristics of the individuals surveyed. There is therefore considerable data on the family size, age and sex distribution, education, occupation, fertility rate, sibling mortality and marital status of heads of household. On malnutrition the survey found general protein deficiency in children because of poor supplementary and weaning food. For adults, the nutritional status of the people in the lowlands was better than that of the hill dwellers. Reasons for these phenomena are discussed. In agriculture, the survey discerned a trend towards commercialisation and a declining acreage for food production for the household. The survey also discovered that there was no relation between income and diet, although cash income resulted in a higher standard of living. The authors attributed this to two factors; the scale and extent of additional income and the lack of nutrition education. Any extra income is first spent on non-food items such as improvement to houses, or purchase of livestock. These findings are similar to those of a later study in the Southern highlands (XIII:353). Unlike this later study, the authors leave out any discussion on the control of the cash income which allows the men to use the cash income on non-food items, leaving the women to provide food for the family on decreasing acreages for food crops.

349. CALDWELL, J.C. (1981), "Maternal Education as a Factor in Child Mortality". World Health Forum, Vol. 2, No. 1, pp. 75-78.

Uses evidence from surveys in Nigeria to show that maternal education is the single most significant determinant of child mortality. This is because of three reasons: (1) educated mothers break with traditional fatalism about illness and adopt alternatives in child care and treatment of illness. (2) The educated mother is more capable of manipulating the modern world. She is more likely to be listened to by doctors and nurses. (3) Education of women greatly enhances the traditional balance of familial relationships where the mother does not have direct responsibility for the welfare of the children. Education converts "maternal indulgence into maternal protectiveness", often resulting in more attention being given to children.

350. CHUNG, D.S. (1975), "Review of On-Farm Grain Storage in Tanzania". Report, Food and Feed Grain Institute, Kangasu State University, No. 49. Excerpted from Abstract in WAERS - 20 (9) Sept. 1978 (abstract No. 5344).

Cereal grains include maize, rice, wheat, grain sorghum and millet. A large percentage of the grain is stored and consumed on the farm - wheat being the prime exception. There are basically six categories of farm storage containers, all involving indigenous materials: (1) in homes above cooking areas, in baskets or in bark containers; (2) ear maize storage on poles; (3) baskets' woven from reeds, bamboo or grass (may be covered with other substance); (4) dried goods for small quantities; (5) mud pots with sealed lids; and (6) metal drums. Main causes of loss and damage are improper and inadequate post harvest grain handling, drying and storage methods. The author points out that there are no formal programmes for improved farm storage. The author does not focus on the significance of women's labour in grain storage. The recommendations presented by Chung are mainly oriented to administrative and technical mechanisms, and will depend for their success on their taking note of women as storers and processors (abstract no. 5344).

351. ECA (1976), <u>Report on the Workshop on Food Preservation and Storage, Kibaha</u>, Tanzania. New York, Economic Commission for Africa. 102 pp.

A workshop on Food Preservation and Storage was organised by the Government of Tanzania with assistance from UNICEF, ECA, and FAO. The 50 participants, largely Regional Secretaries of the Umoja wa Wanawake wa Tanzania (UWT) examined traditional methods of preserving and storing food in the different regions of the country. The aim of the workshop was to equip the UWT secretaries with knowledge and skills needed to conserve surplus food, prevent losses during storage and allow good use of vegetables and fruits available only seasonally. It was hoped that the participants would teach the knowledge gained to village women. The workshop was very concerned with the high rate of child mortality due to malnutrition. It was reported that 150,000 out of 800,000 children die between the ages of 1-5 years; hence the importance of women being taught nutrition, better methods of food preservation and storage and the need for attending clinics. The participants spent most of the period of the workshop carrying out practical demonstrations of improving traditional methods of food conservation. They also recommended better educational opportunities for women, laws to protect food sold in shops and markets and a Board for food surveillance in which women would be fully involved.

352. ISMAIL, EDNA ADAN (1980?), "Infibulation: Breaking the Silence". <u>Spare Rib</u>, p. 17.

Reports on presentation at the African Centre in London on the struggle against female circumcision in Somalia. The form of circumcision prevalent there is infibulation, where the clitoris and labia minora of a young girl are completely cut out, and the larger labia scraped raw and sewn to grow together. Women must constantly have their labia cut open and sewn together again during marriage and child-birth. The author is a midwife who explained how the operation caused infection and death among young girls and grown women. Up until recently, however, the operation was not talked about publicly. The Somalia campaign focuses on the health issue, and argues that there is no reason for the operation: "it is not healthy, not clean, not Islamic, even that it does not guarantee virginity".

Female circumcision is prevalent in many areas of Tanzania, with detrimental effects on the health of young girls and women. Public silence surrounds the issue of female circumcision in Tanzania as in Somalia. However, an important research paper on the subject was presented at a recent conference of Medical Doctors in Dar es Salaam and reported on in the daily Tanzanian Newspapers (XIII:377). More research and public discussion is necessary which focuses on the reasons for the practice of female circumcision in different areas of the country and its impact on women's health, sexuality and fertility.

353. JAKOBSEN, OLDVAR (1978), <u>Economic and Geographical Factors Influencing Child Malnutrition; A Study from the Southern Highlands, Tanzania</u>. BRALUP Research Paper, Dar es Salaam and Trondheim, BRALUP and Dept. of Geography, University of Trond-

heim. 105 pp. No. 52.

Identifies two main causes for underweight among fifty percent
of the children: the traditional habits and taboos that bar
women, specially pregnant women from protein rich food and give
men first right to the food pot, and even more important, the
socio-economic structure that makes peasants sell their crops
in exchange for non-foods or foods with low nutritional status
or turns subsistence farmers into day labourers, thus changing
the power structure in the family in favour of men at the
expense of women and children.

   Crucial "decisions" of the family economy that affect
malnutrition are singled out: (a) decision of men to work the
land or leave it in favour of migration. This forces the women
to do all the agricultural work while at the same time not
benefiting from the husband's migratory work. The only sources
of cash for women are beer selling or work as day labourers.
Failing this, she sells food crops; (b) men's decision to
allocate the amount of land and labour to industrial and food
crops with no respect to family food needs; (c) the decision
to sell or store food crops; (d) the expenditure pattern –
men's preference for items which bring future income or prestige
e.g. cattle, wives, houses, radios etc. The dietary needs of
children are expected to be met by the mother. Monetization
in Njombe was less conducive to better nutrition since areas
with regular cash income were more likely to neglect food
production.

354. JONSSON, U. and OLIVIA MGAZA (1977), "Nutrition, Agriculture
    and Socio-economy. A Report from a Survey in Mvumi Village,
    Kilosa District, Morogoro Region", TFNC Program 15.

The study found a high correlation between low household income
and harvest losses and child malnutrition. Spoilage of crops
due to inability to harvest on time is related to problems of
labour resources, though this is not explained. Poorer households also tended to have more children, and number of children
was related to incidence of malnutrition. Food taboos are also
indicated; they usually concern animal meat or eggs, and pregnant
or lactating women are the ones most affected. No relationship
was found between child malnutrition and housing conditions,
mother's education and mother's marital status. The low
percentage of women who had any education may partly explain
this finding. More serious probing into marital relations
within peasant households is necessary, given the important
role of women as producers and the lack of control they have
over distribution of meat and other protein rich foods.

355. KHONJE, MARGARET (1977), "Trial on Village Integrated Nutrition
    Services". Paper presented to Research Investigators in
    Nutrition Meeting (WHO), National Institute of Nutrition,
    Hyderabad, India 12-17 December, 1977, TFNC.

The activities of the "Trial on Integrated Nutrition Services"
(WHO title - to be referred to below as TINS) consist of maternal
and child health, nutrition, control of communicable diseases and
child spacing. Ten villages are involved, from Mara, Iringa,

Morogoro, Kilimanjaro and Coast Regions, although only one
village is reported on, Boko in Kisarawe District, Coast Region.
The role of the different village-level personnel and institutions in research and action is presented, including the village
peasants themselves. It is pointed out, for example, that a
woman villager would be the more appropriate person to reach
about weaning foods or child spacing, rather than a male village
Medical Aid. The problem of healthy child spacing is related
to high polygamy rates, where "The average man marries a wife
half his age and the wife must have her own offspring in addition to the husband's other children". Malnutrition and disease
among children and infants is related to infection, insufficient
food and specifically to the time and energy mothers take to
seek water.

356. KIMATI, V.P. (1974), "Analysis of Childhood Morbidity and
Mortality in Tanzania", Paper Presented to the Annual Scientific
Meeting of the Association of Physicians in East Africa.
Summarised in East African Medical Journal, Vol. 51 No. 2,
pp. 945-946.

Mortality statistics are generally unavailable because of lack
of compulsory registration of births and deaths. Morbidity and
mortality statistics are only available in hospitals. An
analysis of causes of pediatric admissions at one Tanzanian
consultant hospital revealed severe morbidity in children of
6 months to three years. The three biggest killers were found
to be malnutrition, measles and low birth weights. They were
responsible for 48 % of all mortality and 70.3 % of all morbidity.
The paper emphasises improved nutrition services and family
planning to eliminate these preventable causes of child morbidity
and mortality.
    The complete edition of the paper was not available for
inclusion in this work. It is therefore difficult to assess
if the authors conclusion was preceded by a discussion of the
crucial role of women in nutrition and paradoxically their
inability to provide for the family because of socio-economic
or cultural reasons. In this context see I:23, XIII:353, 378.
Family Planning may protect the health of mothers and children
but it cannot be offered as a panacea for eliminating infant
mortality if social and economic contradictions are not
eliminated.

357. KINGAMKONO, P. (1980), "Infant Formula Marketing and Promotion".
In: Infant Feeding in Dar es Salaam, edited by O. Mgaza and
Han Bantje. TFNC Report No. 44 and BRALUP Research Paper No.
66, Dar es Salaam, TFNC and BRALUP pp. 213-224.

Describes the advertising and marketing policies of infant
formula and foods in Tanzania during the colonial period and
after independence. Shows how until recently multinational
companies had a great latitude in advertising and marketing
infant foods and psychologically reduced breast-feeding to a
backward out-dated practice. Imports of infant foods rose
steadily until 1977 when 1,883 tons were imported at a cost of
approximately 21 million shillings. Even when the quantity was
reduced in 1978 due to adverse economic conditions the cost had

risen considerably. In 1977 advertising of infant foods was
stopped but indirect promotion is still carried out. Imports
of infant foods have dropped only because of general restrictions on imports. It is thus likely that when the economic
situation improves imports of infant foods will rise and
gradually may erode the tendency among the majority of the
mothers to breast-feed and use traditional weaning foods.

By concentrating on the commercialisation aspect of infant
foods and the cost to the country in terms of foreign exchange,
the analysis ignores objective reasons why women use formula
and infant foods, and perceives women only as a means of producing
milk.

358. KIONDO, ANDREW S.J. (1981), "The Health Question in Tanzania:
A Critical Assessment of the Tanzania Medical System in
Relationship to Rural Health Services". Paper presented to IDS
Regional Workshop Research Methodology, Usa River, Arusha, March
30th - April 11th, 24 pp.

Historical analysis of medical services in Tanzania, which
related the health question to broader issues concerning
peasants, the state and capital is presented. Empirical
research was conducted in Maramba Division, Muheza District in
Tanga Region. The Maramba Rural Health Centre did not serve
the whole division, but rather the village near by. For example,
60 % of the patients were from Maramba itself, which has a
population of 3,000 compared to 50,000 in the entire division.
There were no mobile services because fuel was not so allocated.
The preventative aspect of MCH did not function, since people
only attended the MCH clinic when (mainly) children were ill.
Treatment at the centre followed attendance at health education
lectures, which were boring and sermon-like in nature.
Peasants in more distant villages 7 miles or more from the
centre complained that their demands for a village dispensary
had not been met. Distances force many to seek alternative
health services near-by, by buying pills or services of traditional health. Statistical analysis of drug imports and
expenditures at the end of the paper show that hospitals are
allocated more of the drugs. Hence, the vast majority of
peasants in Tanzania have little or no access to medical
services and drugs in spite of the policy proclamations about
preventative medicine and primary health care.

359. KREYSLER, JOACHIM AND SCHULZE-WESTEN, IRMGARD (1973), "Social
Factors Influencing Attitudes of Mothers Towards Nutrition
Services in Rural Population: a case study in Usambara,
Tanzania". Ecology of Food and Nutrition, 2: 49-60.

The study involved a sample of 193 mothers with children age
0-5 years and their attendance at an "under-five clinic". The
mothers fell into two distinct groups, differentiated by
religion and socio-economic conditions. Attendance and
motivation were compared with respect to age of mother, school
education of both parents and occupation of father. The aim
of the study was to discover to what extent the characteristics
of the social status and the beliefs of the people of Usambara
would have to be considered in organizing under-five clinics.

The findings are profusely illustrated with many tables. Some correlation was found between attendance/non-attendance and religion, education and age.

360. KNUTSSON, K.E. and others (1979), Food and Nutrition in National Development; an Evaluation of the Tanzania Food and Nutrition Centre. (TFNC) Dar es Salaam, 146 pp.

Generally useful as a brief overview of the problems of food and nutrition in Tanzania. Among the specific shortcomings of TFNC, the evaluation report identifies the lack of a Food and Nutrition Policy (FNP). It also shows that TFNC studies have not fully incorporated the socio-economic causes of malnutrition, particularly the role of women in food and nutrition programmes. This was especially evident in the draft of the FNP then being prepared by TFNC. The team considered this neglect as serious and asserted that it may serve to increase the hardships of those members of the society who are responsible for both "food" and "nutrition" at household level i.e. the women. It therefore elaborates an argument to prove the negative consequences of this neglect. Most of the aspects of this argument are covered in other studies on women in rural development. However the report does bring out the stark contrast of male bias in agricultural development planning and the female bias in health and nutrition planning - a contrast which would naturally render any comprehensive FNP as useless. Shows that inspite of political statements regarding the need to ensure equality for every "individual", the official attitude in contemporary Tanzania remains much the same as in colonial times.

   The fundamental problem is identified as "the perspective which women hold to themselves in relation to men". In this, the team reveals a major problem of analysis. Is the question of the subordinate role of women, just a female attitudinal problem?

361. MALANGALILA, EMMANUEL GAUDENSIO (1979), "Antenatal Attendance and Mother's Characteristics in Relation to Perinatal Mortality at Rural Dispensaries in Iringa District". Dar es Salaam, University of Dar es Salaam. Mss. Diploma in Public Health. 48 pp. with tables.

The study was conducted in four randomly selected rural dispensaries in Iringa District and involved deliveries from mothers who had attended antenatal clinics at least once during the relevant pregnancy. Correlations were made between perinatal mortality rates and educational level, marital status of mothers as well as the number of visits to antenatal clinics. The mother's age and number of earlier deliveries increased the perinatal mortality rate. Education and marital status appeared to have no statistical significance but mortality rate fell significantly in relation to increasing number of visits to antenatal clinics. The study recommends at least 6 visits.

   No significant difference between deliveries handled by traditional birth-attendants at home and those handled by hospitals were found. This may be so because the high risk cases were diagnosed early at the clinics and recommended for hospital delivery and the home deliveries were therefore mainly non-high risk cases. Nevertheless, argues that with special training and supervision, traditional birth attendants could safely handle non-high risk cases and leave the scarce hospital resources for more difficult case. The study appears to skirt around the questions as to why women attend/do not attend the clinics as often as they should, specially since the question of attendance of antenatal clinics is such a crucial factor in lowering perinatal mortality.

362. MALETNLEMA, T.N. (1977), "The Importance of Nutrition in Socio-Economic Development". Paper presented to the WHO Regional Committee Meeting, Brazzaville 7-14 September, 1977. 25 pp. table, TFNC.

Overview of the contribution of food and nutrition to socio-economic development, the effects of malnutrition, fallacies in the conceptualisation of nutrition, and weaknesses in programmes to improve nutrition. An alternative approach to the problem of malnutrition is outlined. Statistics on the proportion of hospitalised children who are undernourished and of child fatalities due to malnutrition are provided. Malnutrition increases the rate of infertility, miscarriages and intrauterine malnutrition of the foetus.

With the growth of the money economy, nutrition programmes should relate to men as well as women. Maternal and child health services is one of the basic components of community action, and should reach the family level. Food aid is usually for children whereas the mothers are often malnourished, which in turn leads to intrauterine malnutrition of the foetus. Increased food production is one solution, based on integrated community action, involving prevention and treatment, education and job creation. Provision of food let alone vitamin supplements is clearly inadequate, and may lower food production. Two relevant solutions are (1) "food first", not "cash first" and (2) "women in Africa should regain their natural dignity and avoid the superficial aspects of Western culture".

363. MALETNLEMA, T.N. (1976), "Basic Services at Village Level". WHO Seminar on Rural Women Education, Lushoto, 1976. 19 pp. TFNC.

A simply written description of the problems of nutrition and services available at the village level. Nutrition services are integrated with basic health care, beginning at village level with maternal Child Health (MCH) Aids. Malnutrition is related to problems of food production, in turn a result of the historical development of class and the money economy. As surplus foods were generated and appropriated by one class in pre-colonial society (chiefs, kings), others had to produce more and eat less. Colonial rule led to the emphasis on cash crop production at the expense of food crop production, and the loss of female control over household surplus: "The granary has been replaced by a small purse of money permanently attached to the men". One consequence has been malnutrition for women and children, not men.

364. MALETNLEMA, T.N. and BAVU, J.L. (1974), "Nutrition Studies in Pregnancy. Part I, Energy, Protein and Iron Intake of Pregnant Women in Kisarawe, Tanzania". East African Medical Journal, 51 (7): 515-528.

Dietary intakes of 70 pregnant women in Kisarawe showed that the mean intake of protein, energy and iron was not up to the FAO/WHO recommendations. The women on higher intakes delivered larger infants than those on low intakes. Women who said they ate mainly cassava foods showed a lower intake of protein, energy and iron then those who had mixed diets, and this information has been used to divide the women into socio-economic groups I (lower) and II (higher). Argues that maternal malnutrition which affects a quarter of women, could be eliminated by improving communications in the district, and improving the production and utilization of agricultural products.

365. MALETNLEMA, T.N., MHOMBOLAGE and NGOWI, G.E. (1974), "Family Food Consumption Surveys in Rural Tanzania". Tanzania Notes and Records, No. 73: 43-64.

Food consumption surveys in five villages taken from five regions of Tanzania, are described. Claims that some of the protein deficiency is due to food habits based on the principle that "food is made by women for men and often the better share in quantity and quality is given to men". Cites several examples to illustrate this.

366. MALETNLEMA, T.N. (n.d.), "The Role of Medical Staff in Nutrition for Development". Paper presented to the Silver Jubilee of the Physicians of East and Central Africa. 12 pp.

The paper summarises the few main forms of malnutrition: (1) protein energy deficiency - Kwashiorkor, marasmus or a combination of the two, (2) anemia or iron deficiency among pregnant mothers and "under-five" children; (3) vitamin deficiency; (4) iodine and fluorine; and (5) dehydration, not often referred to as malnutrition. The social and economic causes of malnutrition are briefly surveyed, as well as the role of medical services and health education in prevention and treatment. The frequent assertion that food taboos and general ignorance of peasant women and men are the cause of malnutrition is rejected, and it is shown how food practices change with higher incomes, altered village organisation, and so on. Food and nutrition components should become an important part of all health programmes - the Maternal and Child Health Project is an example, which has led to the drastic reduction of protein energy deficiency wherever MCH Services have been established. The tendency to focus community health and nutrition education solely on women is criticised.

367. MEENA, RUTH ELIAWONY (1979), "The Maternal and Child Health Services". Paper No. 4, BW, 9 pp.

The MCH programme depends almost totally on foreign aid, despite the significance of children and the mother as vital national resources. The overall administrative structure of MCH is presented, together with training and other facilities. Equipment is mainly imported, and a large proportion is not in use, partly because of difficulties in maintenance and repair. The marginal significance given to MCH by health and other officials is revealed by the prevalent misallocation of MCH vehicles, which have been appropriated by Ministerial DDD's and other district-level officers for their own use. Medicine and equipment provided by UNICEF have also been misappropriated. The data is drawn from the author's MA dissertation entitled UNICEF and the Tanzanian Child (1979, Department of Political Science, University of Dar es Salaam).

368. MGAZA, OLIVIA and BANTJE, HAN (1980), Infant Feeding in Dar es Salaam. Tanzania Country Report for the IUNS Study "Rethinking Infant Nutrition Policies under Changing Socio-economic Conditions". Dar es Salaam, TFNC and BRALUP. 235 pp.

This study came about as a result of world-wide concern over the shift from breast-feeding to artificial feeding. The material conditions of 228 mothers from 4 areas in Dar es Salaam were surveyed. The sample was taken from two groups each of high income and low income which were further differentiated into employed and unemployed. Two variables were considered as mostly to affect material conditions: household income and female employment. The aim of this part of the survey was to study the impact of mothers' material conditions on their feeding practices, specially breast-feeding. Also studied the impact of formula milk promotion on mothers' attitudes and breast-feeding practices. The findings reveal that only a small percentage of children were fed exclusively on formula or were exclusively breast-fed. The majority are fed on a combination of breast milk and other foods, sometimes including formulas. The duration of breast-feeding decreases with rising income after 12 months. Mother's employment has little effect on the duration of breast-feeding. Rising income also affected weaning foods. About 75 percent of the high income group and 50 percent of the low-income women used feeding bottles. Employed women use them more often than the unemployed. Among the lower income groups the nutritional status of breast-fed children in general seems to be better than those who are bottle-fed. The study claims that there is no direct promotion of formula feeds. However, in private institutions bottle-feeding with formula milk was practised on a routine basis.

There is a considerable amount of data on the conditions of women and children and households in general in Dar es Salaam. Also valuable are the background papers. The editors are not exaggerating when they claim the report to be a "valuable source of data".

369. MGAZA, OLIVIA (1980), "Nutrition and Health Status". In: Infant Feeding in Dar es Salaam edited by O. Mgaza and H. Bantje. TFNC Report No. 484 and BRALUP Research Paper No. 66 Dar es Salaam, TFNC and BRALUP, pp. 126-131.

Discusses nutritional and health problems of pre-school children; breast-feeding practices and weaning foods and habits. The infant mortality rate is 155 per thousand, 50 % of which is due to protein energy malnutrition, which in turn is due to severe

insufficiency in food intake. The overwhelming majority of
women in the rural areas breast-feed their children up to two
years and even in the urban areas only a small proportion of
infants are wholly bottle-fed. Working mothers breast-feed
before and after working hours and use bottle feeds in between.
The weaning period has often been associated with malnutrition
and infant mortality. Porridge made of maize flour or sometimes sorghum and millet is the main meal but few mothers
enrich the porridge with milk, groundnut flour or other legume
flours.

370. MLINGI, B. and F. CHALE (1977), "Research Priorities in Food
Production, Health and Nutrition". Paper presented to Workshop
on African Women and Development: The Decolonization of Research,
Dakar: 12-17 December, 1977. 28 pp. TFNC.

There is a need to Africanise research on food production, health
and nutrition. Research should be oriented towards cutting down
female labour time in various tasks such as head transport of
harvest, food preservation and processing, and promoting
nutrition-rich local foods and production of "ready-made" foods
to reduce cooking time and fuel costs. Food taboos are mainly
for women and children, and their underlying causes must be
researched - one possibility being that men are "greedy" and
want nutritious foods for themselves. Other research priorities
are noted.

371. MOSHA, A.C. (1977), "Grain Legume Utilization for Better
Nutrition - The Tanzanian Experience". Paper presented to the
FAO Expert Consultation on Grain Legume Processing, C.F.T.R.I.,
Mysore, India 14-18 November, 1977, 13 pp., tables, TFNC Pub.
124.

Malnutrition can be combatted by encouraging more efficient
production, processing, storage and utilization of grain
legumes and oil seeds (such as beans, cowpeas, groundnuts,
sesame and soya beans). At the present time however there is
much greater growth in production of maize and other cereals,
and indeed there has been a drop in bean production between
1971/72 and 1975/76. There is a cereals and legumes research
programme run by the Ministry of Agriculture, which is now
emphasising common beans, cowpeas, and green grain, major items
in the national diet. The recommended varieties are bulked and
multiplied into seed that is sold to farmers. Efforts are also
being made to develop instant cereal legume mixtures and
relishes and infant weaning foods which could be produced at
the village level in small industries or at home.
About 30-40 % of stored grain is lost to spoilage agents
like insects, rodents or moulds. The basic reasons include
inadequate drying; storage in sacks, tins, pots and baskets;
and non-use of insecticides. The role of women in legumes
production storage and therefore the need to focus on women in
research, education and development efforts are ignored. The
question here of course is whether women have direct access to
the seeds and whether the monetary aspects lead to production
mainly for sale rather than for home consumption. The author

does not explore these and other economic aspects of the legume
programme.

372. MOSHA, A.C. (n.d.), "Post-Harvest Technology and Nutritional
Aspects of Cereals with Particular Reference to Maize, Sorghum,
Rice and Millet". Dar es Salaam: Food and Nutrition Centre,
TFNC Publication No. 18. 13 pp. biblio. TFNC.

An overview of the technical aspects of harvesting, threshing,
drying and storage pest control, communication and transport,
processing, marketing, consumption and nutrition. The information is valuable for any research on women's role in the
production of the crops specified (maize, sorghum, rice, millet).
At the same time, there is no analysis of the social aspects of
the labour process and the specific and differentiated roles of
men and women are ignored. Identification of problems and
possible solutions are thereby limited in their usefulness (e.g.
discussion of nutrition and caloric losses due to processing
and storage techniques related to women's work).

373. MPANJU, W.F.K. (1979), "Neonatal Complications in Low Birth
Weight Babies in Dar es Salaam". Paper No. 43, BW, 11 pp.

In a comparison of low birth weight (LBW) babies with a control
group, the former were found to have a higher rate of health
complications, especially respiratory distress and jaundice,
and higher mortality rates. Conditions of home and hospital
delivery are analysed to provide an explanation for some of the
findings. Emphasis is put in the conclusion on the need for
adequate antenatal care, which in turn poses the question of
differential access to proper antenatal treatment and the
resources (food, money, "free" time for rest, etc.) necessary
among women of different classes.

374. MWAIKAMBO, ESTHER D. (1980), "A Review of Maternal and Child
Health Services in Rural Tanzania". Paper presented at the
Women's Research Seminar on "Employment, Health, and Education
related to Rural Areas in Kenya, Tanzania, India and Bangladesh"
at "Magleas" July 9-12th Copenhagen, organised by K.U.L.U.,
13 pp.

Argues that high infant, child and maternal mortality rates in
Tanzania are "easily preventable", related as they are to poor
antenatal and post-natal care, unhygienic conditions during
delivery, malnutrition and diseases like measles, polio,
diarrhea, and whooping cough. Figures are given on the primary
health services available in the country, and the presence of
"trained" health services during delivery in 1974. The continued
reliance of the majority of peasant women on traditional midwives
suggests the absolute necessity of providing "modern" training
to these women, so that they can be incorporated into the formal
health sector. This has been done with great success in
countries like Sudan.
    Explains the cause of high mortality rates to be under-
utilization of MCH clinics, due to "ignorance", heavy work loads,
distance, lack of money for transport, husband's refusal to
attend, being "too lazy" and "taboos". The "Blame the Victim"
position underlying such analysis distorts the concrete realities

of peasant women and peasant families today. Again, the oft-stated assumption by medical practitioners and other experts, as well as the World Bank, that the major causes of death are "easily preventable" is a fallacy requiring substantive critique. The primary cause of preventable disease and death is usually attributed to poverty. Is poverty easily preventable? What are the causes of peasant poverty, which lead to inadequate food consumption, poor sanitation, measles, cholera and malaria of epidemic proportions and the death (on the average) of 20 out of every 100 children before the age of five years in Tanzania? These are the kinds of questions which must be asked and answered.

375. NGALIWA, S.J. (1979), Utilization of MCH Clinics and Associated Factors and Effects on Under Five Children at Rural Dispensaries in Dodoma District. Unpublished Ph.D. dissertation, University of Dar es Salaam, 58 pp.

The attendance of MCH clinics over a 12 month period by 628 mothers involving 802 children was surveyed in 4 villages in Dodoma District. Two socio-economic variables, marriage status and education of mothers were considered as likely factors affecting attendance. The study found that of the 802 children about 82.8 % had cards showing that they had attended at least once. However, only 555 had attended over the year considered by the survey and these had an attendance rate of 33.1 % of the required rate. The number of mothers attending the clinic appeared to drop to 50 % by the second half of the first year of the child's life, and to remain at this level for the next four years. Most of the mothers (90 %) were married with about 60 % being illiterate. Unfortunately no correlation is shown between these variables and the discontinuation or continuation of the use of MCH by the mothers. Nor does the study analyse reasons why the attendance drops so drastically. The value of the study is thus diminished by the omission of these relationships.

376. RUTABANZIBWA, JEAN (1980), "Population and Health Planning in Tanzania" ILO and ECA National Seminar on Population and Development, Arusha 17-24 February, 13 pp.

Stresses the necessity of planning health services and programmes in order to meet post-Arusha goals of providing comprehensive basic health services for all the population in conditions of limited resources. The political power of medical doctors helps to explain the initial emphasis on curative services measured by ratios of doctors/nurses/hospital beds to population during the initial post-Arusha period. Such measures ignore the unequal distribution of medical resources and how they are utilized. Regional population figures are matched with health facilities to show the high disparities existent. After 1974 a discernible shift towards preventative and basic health services is notable however in the figures shown.

377. RWIZA, H.T., DAVID R. MSUYA and others (1980), "Complications of Traditional Female Circumcision as seen at Usangi Government Hospital". Paper presented to the Annual Medical Conference, Dar es Salaam.

Female circumcision is practiced in several areas of Tanzania, including Pare, Kilimanjaro, Arusha, Dodoma, Mara and Singida. Three cases are presented, based on hospital admissions to Usangi Hospital, as well as results from interviews of neighbouring adults and an attitude survey administered in a nearby College of National Education and a Private Secondary School. Two of the cases were young girls (8 and 9 years) suffering severe bleeding, anemia and other complications as a result of the complete excision of the entire clitoris and labia minora a few days previous to admission. A young woman suffered severe bleeding after delivery as a result of the tearing of an old post-circumcision scar reaching from the vulva to the urethra. Three other cases were admitted during the same one year period. They recovered as a result of medical attention at the hospital, but the severity of their complications would otherwise have meant possible loss of life.

The adults interviewed stated that the practice of female circumcision is common, especially among Moslems; that it is usually conducted by a traditional expert. The reasons given for the procedure include the following: social acceptability especially to men; to signify ages; to ease subsequent delivery believed to be hampered by the clitoris; to reduce female sexual impulse in order to reduce promiscuity, prostitution and unfaithfulness of wives; to prevent an itching disease called lawalawa and to facilitate future intercourse. These reasons are expressions of patriarchal relations of sexuality and fertility, the woman being perceived as an object, a possession of the father and later the husband, her sexuality to be controlled by men through physical and other means. The complications include frightening children; bleeding; difficult deliveries; diminished sexual impulse leading to the women being "dormant"; tetanus, sepsis and death. All twenty adults recommended that the practice be stopped. Although the young people were generally opposed to female circumcision, a very large proportion believed it was necessary, beneficial and harmless. Significantly more girls were opposed to the practice than boys, and in general Pare boys and girls were more favourable. For example, when asked whether the practice was beneficial or non-beneficial, nearly half of the male youth in the area believed in the beneficial nature of the practice, and more than one fourth of the female youth. The proportions were similar with respect to necessity and harmlessness. The need for more research to take account of varying practices in different parts of the country is stressed. The authors seek to have female circumcision recognised as a national issue requiring a major sustained campaign to eradicate it completely. The irony that although women are most opposed to it, they are the ones who are circumcised so as to please men is noted. The women's movement is encouraged to take up the issue. Also recommends that the problem of female circumcision be integrated into school curriculum in areas where it is practiced.

378. SWANTZ, MARJA-LIISA, HENRICSON, ULLA-STINA and ZALLA, MARY (1975), Social-Economic Causes of Malnutrition in Moshi District. Dar es Salaam, Bureau of Resource Assessment and Land Use Planning (BRALUP), Research Paper No. 38, 85 pp.

An examination of the socio-economic causes leading to malnutrition among children in Moshi District, Kilimanjaro Region, showed how the position of women among the Chagga, the main tribal group in the area, prevents women from fully sharing in the support and care of their family. The Chagga are a patrilinial society in which the superior role of the male and the inferior submissive status of women are strongly rooted and perpetuated through traditional education, beliefs and practices. This is reflected in land, inheritance, and the right to earn cash income. Shows how each of these factors can contribute to the children of the family being poorly nourished, particularly among the low income peasant families. Frequency of pregnancies and its effect on malnutrition of children is also discussed.

379. TANZANIA. MINISTRY OF HEALTH (1979), Inventory of Health Facilities, 1978. Dar es Salaam, 1979. 22 volumes Main Report + 20 regional reports for Mainland Tanzania and 1 for Zanzibar.

Main Report 142 p. comments and tables. The objectives of the inventory were to provide baseline data on all health institutions run by government, voluntary agencies, occupational health services and private practitioners for improvement of services and planning. The data is quantitative, not critically evaluated and covers the following major areas: (a) health facilities, their distribution and physical status (water, sewage, electricity); (b) health manpower; (c) size, staffing and utilization of hospitals; (d) communication; (e) staff quarters; (f) MCH services. The findings reveal significant differences by regions. For instance the population/bed ratio ranges from 455 for Ruvuma compared to 1,558 for Rukwa Region, while others are worse off. There are 51,283 people for every health centre in Ruvuma compared to 94,614 for Coast Region, while dispensaries range from 4,616 people per dispensary in Tanga to 8,484 in Shinyanga. About 60 % of the children had an adequate supply of vaccine but the adequacy varied inversely with the distance from Dar es Salaam.
    Regional volumes. The regional reports are mainly statistical in nature, and include regional maps showing the location of hospitals and health centres; population by type of institution by region and district; population per hospital bed, health centre and dispensary by district; staff according to institutions and population.

380. TANZANIA. MINISTRY OF HEALTH (1980), Evaluation of the Health Sector, 1979. Dar es Salaam, 1980. 2 vols. (Main Report and Appendices).

The evaluation of the health delivery system in the 1970's covers 6 regions - Coast, Dodoma, Kigoma, Kilimanjaro, Mwanza and Ruvuma. The statistics on the physical stock of health facilities in these regions are based on "Inventory of Health Facilities in Tanzania" (379 above). Shows that the increase in population has been faster than the increase in beds. Attendance of health facilities increased but the average number of visits remained the same. It would take the country about 60 years to provide orthodox primary health care facilities i.e. dispensaries and rural health centres. A

drastic and revolutionary change in providing primary health
services is recommended with emphasis on the training of
village health workers, (VHWS) who should be paid a salary so
as to retain them in the health programme. For the cost
conscious, it is shown that the salaries of the VHWS will
amount to less than 4 % the total annual recurrent health care
expenditure.

381. TANZANIA FOOD AND NUTRITION CENTRE (1978), List of TFNC
Publications and Reports, Report No. 297, 38 pp.

A complete listing of publications and reports which are
available to the public, as well as other internal documents.
Many reports concern women directly although they do not
specifically write about women, such as topics concerning
storage technology, food production and food handling, and
nutrition itself. The author index at the back is helpful.

382. WESTERGAARD, MARGARETA (1970), "Mothers' Use of Health
Facilities Provided for Young Children by City Council and
Patterns of Infant Feeding". University of Dar es Salaam,
Sociology Department mimeo, 51 pp.

The research covers attendance at infant welfare clinics in
Dar es Salaam, the proportion of children innoculated with
Triple Antigen, the duration of breast-feeding and the time
of introduction of solid food to children. Compared to a
survey in Kinondoni in 1969, mothers were more likely to
attend the infant clinics, though there were still occupational
and education differences. Occupation is generally defined in
terms of the husband's occupation, broken down into unskilled,
semi-skilled, skilled, white collar low, white collar high.
Children of unskilled fathers were least likely to have
attended child clinics or to have received the triple innocula-
tion. Mothers with no schooling tended not to attend the clinics,
no matter what the occupational level of the husband, except for
the high white collar group. Compared to a 1964-65 study, more
infants were being innoculated with triple shots, indicating
the expansion in provision and use of preventative health.
However, occupation of father made a great difference as to
whether the infant had received the full course of triple
antigen. The majority of all educational and occupational
groups breast-fed their infants up to 12 months of age, with
differentials found for ultimate duration of breast-feeding.
The wives of white collar employees were the most likely to
stop during the first 12 months of age.

XIV. RESOURCES

We have interpreted resources to mean information about (1) materials
useful for study, research and analysis of the situation of women in
Tanzania; (2) women's networks and forms of communication to share
ideas and experiences with each other; (3) institutions and organisations that fund women's research and projects. Eleven of the items
in this section consist of bibliographies; only one of these is
specifically on women in Tanzania (XIV:393). The others have been
selected on the basis of their contribution to stimulating
awareness of the issues, debates and conceptual interpretations and
analyses of the exploitative situations in which women find themselves (XIV:384, 385, 386, 392, 396). Still others have been
selected because they cover materials of relevance to women's
situations (XIV:391, 394, 395).
The choice of these three aspects has been deliberate and in
accordance with our underlying concept that the "women's question"
cannot be understood only by looking at works where the major
emphasis is women. Many of the developmental theories questioned
in Cooper and Young (XIV:385) were not originally posited in the
context of social changes leading to exploitative classes. At the
same time, even where an uncritical approach has been used the
bibliographies are useful in providing an assessment of the scope
of the literature and the extent of interest in the subject.
A few items are included to illustrate the kinds of international
networks and communication tools available to exchange ideas and
experiences (XIV:388-390, 399, 400). These are limited in number
but in themselves provide addresses of women's organizations and
resources that could be used to enlarge the network that one can
draw upon to obtain information and even financial resources to
support research on women as well as women's projects. Two of the
severe constraints to women's projects have been lack of funds and
lack of skills including skills in writing project proposals. In
this context, the information kit for women (XIV:388) and the small
booklet called appropriately women helping women (XIV:399) are
especially useful in a practical way. Since the networks depend on
exchange of ideas and experiences, their full use rests on the
extent to which viable local groups can be established and contacts
made and maintained on a systematic basis.
We had originally intended to have a lengthy section on training
programmes, written materials, etc., which would have provided productive
knowledge and skills of potential usefulness for women peasants in
particular. The confines of space have not allowed us to carry
out this aim. The list of references at the end of this essay give
an idea of what is available and where to find it. Many items are
only available in English. Much more work must be done to produce
and publish Kiswahili pamphlets, posters and books which are simply
written, illustrated with good line drawings, using large typeface
and which are inexpensive. There is also a tremendous need for
research which focuses on the development of labour-saving technology
in cooking, water provision, food preservation and processing and
crop husbandry. In turn such work needs to be popularised through
all the possible forms of mass media.

REFERENCES

Harlan D. Attfield (1977), Raising Rabbits. Vita, Inc., 3706 Rhode Island Avenue, Mt. Rainier, Maryland 20822, USA, 82 pp.

Chuo cha Elimu ya Watu Wazima, Elimu kwa Njia ya Posta (1975), "Kilimo cha Maharage". Somo la 1 (20 pp.), Somo la 2 (10 pp.) Somo la 3 (14 pp.), Dar es Salaam, P.O. Box 9213, Dar es Salaam.

J.F. Hall (1966), Notes on Ox-Training. Dar es Salaam, Ministry of Agriculture, Forests and Wildlife (also in Kiswahili, Ukulima wa Kisasa Series), 14 pp.

D.P. Kirumbi (1976), Ufugaji wa Kuku. Dar es Salaam, Tanzania Publishing House, 101 pp.

Kituo cha Ufundi wa Kujitegemea (n.d.), "Jiko la Kuni/Mkaa" Arusha, P.O. Box 764, Mimeo, 2 pp.

Ulla Lofgren (1974), Play and Play Equipment for Rural Day Care Centres and Nursery Schools in Tanzania. A manual for the Home Economics Training Centre, Buhare, Musoma, Tanzania; Rome, FAO, 55 pp.

T.N. Maletnlema (1971), Utunzaji wa Mama na Watoto Vijijini. Nairobi, East African Literature Bureau.

S. Manase (1980), "Makala ya Shughuli za Uchumi". Dodoma, UWT, 12 pp.

A.C. Mosha (1977), Hifadhi Vizuri Nafaka Yako. Dar es Salaam, Shirika la Chakula Bora Tanzania TFNC, 61 pp.

Ofisi ya Waziri Mkuu (PMO) (1976), Maduka ya Ujamaa. Dodoma, S.L.P. 980, 18 pp.

PMO (n.d.), Kuni kwa Kupikia. Tanzania and FAO with assistance from UNFPA, 6 pp., poster photobooks (other titles: Maji Safi na Salama, Mtoto Mwenye Afya ni Furaha ya Wazazi, Mtoto Wako Akiwa Mgonjwa, Mapato Mengine ya Fedha)

Eva Sarakikya (1978), Tanzania Cook Book. Dar es Salaam, Tanzania Publishing House, 165 pp.

Taasisi ya Elimu ya Watu Wazima, Idara ya Elimu kwa Umma (1974), Chakula ni Uhai. Dar es Salaam, 96 pp. (see also Mtu ni Afya, Misitu ni Mali).

David J. Vail (1975), Technology for Ujamaa Village Development in Tanzania. Maxwell School of Citizenship and Public Affairs, Syracuse University, 64 pp.

Uno Winblad and Wen Kilama (1980), Sanitation Without Water. Stockholm, SIDA (free copies available from SIDA, S-105 25 Stockholm, Sweden, and SIDA, Dar es Salaam Office), 133 pp.

---

383. ALASEBU GEBRE-SELLASSIE (1979), The Situation of Women in Africa: A Review. UNICEF and EARO. 65 pp.

Analyses the situation of women in Africa and assesses the impact
of this situation on the well-being of the children in that
region. The following aspects are covered: socio-economic
conditions, tradition and law, social change, population,
education, health and water. Comparative data for women in
Africa presented in the form of tables in the text itself and
as appendices. Appendix 2 outlines women's projects in various
African countries and their funding agencies.

384. BUVINIC, MAYRA (1976), Women and World Development, An
Annotated Bibliography. Washington D.C., Overseas Development
Council, 162 pp. 381 items.

Clusters studies on women according to the following subject
areas: general studies on women in development; the impact of
society on women's roles and status; the individual in society;
socio-economic participation of rural women; education and
women; women's work and economic development; women and health,
nutrition, and fertility/family planning; women's informal and
formal associations; women, law and politics. Special issues
of journals and periodicals on women and development, and
bibliographies related to women and development are also
listed in the annexes. There is an author index, and items
are clustered by region within each subject area. The annotations
include commentary on the materials, and are critical of all
examples of "male ideology" as it pervades the content. Provides
a critical review of research on women, which includes discussion
of the problems in using concepts like status and role. The
bibliography is useful in developing an idea of the kind of
research taking place all over the world. However, the very
scope of its endeavour has meant that it provides limited input
on any one region, particularly on Africa.

385. COOPER, ADRIENNE and KATE YOUNG (1980), "Women in Social
Production: An Annotated Bibliography". University of Sussex,
Institute of Development Studies, Draft presented to Study
Seminar 97, Women in Social Production in the Caribbean, Puerto
Rico, 94 items, 55 pp.

Explores the recent literature on Social Production which
examines "the relations of distribution and exchange within the
household and relations of power and dependence within the
family" as these, "affect the sexual division of labour in the
work force and structure women's role in production". Hence,
both economic and so-called "extra-economic" activities are
included in the conceptualisation of social production. Not
all of the items are specifically focused on the women's
question. Many are included which clarify the understanding
of social transformation and exploitative class and gender
relations. The bibliography is useful in familiarising the
reader with the kinds of debates which have arisen in feminist
and historical materialist circles in England and North America.
These debates are highly relevant to analyses which have developed
in Tanzania concerning similar problem areas.

386. FORTMANN, LOUISE (1979), Tillers of the Soil and Keepers of the
Health: a Bibliographic Guide to Women and Rural Development.

Bibliography series. Ithaca, N.Y., Cornell University, Center
for International Studies, 432 items, 53 pp.

The items are selected on the basis of what the author considered
would be relevant to people who are teaching about women and
rural development, undertaking research, or running or designing
programmes in the field. Its primary focus is the third world
and the emphasis is on recent literature arranged in the following
order: Bibliographies; readers, general; agriculture; economic
participation; education; law; family; population; ethnography.
Most of the items are not annotated. The only exception is the
second section entitled "readers" - where a table of contents
is provided for the 10 items included in this section.

387. HAFKIN, NANCY J. (1977), Women and Development in Africa: An
Annotated Bibliography. Bibliography Series No. 1, Addis Ababa,
ECA, ECA/SPD/ATRCS/BIBLIOGR/77, 568 items, 177 pp.

The bibliography covers materials on general studies on women
and development in Africa, rural development and women, population
studies, education and training, urban development and women,
situation of women and women's organizations. There are country
references and author indices, which allow the reader to quickly
trace relevant materials. The bibliography is particularly
thorough regarding materials produced by UN and other international agencies.

388. INTERNATIONAL WOMEN'S TRIBUNE CENTRE INC. WITH AFRICAN TRAINING
AND RESEARCH CENTRE FOR WOMEN (ATRCW) (1981), Information Kit
for Women in Africa. Addis Ababa, UN/ECA, loose-bound folio
and mimeo available. Free distribution from ATRCW or UNDP,

Provides an introduction to the range of resources and activities
"for, by and about women engaged in development programmes
throughout Africa. Most importantly, the kit is aimed at
strengthening and stimulating the on-going exchange of ideas,
experiences and resources among women within the region". There
are four sections, (A) Funding and Technical Assistance
(Proposal Writing, Funding Sources), (B) Women's Projects,
(C) ATRCW Publications and (D) ATRCW Information. A useful
collection of information for those interested in doing research
or developing programmes or projects oriented towards women.

389. ISIS, (Via della Pellicia 31, 1227 Carouge, Geneva).

"ISIS is a resource and documentation centre in the international
women's liberation movement. It was set up in 1974 by a
collective of women to gather materials from local women's
groups and the feminist movement and to make these resources
available to other women". It also co-ordinates the International Feminist Network (IFN) a communication channel through
which women can mobilise international support for each other.

390. ISIS International Bulletin. No. 11, Spring 1979. Rome, ISIS.
Distributed free to third world subscribers (address as in 389).

This is a quarterly periodical which reproduces theoretical
and practical information and documentation from women's groups
and movements around the world. It includes articles, resources,
listings as well as reports and notices about what is going on

in the movement in other countries and continents in order to
help in the exchange of ideas, contracts, experiences and
resources among women and feminist groups.

Each number of the bulletin focuses on a single issue
concerning women. The theme of number 11 was "women, land and
food production". Other topics covered included:
1. The International Tribunal and Crimes Against Women.
2. Women in the Daily Press.
3. Women in Liberation Struggles.
4. Battered Women and the Refugee.
5. and 6. Feminism and Socialism.
7. and 8. Women and health.
9. Women in South Africa.
10. Women workers.

391. KOCHER, JAMES E: (1976), A Bibliography on Rural Development
in Tanzania. Cambridge, Harvard Institute for International
Development, 353 items, 30 pp.

Rural Development is understood to mean both increased production
of agricultural and other rural economic activities and the
progressive enhancement of the material well-being of rural
people as a result of the provision of education, improved
health and better nutrition. These aspects are covered in the
bibliography under 7 sections; general references, ujamaa,
rural development policy, planning and production, rural social
characteristics and services, history of rural or agricultural
development and "related topics".

392. KRATOCHVIL, LAURA AND SHAUNA SHOW (1974), African Women: A
Select Bibliography. Cambridge, African Studies Centre, 1210
items.

The items are mainly drawn from the materials available at
Cambridge, and cover both published works and unpublished mimeo
papers generated in Africa as well as abroad. Items are
clustered by the subjects: general, the arts, development
studies, economics, elites, family, legal position, ornamenta-
tion, politics, religion and ritual, sexual relations, urban
studies, women's organizations and youth, with many sub-headings
as well. There are regional and author indices which allow the
reader to quickly search for relevant materials in conjunction
with the subject index. The bibliography is extremely thorough
and up-to-date (that is, as of time of publication, 1974),
including materials produced from ERB, BRALUP, social science
conferences, as well as East African periodicals and so on.

393. MASCARENHAS, OPHELIA and MARJORIE MBILINYI (1980), Women and
Development in Tanzania: an Annotated Bibliography. Bibliography
series, No. 2. Addis Ababa, African Training and Research
Centre for Women, UNECA. 200 items, 155 pp.

Communicates information about women's studies and women's
projects in Tanzania. Directed to scholars as well as people
actively involved in women's programmes. Includes scholarly
empirical and theoretical sources as well as report literature
discribing experiences with women's organisations and projects,
and a small number of research and planning materials that are

not focused   specifically on women but which raise issues
significant to women and where the exclusion of the women's
question is therefore doubly questionable. A critical evaluation
of the work is included in the annotation within the theoretical
framework of "sexual division of labour" and "patriarch relations".
These concepts have been situated in specific social relations
such as matrilineality or patrilineality as well as within the
world capitalist economy.

The content of the bibliography is divided under the following
categories: general materials not specific to Tanzania; general
materials on the situation of women in Tanzania; case studies
(anthropological); women peasants; women workers; women's
projects and cooperatives; ideology; education; legal system;
politics; biological reproduction and sexual relations; child
care; family and domestic labour; and health and nutrition.

394. MASCARENHAS, OPHELIA (1981), Source Materials for Issues in
Population and Development in Tanzania. Produced under contract
to UNFPA, 341 items, 156 pp.

A workshop was held in Arusha in August 1980 to discuss the use
of population data in planning. The workshop recommended that
there was need to prepare a definitive "status report" on
population and development. The present annotated bibliography
was commissioned to provide the authors of this report with
information on primary and secondary source materials. The
bibliography includes a selection of key works on population
theories and methodologies for interpretation of demographic
data, census data and methodology; mortality; fertility and
socio-economic development; migration and its consequences;
urbanisation; rural development and settlement patterns; women
and development; food and nutrition; family planning; family
life education and child care; health and ecology; employment,
education and manpower planning; and finally, population and
the planning process. The underlying principles affecting the
selection of materials as well as the annotations are two-fold;
that one must not be side-tracked by the Malthusian school of
thought that population control alone will eliminate poverty
and underdevelopment; that, nevertheless, the country must take
cognizance of the implications of the present growth of
population and its characteristics to national goals like
universal primary education, health services and clean water
for all, in the light of worsening terms of trade and falling
productivity.

395. OMARI, C.K. (1973), Bibliography on Family Life Education in
Tanzania. Dar es Salaam, available from FAO Office, 438 pp.

An extremely thorough review of literature on the following
topics: (1) child care and development; (2) family relationships; (3) health; and (4) population. A useful pattern of
notation is used for each item, which gives the reference
itself, its library classification (the reader can jot down
the catalog number and head straight for the shelves - most
items are drawn from the University Library), the objective
of study, sample upon which it was based, the research
techniques used, a summary of findings, recommendations made

and comments of the author. Includes a wide range of materials, some concerning the economy of different pre-colonial societies, female initiation rites and so on. Although published so far only in English, Swahili materials are included.

396. RIHANI, M. (1978), Development as if Women Mattered: An Annotated Bibliography with a Third World Focus. London, Overseas Development Council. Occasional Paper No. 10. Published by Transcentury Foundation, 1789 Columbia Road, N.W., Washington D.C. 20009, USA, 138 pp.

The bibliography is arranged by topic with entries sub-divided by region. Since there is only an author and not a country index, to find entries on Tanzania, the reader would have to go through the African section for each topic entry by entry. The topical organization includes general materials, women in culture and society, socio-economic participation, women and migration, formal and non-formal education, rural development, health, nutrition, fertility and family planning, formal and informal associations, communications and impact of development and modernization. An introductory essay includes a section of findings and recommendations that challenge some prevalent assumptions on women's roles.

397. SNELL, JOHN P. (1980), Tanzania: An Annotated Bibliography on Population in the Context of Rural Development. Rome, FAO, Population Documentation Centre. 242 items, 75 pp. plus author and subject annexes.

Materials were selected on the following basis (1) published no earlier than 1975 (2) primarily concerned with rural populations and (3) printed outside Tanzania. The emphasis of the work is more on rural development than on population but even here the coverage is handicapped by the three criteria for selection. Although there is no attempt at critical evaluation of the works included in the bibliography, the annotations are fairly extensive and quite adequate to get a gist of the content of the material surveyed. A wide range of topics of relevance to rural development are included under the following headings: demography, research, methodology; population; social organization; culture; education; informa- tion; economy; administration; legislation; government policy; psychological factors; life; health; fertility; family planning; migration; population dynamics. Each heading is further subdivided into 3 or more sections.

398. TNR, Tanzania Annual Bibliography, compiled by Andrew Roberts, Bryan Langlands, and Ophelia Mascarenhas. Published in different issues of TNR, Dar es Salaam. The Tanzania Society.

The annual bibliographies cover a wealth of material, published and unpublished, which are now clustered in the following subjects: general; agriculture; anthropology; archaeology; botany, climatology; demography; economics; education; environment; geology; history; hydrology; languages; law; literature; medicine; nutrition; political science; religion; sociology; soil science; veterinary science; zoology; with sub- headings for some topics. It is possible to search through and

find materials on women, but having a specific heading on women
would be a major achievement. The first bibliography was
published in TNR No. 65, June 1967, and covered materials
produced in 1959 through 1964. There are bibliographies
thereafter in nearly every successive issue, the latest being
1975 published in No. 81 and 82 (1977). A new issue is soon
to be published however, and a five year special TNR issue
(1977-1981) is under preparation.

399. WORLD CONFERENCE ON THE UNITED NATIONS DECADE FOR WOMEN (1980),
Women Helping Women. UN. Document No. DP1/671-40998. New York,
24 pp. (for information on obtaining, see 400 below).

This booklet describes a variety of women's projects which have
been successful in a number of countries in Asia, Africa, South
America and Europe. These projects were funded by NGOs both
national and international. Although not specifically on
Tanzania, many of the projects are suitable for experimenting
in Tanzania. In addition, the booklet gives useful hints on
the kinds of NGOs that are likely to assist women's projects
in Tanzania.

400. WORLD CONFERENCE OF THE UNITED NATION'S DECADE FOR WOMEN:
Equality, Development and Peace (1980), Women 1980. Nos. 7 and
8, New York (available from Information Officer, World Conference
of the UN Decade for Women, DESI/DPI, Room 1061, UN Headquarters,
New York, New York 10017, USA), 8 pp.

This newsletter distributed free provides information on the
latest developments within the United Nations system and the
world concerning issues related to women. Issue No. 7, for
example, focuses on the new International Development Strategy
(IDS) formulated by the recent special session of the United
Nations General Assembly held to discuss economic development.
For the first time the strategy explicitly includes women "as
an integral part of the main body of the strategy - in the areas
dealing with industrialization, food and agriculture, science
and technology and social development".
    Lucille Mair, the Secretary General of the World Conference
of the United Nations Decade for Women, noted in her address to
this special session of the General Assembly that "Their (women's)
status, too often one of inferiority and dependency, supplying a
vast reservoir of cheap unskilled labour, is inextricably linked
with a chain of economic relationships forged in the international market system... such relationships have been either
undervalued or ignored in the past, to the detriment of past
development strategies", particularly in agriculture. First
priority must be given to the special requirements of rural
women peasant producers. She also argued that women are
particularly vulnerable in manufacturing and other areas of
wage employment, vulnerable to fluctuations in international
monetary business cycles and to the policies of transnational
corporations, especially in investment and labour practices and
the transfer of technology.
    Issue No. 8 announced that the United Nations General
Assembly endorsed the Copenhagen Programme of Action for the
second half of the UN Decade for Women on December 11th, 1980,

and urged governments to implement it and other decisions of the
Conference Proposals for the Programme of Action to be made by
the Secretary General to the 1981 session of the UN Economic and
Social Council. Provides information about possible sources of
funds for developmental projects, like the Voluntary Fund for
the UN Decade for Women, which is open to innovative and small-
scale projects. The UNDP offices in Dar es Salaam and Arusha
can provide more information, or one can write directly to the
Voluntary Fund for the UN Decade for Women, Room DC-1002, One
United Nation's Plaza, United Nations, New York, New York 10017,
USA.

AUTHOR INDEX

Key to section location of item numbers:

Tanzania, Prime Minister's
    Office - 58-63, 166, 226,
    232, 260, 296, 297, 298, 371
Tanzania Food and Nutrition
    Centre - 381
Tanzania National Council of
    Social Welfare Services- 342
Tanzania National Scientific
    Research Council - 343, 344
    See also UTAFITI
Tesha, Nancy - 179, 326, 345
Tinker, Irene - 17
Tobisson, E. - 134

UMATI - 314-317
Umoja wa Wanawake (UWT) - 261-266
United Nations - 18
United Nations Children's Fund
    (UNICEF) - 232, 233, 346,
    347
United Nations Economic
    Commission for Africa
    (UNECA) - 19-22, 351
United Nations Fund for
    Population Activities (UNFPA)
    - 278
United Nations Protein
    Advisory Group - 23
United Nations Research
    Institute for Social
    Development (UNRISD) - 24
University of Dar es Salaam - 166
University of Dar es Salaam
    Education Department - 205
UTAFITI - 64, 65

Virji, Parin J. - 162
Vitta, Paul B. - 66
Vuorela, Ulla - 70, 135, 136,
    270, 318

Walji, Parveen - 289
Warioba, E. - 334
Wembah-Rashid, J.A.R. - 83
Westergaard, Margareta - 163, 382
Wilson, G. McL. - 84
World Bank - 25
World Conference of the United
    Nations Decade for Women
    - 399, 400
Wright, Marcia - 26, 85

Young, Kate - 385
YWCA - 180

Zalla, Mary - 378